Pelican Books

Crisis and Conservation:
Conflict in the British Countryside

Charlie Pye-Smith was born in Huddersfield in 1951. He studied biology
at Newcastle upon Tyne University where he received his B.Sc. in 1974.
He later studied conservation at University College, London, gaining his
M.Sc. in 1979. He has had varied experience in the conservation field:
in 1974 he was co-leader of an expedition to Kenya to study the problem
of the protection of coral reef; from 1977 to 1978 he was a Research Associate
at the University of Edinburgh under contract from the Nature Conservancy Council; he was the first editor of *Ecos*, the magazine of the British
Association of Nature Conservationists, and was a regular contributor to
Vole. He writes articles for other magazines and newspapers. He also worked
for a year at the Beamish Museum studying the social history of mining
villages in Durham and spent about fifteen months working on farms, mostly
in Yorkshire but also for a short period in the Pyrenees. He spent a long
period rambling through Africa and travelled through Egypt, Sudan,
Ethiopia, Uganda and Kenya. He is currently working on a book on
agricultural reform.

Chris Rose was born in London in 1956. He was educated at the universities of Aberystwyth and London where he studied ecology and conservation.
He first became interested in wildlife through drawing birds, an activity
which was encouraged by his parents. When he became involved in conservation he discovered that the real problems of wildlife and the countryside
are more political than ecological. He has worked for public and voluntary
sector conservation organizations, and done odd jobs in teaching and
journalism. He was a founder member of the British Association of Nature
Conservationists in 1979 and the London Wildlife Trust in 1981, for which
he subsequently worked as Conservation Officer. He now works as a
campaigner for Friends of the Earth. He lives in Richmond with his wife
Sharron.

CRISIS AND CONSERVATION: CONFLICT IN THE BRITISH COUNTRYSIDE

Charlie Pye-Smith
and Chris Rose

Penguin Books

Penguin Books Ltd, Harmondsworth, Middlesex, England
Penguin Books, 40 West 23rd Street, New York, New York 10010, U.S.A.
Penguin Books Australia Ltd, Ringwood, Victoria, Australia
Penguin Books Canada Ltd, 2801 John Street, Markham, Ontario, Canada L3R 1B4
Penguin Books (N.Z.) Ltd, 182–190 Wairau Road, Auckland 10, New Zealand

First published 1984
Copyright © Charlie Pye-Smith and Chris Rose, 1984
All rights reserved
Made and printed in Great Britain by
Richard Clay (The Chaucer Press) Ltd,
Bungay, Suffolk
Filmset in Monophoto Baskerville by Northumberland Press Ltd, Gateshead

Contents

Maps

List of Abbreviations

ADAS	Agricultural Development and Advisory Service
AONB	Area of Outstanding Natural Beauty
BANC	British Association of Nature Conservationists
BASC	British Association for Shooting and Conservation
BES	British Ecological Society
BTCV	British Trust for Conservation Volunteers
BTO	British Trust for Ornithology
CAP	Common Agricultural Policy
CAS	Centre for Agricultural Strategy
CLA	Country Landowners' Association
CoEnCo	Council for Environmental Conservation
ConSoc	The Conservation Society
CPRE	Council for the Protection of Rural England
CRC	Countryside Review Committee
DoE	Department of the Environment
DoT	Department of Transport
EEB	European Environment Bureau
ENDS	Environmental Data Services
FNR	Forest Nature Reserve
FoE	Friends of the Earth
FWAG	Farming and Wildlife Advisory Group
IDB	Internal Drainage Board
ITE	Institute of Terrestrial Ecology
IUCN	International Union for the Conservation of Nature and Natural Resources
LDC	Land Decade Council
LNR	Local Nature Reserve
MAFF	Ministry of Agriculture, Fisheries and Food
MNR	Marine Nature Reserve
NCC	Nature Conservancy Council
NFU	National Farmers' Union
NNR	National Nature Reserve

NRA   Nature Reserve Agreement
NWC   National Water Council
PI   Public Inquiry
RLDC   Regional Land Drainage Committee
RSNC   Royal Society for Nature Conservation
SDD   Scottish Development Department
SERA   Socialist Environment Resources Association
SPNR   Society for Promotion of Nature Reserves
SSSI   Site of Special Scientific Interest
WWF   World Wildlife Fund

Acknowledgements

Of the many people who have given us valuable information and advice we would particularly like to thank Philip Lowe of the Bartlett School of Planning, University College, London, and Richard North. Philip Lowe read parts of Chapter 3 when in manuscript form and pointed to various inconsistencies and errors. Throughout the writing of this book Richard North has given us considerable encouragement and help and we owe him our special thanks.

While those who the world trusted as its leaders were pinning their faith and their credibility to their naive apprenticeship to none other than the sorcerer's apprentice himself – high technology – we despised environmentalists were busy getting ready for the day when it would all end in tears. That day has now unhappily arrived ...

MAX NICHOLSON, 1979

Conservation is not worth having if it merely shifts hardships from rich to poor, or from later to now. Growth is not worth having if it merely speeds up the rate at which the rich can guzzle resources which the poor need both now and later. Most questions about whether or not to save or use resources (growth questions, conservationists' questions) are really about who should use the resources. They are like any other questions of distributive justice.

HUGH STRETTON, 1976

One

Introduction

Britain's countryside has survived ice ages, wars, plagues, famines and the vagaries of one of the world's most unpredictable climates. It has accepted the growth of towns and cities and borne the pressures of population to emerge tattered, yet rich and varied. The ages of canals, railways and even motorways have left only minor scars on the landscape. In fact the rich mosaic of habitats and great variety of landscapes are probably unparalleled anywhere else in the world. Or this, at least, was the case until the last few decades.

Today it is more than just a few lesser-known species of insects or obscure plants that are threatened with extinction, and it is something much greater than a little-known view or infrequently trodden path that is being destroyed by the drastic changes which now sweep across Britain's countryside. Indeed we are too late to save the countryside that existed a mere ten years ago. Of the pieces of countryside recognized by the government as being nationally important for conservation more than one in ten is damaged or destroyed each year. The main culprits, as this book shows, are the farming, forestry and water industries and the interest groups which support them.

We preface our discussion of how and why these three industries are destroying so much of our wildlife with a brief historical sketch of Britain's vanishing wildlife and the centuries-old struggle for the rights to use land. We then devote a chapter to the planning system, one of whose purposes is to resolve conflicts between the need to conserve our environment and the necessities of economic development. In particular we point to the inadequacies of British planning law and the impotence of planners which results from farming and forestry activities being exempt from any form of controls.

That so much of our flora and fauna has been lost since the last

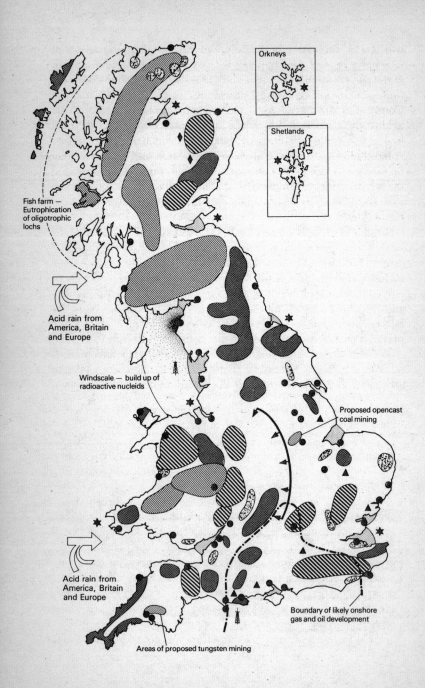

Orkneys

Shetlands

Fish farm —
Eutrophication
of oligotrophic
lochs

Acid rain from
America, Britain
and Europe

Windscale — build up of
radioactive nucleids

Proposed opencast
coal mining

Acid rain from
America, Britain
and Europe

Boundary of likely onshore
gas and oil development

Areas of proposed tungsten mining

war is some indication of the failure of the conservation movement to achieve its aims. In Chapter 4 we look briefly at the development of the conservation movement and discuss why the state's conservation agencies – the Nature Conservancy Council (NCC) and the Countryside Commissions – have been fighting a losing battle against the farmers and foresters. In Chapter 5 we take a detailed look at the wildlife, habitats and landscapes which are under threat. A handful of species have already disappeared and hundreds may be extinct by the end of this century if the present onslaught on the countryside continues. In the final chapter we offer some solutions which, we believe, may help to save the countryside from further destruction.

Throughout the book we refer to the many organizations involved in the British conservation movement. Rather than describing the origins and aims of each within the main body of the text we have included short profiles of the most important groups in Appendix 3. Appendix 2 consists of a short essay on how to start a pressure group, and Appendix 4 covers all the designations – for example, National Parks, Nature Reserves, Heritage Coasts and so on – which have played a part in the battle to save the British countryside.

We are writing at a time when the conservation movement is in a state of some confusion. Until recently many conservation groups expended much of their energy on fighting for their own

Map 1 Threatened Britain. This map shows some of the major threats to Britain's countryside and wildlife that will probably arise within the next ten or twenty years. It is based on current trends and takes no account of any adverse new technologies or land-uses. Areas left blank are largely those in which no significant tracts of habitats survive.

★ Most probable areas of major oil pollution

Threatened wetlands

Major remaining areas threatened with agricultural intensification

▲ Major areas of remaining threatened heathland

Areas most threatened by expansion of conifer plantations

Main areas where semi-natural woodland will probably be converted to plantations

◆ Proposed Cairngorm ski development

◀ Westward spread of hedgerow destruction

Threatened estuary of international ornithological significance

● Possible nuclear power sites

Likely offshore new gas/oil development

survival, trying to raise membership to keep afloat, while battling against organizations and individuals infinitely more powerful than themselves. Over the last ten years, however, conservation has attracted massive support and public sympathy. Over 3 million people in Britain are paid-up members of conservation groups and there is widespread sympathy for the general aims of conservation. But despite the burgeoning environmental movement many of its participants are experiencing deep frustration, having realized that winning public support and building large memberships have done practically nothing to stem the destruction of wildlife and the countryside.

If the conservation movement is to succeed it must enter a new phase of development. It must address itself to the practical issues which affect everybody's daily lives, something which it has studiously avoided doing in the past. It is for this reason that we highlight the importance for conservation of property rights and advocate radical reforms not only in the way land is used but by whom it should and could be used. And it is for this reason that we stress the benefits for employment which could follow from land reforms.

Our experiences in conservation have convinced us that the movement will not flourish in the 1980s and beyond unless it first comes to terms with some very basic political problems. The effective conservation of the countryside demands dramatic changes in the workings of the farming, forestry and water businesses in particular. The changes will be vigorously opposed by the powerful vested interests which use land as a means to realizing purely financial goals. The countryside is now a battle ground for chemical companies who wish to see it dosed with their particular brands of chemical, and for multinational corporations, pension funds and other city institutions which demand fixed rates of return on farming and forestry for investment purposes. Individual farmers and farm managers are now technocrats running outdoor and indoor food factories: the rural idyll is dead. The National Farmers' Union (NFU) advises the Ministry of Agriculture on acceptable levels of subsidies and grant aid to farmers, while the Forestry Commission provides public money and tax incentives for landowners to convert ancient woodland into monotonous plantations of Christmas trees and other fast-growing softwoods. The 'countryside' has become almost irrelevant to the industrial techniques of food and timber production, except perhaps for advertising the final product.

What is so sad is that many conservationists, and particularly those in the greatest positions of influence, have persistently clung to the belief that farming and conservation share the same interests, aims and objectives, and that conservation cannot succeed except by persuading landowners and land-users to set aside small patches of land for wildlife. While the conservationists have pursued this softly-softly approach of 'consensus, cooperation and compromise' (a formula cooked up by civil servants; see p. 73), the landowning interests have done just the opposite. They have pressed ahead with bigger and more profitable schemes. They have drained great tracts of marsh, replaced woodlands which have survived since Norman times with prairies of wheat and barley, flooded whole valleys with water for which tomorrow we shall have no use, and ploughed up some of our finest heaths and downs. The lobbies responsible for this state of affairs have carried on a successful propaganda war with the conservation movement. Meanwhile the NCC, the Countryside Commissions and the County Naturalists' Trusts are dominated by people who are themselves farmers, foresters and landowners.

Conservation raises some very basic questions about the rights of people to use or abuse the land they own. We start from the premise that wildlife and nature are part of our common heritage: we all have a vested interest in the survival of the countryside. To be a predominant force in the way we all lead our lives conservation will have to argue its value in both social and economic terms. There is little point, after all, in cleaning up our polluted rivers and saving our woods and estuaries if only a few have the means to enjoy them. Not long ago conservationists were widely regarded as a bunch of harmless eccentrics. Today they are part of a social movement which derives its support from all sectors of society. Conservation, like this book, is as much about people as about the wildlife and landscape which surround them.

Vanishing Wildlife: A Brief Panorama

Ten thousand years ago the last of the glaciers which at one time had covered the whole of Britain began their final retreat towards the Arctic. As the ice melted, plants colonized the sand and clay left in their wake. Our present wildlife is an inheritance from those early centuries after the Ice Age. The first forest clearances were carried out by Neolithic man, and since then the landscape has undergone continuous transformations. However it has only been in the present century that man has had a truly catastrophic impact on flora and fauna.

Despite the scale of forest clearance, many species of the original natural forests survived man's ways of farming and woodmanship right up to the twentieth century. But now intensive agriculture and industrialization are reducing this large and ancient company of survivors to a precious few. Though only one species has been totally lost in recent years, an increasing number are at risk. The large blue butterfly became extinct in 1979 after a long and slow decline due to changes in its habitat (see p. 94). During the next few years we shall probably have to write obituaries for many more species, and among the butterflies these may include the high brown fritillary, the silver spotted skipper, the glanville fritillary and the heath fritillary.

The larger beasts were hunted to extinction long ago. The harmless beaver was exterminated as early as the twelfth century, while the last wild bear had disappeared several hundred years before. The now totally extinct cattle of Europe, the mysterious aurochs, had certainly vanished by the Middle Ages, and the wild boar finally became extinct in Britain during the eighteenth century. The last wolf in the British Isles was killed in Ireland around 1786.

These animals were beasts of the primeval forests, fens and marshes that were felled and drained to form the intimate British countryside. Several writers have labelled this lost natural forest the 'wildwood'. While none of it remains intact, many small woods and deer parks are its direct descendants, leaving us with a ghostly and fragmented image of primeval flora and fauna in the form of 'ancient woodlands'. These woods are among the most prized and threatened habitats left in Britain. Those species which inhabited the forest glades and the clearings resulting from natural landslides, or which clung to river banks and colonized areas blasted by lightning, found a new home in meadows and grasslands created by pastoral man. Along with plants and animals from cliffs and sand dunes they have formed the characteristic communities of meadows and downland. Even these habitats are now disappearing at an alarming rate as a result of modern farming techniques (see p. 93). However, many species from the wildwood can only survive within continuous woodland cover. Incapable of migrating into more open habitats, their fate depends entirely on the survival of ancient woodlands.

With a pedigree that goes back to the Ice Age, ancient woodlands are much more than just collections of plants and animals. They are living records of past events, both social and natural. Before iron and steel became widely available for the manufacture of domestic, agricultural and industrial implements, the woods were the economic mainstay of towns and villages. They were cropped to make everything from broomsticks and beanpoles to spoons and water-pipes, and larger timber was taken for industry and the building of houses, ships and workshops. The woods provided medicinal herbs and harboured game. Villagers used them to graze cattle and pigs and the harvest of nuts and fruit was a valuable addition to the rural economy.

Many of our place names, our crafts and traditions, and even surnames and figures of speech, are those of a nation whose history has been one of continuous woodmanship – continuous, that is, until the twentieth century. When modern agriculture or forestry eliminates a remnant of the wildwood it removes not just the descendants of the primeval flora and fauna but an irreplaceable organic record of people's lives and their work. Moors and heaths, chalk downland and old meadows can hold similar secrets, but none is so rich and so completely impossible to re-create as ancient woodland.

Most of our towns and villages and some of our woods can be recognized from the 1086 survey of the Domesday Book. Some individual woods may have been continuously managed since the Roman Conquest and many more since Saxon times. The Norman Domesday survey shows Huntingdonshire, a fairly typical county of the fertile English lowlands, to have had about 7 per cent woodland cover, made up of the 'waste' (the wildwood) and defined areas of woodpasture or coppice (see p. 78). Thus much of the wildwood had already been lost but the pattern of woodland change was very slow until this century. The Board of Agriculture Survey of 1905 found that about 5 per cent of England was still covered in woodland (nearly all of it ancient), representing very little change in nearly a millennium. Despite great changes in Britain's social and economic development, an astonishing wealth of such ancient countryside remained right up to the Second World War. Since then the losses have been enormous.

Between 1946 and 1975, 42 per cent of the Northamptonshire

tract of ancient woodland known as Rockingham Forest was grubbed up to make way for arable crops, conifer plantations and mineral extraction. During the same period Lincolnshire lost 46 per cent and Cambridgeshire 36 per cent of their ancient forest, while almost half was lost in Suffolk. Dr Derek Ratcliffe, the NCC's Chief Scientist, wrote in evidence to the Select Committee of the House of Lords on Forestry in 1980 that 'the material demands of society are likely to eliminate the rest of such woodlands outside nature reserves or other specially protected areas by the year 2025'.

What has survived man's use for centuries is now being swept away in a few decades. For many, this loss represents more than just the decline of a natural asset. 'It is an uncanny experience,' wrote the Cambridge woodland ecologist Oliver Rackham, 'to trace an identifiable wood or hedge through five or seven centuries, and on going to the spot to be just in time for the dying embers of the bonfires in which it has been destroyed.' Most such losses result from the fact that landowners stand to make more money from converting their woods to cornfields (with generous government subsidies) or to conifer plantations (again with subsidies and tax concessions; see p. 42).

When Dr David Goode and Angela King began to release the findings of an NCC survey on habitat loss in 1980, conservationists were shocked to find that not just 4 per cent of Britain's 3,000-plus Sites of Special Scientific Interest (SSSIs, the key conservation areas) were suffering serious damage or being completely destroyed each year, as had previously been suspected. The figure was actually nearer 12 per cent, and in Dorset a third of such sites had been damaged or destroyed in the twelve months previous to the survey. Building and urban sprawl, for so long the bogeymen of conservation and farming lobbies, accounted for almost none of the losses. In fact, in urban areas planners could be relied on to safeguard nearly all SSSIs. The culprits were almost always modern agriculture and forestry, two activities which until recently had been seen as wholly compatible with conservation.

In south-east Scotland, 88 per cent of the lowland heaths were destroyed between 1960 and 1980. In Wales, the Powys Assistant Regional Officer of the NCC found that the whole stock of semi-natural vegetation – the habitats ranging from riverside marshes to woods and unsown grassland – was being eroded at such a rate that by the end of the century only half of that present in 1971 is likely to remain.

In Dorset 32 per cent of the SSSIs were damaged or destroyed in a single year, including many of Thomas Hardy's celebrated heaths. By 1980 the delicate feather mosses and peat bogs of Lancashire had been reduced to less than 1 per cent of their 1865 extent. Between 1937 and 1971, 47 per cent of Wiltshire's rolling chalk downland, the richest of all open habitats for flowers, was ploughed up, mostly to grow cereals, often with massive aid from the tax-payer. Indeed, since 1971, twenty-nine of the remaining fifty downland wildlife sites in Wiltshire have been so seriously damaged, for example by fertilizers and pesticides, that they will never recover their characteristic species.

On the windswept marshes of the coastal estuaries losses of salt-marsh and intertidal feeding grounds for waders have been comparable. A survey by the Royal Society for the Protection of Birds (RSPB) in early 1982 revealed that 32 per cent of the grazing marshland of the North Kent Marshes had been converted to arable since 1969.

With these drastic habitat losses (described in greater detail in Chapter 5) individual species inevitably suffer too. For example, the beautiful snake's-head fritillary is a plant of damp alluvial meadows, and is disappearing at a rate of 8 per cent a year. During the fifty years up to 1980 its known range was reduced from 116 sites to a mere seventeen. Hundreds of other once-common species have similarly become rarities as their habitats have been destroyed in recent years (see, again, Chapter 5).

A great number of Britain's plants and animals are to be found on the continent. Their extinction in this country, it is sometimes foolishly suggested, is of little importance. It is only a short step from that argument to the assumption that we have little, if anything, of international significance to conserve. But that is not the case. While they have close relatives abroad, many British species are now distinct races after many generations of independent evolution, and the communities in which they live are quite unique in themselves. Furthermore, agricultural change is threatening them just as much in Germany, France or Spain as it is here. Writing in a paper submitted to the Great Britain Nature Conservation Strategy Working Group in 1982, the NCC's Chief Adviser, Professor Norman Moore, remarked of Britain's wildlife:

From the world point of view its outstanding features are:

(a) the humid deciduous woods of the west with their exceptionally rich bryophyte flora;
(b) the wide range and extent of heathlands – several types are confined to the British Isles;
(c) the immense variety of habitats in a relatively small area due to an unusual range of geological formations and of climate. As a result Britain supports both arctic-boreal species and mediterranean/lusitanian ones;
(d) the relative mildness of its winters makes Britain a particularly important wintering area for many bird species of the far north ... Finally, the main range of a number of important species is centred on Britain, e.g. bell heather, bluebells, grey seals and gannet.

Yet all of these habitats, and virtually every species that depends upon them, are under great threat.

Agriculture, as modern farming's apologists are fond of saying, was largely responsible for creating the countryside. That is quite true. It was a slow process that took over 2,000 years. Many species found ways to live within man's landscape and many were actively encouraged. But modern agricultural and forestry techniques are changing so fast that the majority of these survivors could be wiped out unless we act now. The changes wrought in the countryside during the last thirty years have been so rapid that many people have failed to grasp their true dimensions. The farmers and foresters are a tiny minority (0·02 per cent) of the British people, yet in their quest to turn the countryside into a food and timber factory they have been aided and abetted by successive governments which have been loath to impose any sanctions on their destructive activities.

Locking Up the Common Ground

The struggle between the landless and the landed goes back over 1,000 years to the time when common lands, as their name implies, were common property. The campaigns and concerns of environmental groups today should be seen in the context of the centuries-old conflict over land rights, not least because the demands of landscape and wildlife conservation and the future solution of environmental problems call for radical changes in the present use of land in Britain.

The philosopher Bertrand Russell observed that twentieth-century attitudes to landownership in Britain occupy in the public mind a place similar to the unquestioning acceptance by the people of the Divine Right of Kings before 1653. Since the Second World War the belief that the fate of rural land should be determined by market forces and the whims of those who own it has been reinforced by governments which have left agriculture and forestry outside the framework of democratic planning controls. This is in sharp contrast to the property rights of town-dwellers. To add a garage to a house the owner must apply for and obtain planning permission from the elected local authority. But to plough up 100 acres of ancient pasture or oak forest the landowner requires no permission. The only real sanction over his activities is his conscience.

Bemoaning the enclosure of a Northumberland common in the 1820s, the engraver Thomas Bewick termed it 'the poor man's heritage in ages past'. In fact it might have been more accurate to say it was all that remained of his heritage, because by the nineteenth century almost all land had been fenced off and made private. As the landscape historian W. G. Hoskins has observed, common rights 'probably antedate the idea of private property and are therefore of great antiquity'. Indeed, even at the time of the Domesday survey in 1086, when the manorial system was already well established, the lords' claims to 'private' land were far from secure.

Commoners' rights included access to more or less everything a family needed and which was available from the wildwood or 'waste'. Most important was the right of pasturage for sheep, goats, cattle, horses or geese. Acorns and beechmast were consumed by commoners' pigs (the right of pannage), while on peaty ground commoners could cut turf for fuel or roofing (the right of turbary). The rights to collect firewood were also attached to most common land (the right of estovers). The commoners' rights to use land maintained the strong social contract between man and the land, thus more than just access to open space was lost when the British countryside was enclosed. Today a mere 1½ million acres of common land remain in England and Wales.

The enclosure process began gradually, although four-fifths of our ancient commons had been enclosed before the famous Enclosure Acts of the eighteenth and nineteenth centuries. All medieval manors employed a 'woodward' whose job it was to safeguard the 'spring' (young trees in the wildwood) from the depredations of the commoners. In addition, the 'hayward' tried to protect the common hay crop until the time when it could most profitably be harvested. The grazing of commoners' animals also conflicted with the objectives of woodland management as perceived by the nobility, and in 1483 Edward IV passed a statute authorizing the enclosure of woods for seven years after cutting (coppicing), 'with sufficient hedges able to keep all manner of Beasts and other cattle out of the same ground for the Preservation of their young spring'.

Although they retained some of their rights, this statute signalled the beginning of the end for the commoners' system. It enabled the manorial lords to organize trade of wood and timber with the nearest cathedral towns and cities. During the following centuries, and well before the process was finally legitimized in the Parliamentary Enclosure Acts, the rural economy changed from one based upon the exchange of goods and services to one based on money and the private ownership of land.

By the time of the Civil War (1642–50) half of England's agricultural land had been enclosed and the dispossessed peasants were forced to sell their labour rather than their produce to the rising class of tenant farmer. The few attempts by the peasants to regain their land were mercilessly put down and all failed. Meanwhile, many commoners' rights – for instance to coppice woodland – fell into neglect. By the nineteenth century the local squires or lords of the manor were assuming ownership and auctioning plots of coppice to the highest bidder.

During the eighteenth and nineteenth centuries 4,000 Parliamentary Enclosure Acts affected a further 6 million acres of land. They were inspired by the Agrarian Revolution which began around 1750. The principal justification for enclosing and improving the commons was economic: they could be farmed more productively. Reporters of the Board of Agriculture, sent round the country to study the state of the commons in the 1790s and early 1800s, were unanimous in their condemnation of the management of the lowland commons. They saw them as overstocked and in need of 'improvement'.[1] This was just what the politically dominant landowners wanted to hear; the report ignored all social considerations apart from their own. The increase in agricultural productivity was of no benefit to the farm worker of the nineteenth century. By the 1830s over 300,000 people from the 686,000 families of agricultural workers were on poor relief. Many of those employed by the landowners were little better off.

At the same time people were leaving the land for the cities. At the beginning of the last century, a third of all British workers were employed on the land. By 1850 this figure had dropped to a fifth; by 1900 to a tenth. The rapid growth of the industrial working class was a result of a burgeoning population and the migration of the landless and workless farm labourers to the centres of industrial expansion.

The struggle for land rights was taken up by the inhabitants of the growing industrial towns. 'It is an historic irony,' wrote E. P. Thompson in *The Making of the English Working Class*, 'that it was not the rural labourers but the urban workers who mounted the greatest coherent national agitation for the return to the land ... Faced with hard times and unemployment in the brick wastes of the growing towns, the memories of lost rights rose up with a new bitterness of deprivation.' A massive return to the land never materialized but many people tried to escape from the miseries of the industrial towns by taking to the countryside for recreation. For the last 150 years people have campaigned for the right of access to uncultivated land. The demands for access to land outside the cities contributed to a growing interest in natural history and thus the rise of the landscape and nature conservation movements.

By 1850, half the remaining lowland commons in England were to be found within fifty miles of London. In 1773 the Report of the Revenue Commission found that the commons of Epping Forest amounted to some 9,000 acres and were extensively used by Londoners. Despite a recommendation by the Commission that the area should remain open, some 2,000 acres were taken into private ownership in the fifty years that followed and by 1867 the Forest was reduced to its present size of 6,000 acres. In 1865 and 1866 the Lord of the Manor of Loughton enclosed over 1,000 acres at one fell swoop, leaving a mere 9 acres for the recreation of villagers. There the matter might have rested had it not been for three members of the Willingale family. Having witnessed the enclosure of the Forest and the felling of trees, the family determined to exercise the commoners' ancient rights. Led by Thomas Willingale, a Loughton labourer, the family proceeded to lop the hornbeam pollards for firewood. The Willingales were arrested and sentenced to three months' hard labour but their case was taken up by the Commons Preservation Society, which had been formed in the previous year to act as a pressure group to fight for commoners' rights. After protracted wrangling, during which Father Willingale expired, an injunction was granted in 1874 to stop the enclosures. The lords of the Forest were ordered to remove all fences erected after 1851, but persistently refused to do so. In 1879 5,000 people turned up in Epping to protest by exercising their right to lop trees. Two years later Queen Victoria was compelled to declare the Forest open to the public 'without let or hindrance'.

The Commons Preservation Society also played a key role in saving Hampstead Heath from development. Among the Society's more eminent members were the architect Robert Hunter, who became its Secretary, and the philosopher John Stuart Mill. Thirty years after the Commons Preservation Society was founded, Hunter joined with the reformer Octavia Hill and the Lake District vicar Hardwicke Rawnsley to form an organization which could own land as well as campaign. This was the National Trust, which is today the largest landowner in England after the Crown and the Church. The early activists of the Trust included William Morris, the anarchist craftsman, John Ruskin, a philosopher of the Romantic Movement, and Thomas Huxley, the eminent biologist and champion of Charles Darwin. By now it was clear that in the Home Counties the fight to save the commons had shifted from the dispossessed labourers to well-organized groups of middle-class urbanites.

However, the most famous access battles were fought around the industrial towns of northern England and southern Scotland. 'Every weaving district,' wrote E. P. Thompson, 'had its weaver poets, biologists, mathematicians, musicians, geologists, botanists.' Such self-educated workers formed the rambling clubs in the north, and they were closely linked to the early trade union, cooperative and labour movements. Once again the battle for access centred on the commons, which in the north lay mostly on the moors and mountains. The landowners of the Peaks, the Pennines and the North York Moors zealously kept people off their grouse moors and fought the urban ramblers as vigorously as their ancestors had evicted the rural peasantry.

Despite much establishment opposition, the access movement steadily gained credibility and influence. From 1884 onwards a succession of Access Bills were put before Parliament, although it was not until just before the Second World War that one succeeded, and even that was a very poor affair. The *Manchester Guardian* of

21 April 1925 summed up the widespread liberal revulsion at the intransigence of landowners and apathy of the government:

> There is something wantonly perverse and profane in a society in which the rights of property can be used to defeat the emotions in which mankind has found his chief inspiration and comfort. If ever any truth lurked in the phrase 'the rights of man' those rights should surely include the right to climb the mountains, and the right to dream beside the sea.

Impatient with the access lobby's lack of success, Bernard Rothman, an unemployed mechanic from Manchester, gathered together friends from the British Workers Sports Federation to organize a mass trespass in April 1932. Five hundred people walked past the stick-wielding police and gamekeepers on to the forbidden heights of Kinder Scout in the Peak District. The six ringleaders were arrested and charged with 'riotously assembling to disturb the public'. One was acquitted but the rest received a total of seventeen months' imprisonment. Howard Hill recalls in *Freedom to Roam* that the police evidence 'was calculated to play on the political prejudices of the jury, which was made up of two Brigadier-Generals, three Colonels, two Majors, three Captains, two Aldermen, all country gentlemen'.

In 1949 Parliament passed the National Parks and Access to the Countryside Act, which established the forerunners of the Nature Conservancy Council and the Countryside Commission and laid down legislation for the creation of National Parks and National Nature Reserves. According to the Labour government it was 'a comprehensive charter of rights for all lovers of the open air'. However, Lewis Silkin, whose responsibility it was to steer the Bill through Parliament, had made significant concessions to the landowners. In 1981 the Wildlife and Countryside Act became law and again the landowners triumphed (see pp. 200–202). Reflecting on the findings of the 1878 survey of landownership, which revealed that over four-fifths of Britain was owned by just 7,000 men, the sociologist Howard Newby wrote that 'landownership not only represented a major source of wealth but was also virtually [an indispensable condition] of political power and prestige'. Although the power of the landowner has waned it is still remarkably evident in the Houses of Parliament. Over three-quarters of the members of Mrs Thatcher's 1981 Cabinet were owners of rural land.

'Holding the line', 'turning the tide', 'stemming the flow': these are the sort of expressions frequently used both to suggest the gravity of the plight of wildlife and landscape, and to hold out some hope of imminent improvement.

As the reader will have realized by now, this is a gloomy book. After the privatization of the heritage, and then its dismemberment, what is the conservation movement achieving? Environmentalists continue to press for reform through legislation – to rein in the excesses of private landowners – but they have also resorted to private landholding themselves. The details of the conservation estate – from the tiny army of County Naturalists' Trust reserves, often no larger than a copse or single field, to National Nature Reserves and National Parks – are given in Appendix 4. But of the third or more of Britain's land surface which is not beyond redemption for conservation purposes, the government and non-government agencies have managed to give permanent protection to only around 1 per cent, with about 5 per cent having some nominal protection. Drastic reform – or revolutionary change – is therefore clearly needed if the agents of destruction are not to outstrip the work of conservation agencies in the race for the final acres.

Two

Agents of Destruction:
The Farming, Forestry and
Water Industries

There is no room in this book to detail the losses of species, habitats and countryside which can be specifically laid at the door of such industries as those involved in the development of nuclear power, in the oil industry and in transport development. All have, from time to time, caused environmental problems of great severity. In this chapter we have taken the three main industries which are virtually entirely dependent on the countryside and which are posing the greatest threats to wildlife and countryside. Each industry is guided by massive bureaucracies whose main purpose is to promote a continual increase in the supply of their products, apparently without regard to whether or not we need them, and despite the environmental and social problems which their never-ending expansion has engendered.

Agriculture out of Control

Excluding nuclear war or monumental Acts of God, modern intensive agricultural practices will continue to be the most immediate and significant threat to wildlife and landscape in Britain. Farming today is big business. The farmer is no longer the fence-gazing rustic, if indeed he ever was; he is a capitalist whose practices are determined by the markets of the big cities. Since the last war successive governments have poured money into boosting agricultural productivity, with the ostensible aim of making Britain self-sufficient in temperate food products. The resulting intensification, particularly in the lowlands, has had a major impact on both rural communities and our wildlife.

The agricultural revolution which now transforms rural Britain had its roots in the dark days of the last war when the German

U-boat blockade prevented shipments of foreign food from reaching our shores. Agriculture had been in a state of decline since midway through the last century and by 1939 we were importing over two-thirds of our food, most coming in cheaply from the Empire.

In 1942 the Committee on Land Utilization in Rural Areas (in the Scott Report) laid down policies which were to guide future agricultural expansion. The Committee considered future needs of countryside conservation and saw no inevitable conflict between farming and other interests: 'The beauty and pattern of the country-side are a direct result of the cultivation of the soil and there is no antagonism between use and beauty.' The central recommenda-tion of the Scott Report was that Britain should aim towards self-sufficiency. The latest major government policy statements, *Food from Our Own Resources* (1975) and *Farming and the Nation* (1979), did little more than reiterate the philosophy of the Scott Report. Britain would continue to expand production at a rate of $2\frac{1}{2}$ per cent a year (it is a mystery why the government hit on this figure rather than, say, 2 or 3 per cent). No account was taken of the fact that the EEC, of which we are a member, is collectively self-sufficient in virtually every temperate food product.

The Scott Report was an inspired blueprint for feeding the nation, and members of the Committee can be forgiven for failing to fore-see the bitter clashes which were to arise between farming and con-servation over the next four decades. Such charity, however, cannot be extended to the civil servants who drew up the latest policy state-ments: agricultural developments in the 1960s and 1970s had left much of southern and eastern Britain assuming the monotony of a Canadian prairie, yet the Ministry of Agriculture, Fisheries and Food (MAFF) chose to ignore all pleas for agricultural reform.

So why have successive governments been so reluctant to recognize the detrimental impacts of recent agricultural intensifica-tion on the countryside? And why have they chosen to press for further expansion, despite our being party to the Common Agri-cultural Policy (CAP), and with total disregard for existing sur-pluses? The answer lies partly in what the agricultural economist Professor Gerald Wibberley calls the 'dangerous philosophy of agri-cultural fundamentalism'. This he defines as 'an uncritical accep-tance of the activities and methods of those who hold agricultural land [and] a belief that the countryside is dominated by people and groups who inherently conserve rural land in the long-term interests of society'. The agricultural lobby has a uniquely powerful sway within government and cabinet (see p. 22) and the urban population, physically alienated from the countryside, tends to assume that 'farmers know best'. Thus the agricultural industry has been able, with the minimum of public scrutiny, to increase productivity and profitability regardless of economic and strategic needs and the environmental and social costs.

Agriculture is almost entirely exempt from planning controls, with a consequent lack of constraint over what landowners can do to their land. Recent calls by conservationists for some form of planning controls have been powerfully resisted by MAFF and the two most powerful farmers' pressure groups, the NFU and the Country Landowners' Association (CLA). Although these groups have so far successfully resisted attempts to introduce planning controls there is some indication that farming interests now recognize that some agricultural activities are damaging to wildlife and landscapes. The NFU and the CLA jointly produced with the NCC and the Countryside Commission a leaflet entitled *Caring for the Countryside* (1977), though cynics may be forgiven for interpreting this as no more than a token gesture. In 1978 the Advisory Council for Agriculture and Horticulture in England and Wales recognized that there was 'a widespread feeling that agriculture can no longer be accounted the prime architect of conservation nor farmers accepted as natural custodians of the countryside'. The report recommended that the 5,800 members of MAFF's Agricultural Development and Advisory Service (ADAS) should widen their role to give advice to farmers on conservation matters as well as food production. Subsequently the Conservatives cut the service and there is little chance of it taking on this additional role.

Productivity and Fuel

The Countryside Review Committee, in a recent discussion paper, *Food Production in the Countryside* (1978), expresses the health of the agricultural industry thus: 'The productivity record is impressive. Since the mid-1950s, at constant prices, there has been an increase of 75 per cent in the agricultural gross product with a work force reduced by 50 per cent. Total labour productivity has nearly quadrupled over the period.'

Eighty per cent of the British land surface is farmed by less than 3 per cent of the civil work force (compared to an average of 8 per cent for the rest of the EEC) and the increase in productivity since the war – we are now 75 per cent self-sufficient in temperate foods – has been accompanied by a dramatic reduction in the labour force.

Between 1939 and 1970 the agricultural labour force fell from around a million to 300,000. The numbers working in agriculture have continued to fall each year. In May 1982 just under 50,000 unemployed agricultural workers were competing for less than a hundred job vacancies. In 1982 the number of farmers was estimated to be 205,000, of whom just over half could be counted as full-time farmers making a significant contribution to agricultural output.

At first sight the industry's productivity record is impressive. However, the figures do not include the social, environmental or energy costs.[1] The industry has become an exceedingly poor employer at a time when over 3 million are unemployed in Britain. Farm workers have either been squeezed out by the machine or they have left in search of higher wages in industry (earnings of farm workers – a highly skilled group of people – are still approximately 30 per cent below the average in industry). Furthermore, many small farmers have been forced to sell their land as government policies favour large holdings.

The energy costs of modern agriculture are also considerable. While farming in Britain consumes 4 per cent of our fuel, food production (including processing, packaging and associated transport) consumes a hefty 13 per cent. Yields per man and per acre have rocketed with the introduction of modern fertilizers and pesticides (most of which are oil-based), but the energy costs of intensive agriculture now exceed the energy value of the food produced, prompting one ecologist to remark that we no longer eat potatoes made from solar energy, but from oil. Sir Kenneth Blaxter, director of the Rowett Research Institute, told the Oxford Farming Conference in 1978: 'Our present farming methods have developed because oil has been cheap. Farmers have been quick to realize the large marginal returns which have accrued from increased investment in mechanization, fertilizers and agro-chemicals. The question is how such increases in costs can be offset in the future if, as oil runs out, all energy sources become more expensive.' In view of the warnings of Blaxter and many others the Ministry of Agriculture has been remarkably complacent about the industry's over-reliance on high fuel inputs. With over a quarter of farmers' incomes now going on paying interest on bank loans this aspect of farm expenditure will become increasingly significant.

Public Money: Private Profits

Productivity is also boosted by large injections of public money by the government and the EEC. In *Agriculture: The Triumph and the Shame*, Richard Body, the Conservative MP for Holland with Boston, estimates the overall public expenditure on agriculture to be of the order of £3,350 million per year, which works out at around £13,000 per farmer. (It is, perhaps, invidious to give an average per farmer as many farmers, particularly those with small holdings on poor land, hardly benefit at all from this public money.) Where the food production is added to a surplus, or prices are held down to boost consumption, we are not farming in order to eat but to benefit the farmer. Increased production also means eliminating rough grazing, hedgerows and wildlife habitats from existing farmland, and expanding in marginal areas to bring new land into production.

Before Britain joined the EEC, the government used a system of negative controls and positive inducements in order to encourage increased output. These could include, for example, quotas on the acreage a farmer could allocate to certain crops, price support systems for particular products, and direct grants for, say, draining meadows and grubbing up hedgerows. Since entering the EEC Britain has switched to its system of intervention prices. Once the open market price for a product falls below the determined intervention price, the EEC has to buy off all produce offered to it at that price. Inevitably this has encouraged over-production and led to the infamous wine-lakes, butter-mountains and so forth. The Common Market countries now produce surpluses of sugar, poultry meat, dairy products, barley, wheat and wine; 70 per cent of the EEC budget now goes on the Common Agricultural Policy expenditure, and much of this goes on dealing with surpluses. The European Agricultural Guidance and Guarantee Fund (FEOGA) was estimated to be over £9,000 million in April 1983 for the following year. By July it was realized that this was an underestimate and another £1,090 million was added to this huge cost.

Power and Influence

Of course the grant and price structure of farming could be adjusted to encourage farmers to produce less of those foodstuffs which are in surplus, and to conserve the countryside. The fact that it does not is due to the influence of the farming lobby within government. Few other sections of the community, comparable in terms of the number of individuals involved, exercise as much power over government decision-making as do farmers and landowners. Many are in positions of power themselves, and the implications of such influence for the resolution of land-use conflicts are profound.

On entry into the House of Commons all MPs must declare their business interests. The one glaring anomaly is that the ownership of land or farming interests are exempt. This gives some indication of the House's privileged attitudes towards the farmer. The proportion of farming MPs is large, especially when one remembers that less than 1 per cent of the population owns and farms land. Take, for example, 1972: ninety-five MPs, of whom eighty-three were Conservatives, either were or had been landowners or farmers. As previously mentioned, over three-quarters of Mrs Thatcher's 1981 cabinet were landowners, and conservationists are seldom surprised that such a landowner-biased institution is normally more interested in bolstering the farmer's profit margin than in protecting our dwindling wildlife.

The power of the agricultural lobby within Parliament is further emphasized by the existence of a Ministry whose sole function is to look after the farming and fishery industries. Good administration, it can be argued, cannot flow from a government Ministry charged with both promoting and controlling an activity, in this instance farming. Yet that is exactly what happens. The farming lobby may point to the NCC and the Countryside Commissions as the departments charged with exercising controls over agriculture. However, the NCC with a budget of less than £10 million has no control, indeed negligible influence, on farming concerns. Furthermore, farming practices, unlike all other industrial developments, are not subject to any scrutiny under the planning system.

Farmers are well served by both the NFU and the CLA, and MAFF policy is often little more than an official government statement of the desires of the NFU. In addition, Shoard has calculated that one civil servant looks after the needs of twenty-one farmers.

The power of the farming lobby is felt not only in central government but also in local authorities. In 1967 the Maud Committee on Local Government Reform found that farming was the dominant occupation of rural district councillors, with 35 per cent of all rural district council members in England and Wales being farmers. Howard Newby and a team of sociologists at Essex University found that similar patterns of dominance exist in their case study of Suffolk County Council. Farmers comprise just 1·2 per cent of the county's population, yet in 1971 16 per cent of county councillors were farmers.

Technological Farming and its Impacts

The internal combustion engine has liberated the farm worker from the back-breaking tasks once performed with the horse and by hand. The farm worker on an arable farm today spends most of his time working machines. The modest tractors of the 1950s and 1960s are now used mainly for light work on dairy farms and in the uplands, while the lowland plains are cultivated by huge tractors and caterpillar engines. By 1971 Britain had the highest density of tractors in the world, with one for every thirty-six acres of arable land.

All the indications are that farm machinery will continue to change both in size and versatility. John Matthews of the National Institute of Agricultural Engineers has predicted that by the year 2030 the farmer will only see a plough or a combine in a museum. He will cultivate his fields from a cab on a sixty-foot-wide gantry which will till, sow, spray, irrigate and harvest the crops. The stock farmer, according to Matthews, will probably manage his animals with robots. If he is right we can presumably expect the farm worker to become extinct in the near future, in which case the government's standard measure of agricultural success in terms of productivity per man will be even better than it is today!

Disappearing Hedgerows

Bigger and more powerful machines have enabled the farmer to cultivate more land at greater speeds. The unwieldiness of the new machines provides a further inducement to increase the size of fields by ripping out hedgerows and boundary trees.

The plight of Britain's hedgerows is well known and their demise in our lowland landscape has been partly due to encouragement by MAFF to remove them. Until 1972 MAFF gave grant aid of one-quarter to one-third of total costs to farmers who removed hedges. Since 1950 hedge removal added 100,000 ha to arable land. Up to the mid-1960s hedgerows were being removed at a rate of around 8,000 km a year; of this total MAFF, through grant aid, was responsible for the removal of approximately 1,200 km per year. The government support of this destruction inevitably led many farmers to believe that hedgerow removal was an integral part of good farming.

Some counties, particularly those in the south and south-east, were more affected than others. For example in Huntingdonshire field size more than doubled from an average of 7·7 ha to 18 ha between 1945 and 1972. During this period an average 28 m of hedge per ha were removed. By 1972 only 20 per cent of hedgerow trees present in 1945 remained.

As far as the farmer is concerned hedges serve little purpose. They are expensive to maintain as stock barriers and less convenient than post-and-wire or electric fences. They also take up space which could otherwise be put to cultivation. (We discuss their importance as wildlife habitats in Chapter 5.) The effect of hedgerow removal on landscape is all too obvious.

The Chemical Armoury

Pesticides, fungicides and herbicides have helped to revolutionize farming. They have largely released us from the threat of disasters such as the potato blight epidemic which led to the emigration or death by famine of half the population of Ireland in the mid nineteenth century. There is no doubt that chemical pesticides and inorganic fertilizers have enabled farmers to increase crop yields dramatically. In 1952 the average yield per ha for wheat was 2·85 tonnes. By 1982 the figure had risen to 6·4 tonnes, with the British record now standing at 13 tonnes per ha.[2]

Before the last war most lowland farms were mixed and stock manure was used to fertilize the arable fields. Crop rotation also ensured that there was no loss in soil fertility. The trend since the last war has been towards increased specialization, with arable crops being concentrated where they grow best, in a belt down the east of England, and dairy farming predominating in the damper west.

The hills of the north and west are given over mainly to sheep farming. This increase in specialization, with manure being produced where it is often not needed, combined with the availability of cheap (pre-1973 oil crisis) fertilizers, led to massive amounts of inorganic fertilizer being poured on to the land. Between 1953 and 1976 the use of nitrogen-based fertilizers rose eight-fold. Over a million tonnes are annually applied to British farmland, one of the consequences being the elimination of many herbs from low-nutrient soils (see p. 92) as well as the eutrophication of some fresh waters (see p. 104). In 1981 British farmers spent £794 million on fertilizers and lime (but only just over £1,000 million on wages!).

In the last century only a few very crude and often toxic chemicals were available to control crop pests, the most notorious being the extremely dangerous hydrocyanic gas and copper arsenate (Paris green). The safest and most effective pesticides up to the last war were two natural derivatives of plants, Derris and Pyrethrum. These were superseded during the war by the highly effective (and long-lasting) DDT, a complex organochlorine. In 1939 the farmer had sixty-three pesticide products to choose from; by 1980 the number had risen to over 800.

As long ago as 1945 the ecologist Kenneth Mellanby warned that although DDT had low immediate toxicity (comparable to aspirin) it accumulated in the body fat as the metabolite DDE which could have severe physiological, and thus ecological, consequences. Passing through the food chain from a coating on plants to insects, then through to birds and predators, DDT and similar organochlorines proved to have the effects feared by Mellanby. By the time Rachel Carson published *Silent Spring* in 1962 restrictions on the use of DDT were already being considered. As it caused the thinning of egg shells and reduced fertility in birds of prey, DDT led to the extinction of the peregrine falcon over much of the British Isles. Today its population is still reduced by 75 per cent of its pre-DDT level (see p. 100).

Though public pressure forced the government to accept that DDT should be restricted in use and banned as a dressing for wheat seed, concern has been revived by recent revelations that more and more DDT is being employed by horticulturalists. In 1978 Joyce Tait, a researcher with the Open University, found that every one of eighty-four vegetable farmers interviewed in Lincolnshire admitted to using DDT. Overall, 5 per cent more organochlorines were used in the second half of the 1970s than in the first half. Yet in 1969 the government had conceded, in line with the advice of its own Advisory Committee on Pesticides, that the use of organo-chlorines 'should cease as soon as possible'. DDT is just one example of the many dangerous chemicals which became part of the farmers' anti-pest arsenal after the last war.

In Chapter 5 we mention various species and habitats which have suffered as a result of modern chemical farming. In many instances it is the sheer quantity of fertilizer and pesticide applied as much as the nature of the chemicals involved that threatens wildlife. Dr George Cooke, the Chief Research Scientist of the Agricultural Research Council, warned in 1981 that the indiscriminate use of pesticides has led to a build-up of pest resistance which is now the most serious threat to pest control. The Royal Commission on Environmental Pollution has identified at least ten serious pests which have developed resistant strains. With better spraying techniques, according to Cooke, the amount of pesticides used by farmers could be reduced 1,000 times. Another major problem with pesticides is that they kill many more species than those for which they are intended. Though the Royal Commission on Environmental Pollution recommended in 1979 that MAFF should develop more efficient ways of applying pesticides little progress has been made. Farmers spend more than half a billion pounds per year on pesticides; it would benefit them as well as our wildlife were they to take heed of the advice of Dr Cooke and the Royal Commission.

The Improvement of Marginal Lands

Farming at the edge of profitability – on dunes, downs, heath, moor and anywhere else with poor soil and growing conditions – has always been a risky business. In past centuries marginal land was opened up by the plough or intensively grazed, then left to revert to scrub or heath in hard times, only to be reclaimed again when economics favoured expansion. This cycle has now been replaced by a one-way process. The farmer now has the technological ability to reclaim land and artificially maintain, in a fertile state through the use of chemicals, what was formerly poor land. Similarly, modern drainage techniques enable the farmer to drain marshes and keep them drained.

As long ago as 1939 government grants were introduced for the ploughing up of ancient grassland. It was, in the circumstances of war, a sensible and inevitable decision. Apart from the fact that Britain had to produce more food during the war, the number of farm horses had fallen from a recorded maximum of nearly $1\frac{1}{2}$ million just before the First World War to just 650,000. Two million acres of grassland set aside for grazing horses was thus under-utilized.

Today there may be around 25 million acres of grassland (excluding rough grazing) but much is in the form of high-productivity, chemically treated temporary grass leys. They are sown with mono-cultures such as Italian rye grass and are particularly responsive to nitrogenous fertilizers. This grassland is best cut for silage and fed to animals kept indoors in the winter; some farmers now zero-graze their stock, keeping animals indoors throughout the year.

Traditional meadows, the ancient grasslands, can be converted to high-productivity grasslands dominated by just a few species by the use of selective herbicides and the application of fertilizer. This trend, together with the increase in ploughing out ancient grass-lands, has led to the disappearance of floristically rich grass meadows over much of the country. The incentives to improve marginal land are big. At 1978 prices a farmer who enclosed and converted heather moorland in Exmoor National Park for grazing could expect to earn an extra £50 per ha per annum. As a result 20 per cent of moorland on Exmoor has been lost since 1960. For the same reasons the amount of old-fashioned permanent grassland on farms in Piddlehinton in Dorset was halved between 1920 and 1970. This is typical of what is happening throughout Britain.

The acreage of land drained each year in Britain has risen six-fold since 1950. Every year about 250,000 acres are permanently dried out at a cost of £23 million, most of which is tax-payers' money dished out by MAFF. Wetland habitats are now among the most threatened in Britain (see p. 102).

Seventy per cent of all the wetlands in Bedfordshire have been lost this way since 1950. The purpose there, like elsewhere, is to bring more land into production. Large-scale works are eligible for up to 80 per cent grant aid from MAFF, and farmers and Internal Drainage Boards (see p. 38) can claim up to 50 per cent of costs for schemes involving the installation of under-drainage. Conserva-tionists fear that it is over-capitalization (for example idle machinery) rather than rational agricultural policy that often deter-mines whether land is drained. As far as profits are concerned, figures calculated for the Somerset Levels – one of the great conservation areas – show why farmers are keen to drain marshland. A farmer draining the Levels would increase his income by £75 per ha if the land were used for dairy farming, or £100 if it were turned to arable production.

The Urbanization of Farmland: Does it Matter?

Each year the urbanization of farmland takes 15,000 ha of land out of agricultural production. There is an argument – popular in agricultural circles – which ties this loss of farmland into the same equation as the reclamation of marginal lands, the heaths, moors and marshes discussed in the last few pages. Put simply, it is claimed that the loss of productive land around our cities, itself a result of developers being forced out of towns and cities while land within them is allowed to remain derelict and idle, inevitably leads to the destruction of areas important for wildlife and landscape beauty. This argument has been championed by the expansionists in the agricultural lobby and given academic respectability by geographers like Alice Coleman of King's College, London, and pressure groups like the Land Decade Educational Council.

Coleman has argued that much of the blame for land waste and loss of farmland to urbanization can be attributed to bad planners and the failure of the planning system. She has been the intellectual guru of the Land Decade Council, an unmistakably right-wing alliance of landowners and academics whose main concern is the urban threat to farmland. Coleman is undoubtedly right to point to the ways in which we waste land in Britain. However, the emotive way in which she has sought to attack the planning system and champion the free-enterprise use of the countryside (by farmers, of course) has brought her many critics. She talks of the countryside being more and more 'infested by diffuse urban sprawl'; of wasteland, derelict land and scrub 'advancing like a cancer' across what was formerly productive land; and of the planning system which has 'almost totally failed to achieve any compatibility of planning aims'.

Graham Moss, also one of the leading lights of the Land Decade Council, has claimed that 'rural areas have poor political representation compared with urban areas'. However Philip Lowe, in an issue of *Town and Country Planning* (Autumn 1980) devoted to assessing the views of the Land Decade Council (LDC), has countered with the more accurate observation: 'Nothing could be further from the truth: rural pressure groups and lobbies proliferate and seem increasingly effective in presenting the problems and needs of the countryside.'

The agricultural economist Gerald Wibberley identifies the views of the LDC as part of the agricultural and rural fundamentalism mentioned earlier. He points to the simplistic way in which LDC writers in their *Land Use Perspectives* cling to an outmoded man/land ratio perspective.

There is enough evidence around the world to make most thinking people realize that there is no simple meaningful relationship between the area of land in a country and the fortunes of the people who live in that country. The simple man/land ratio concept has been abandoned by all reputable geographers but still seems to appear in a dangerously simple form in this particular country of ours.

Drawing on the comprehensive studies of his colleague Dr Robin Best, Wibberley argues that the land taken from agriculture for urban use poses no real danger to the farming industry.

Wibberley points out that the

relative efficiency of land use in our 'farmscape' [Coleman's expression] or agricultural areas is so low that, of the future food needs of the British population by the year 2000, only 10 per cent of these needs will be related to the land which is likely to be urbanized between 1965 and 2000. In other words, 90 per cent of the extra agricultural output we may need if we go more self-sufficient in food will have to come from changes in the way in which our existing farmland is used.

Studies at both Wye College and at Reading University, according to Wibberley, 'give no support to the suggestion that losses of agricultural land to the urban sector constitute a main threat to the food supply of Britain'.

Bryn Green, in his book *Countryside Conservation*, suggests that the pessimistic prognosis of the agricultural lobby, supported by the likes of Coleman and the LDC, are also difficult to understand for reasons beside the simple fact that increase in agricultural output far outstrips any losses in production due to urban land-take. He argues that they postulate excessive increases in population and food demand for an already overfed and now stabilizing population. Britain, according to Professor Kenneth Mellanby, author of *Can*

Britain Feed Itself? could be self-sufficient without any increases in productivity if we moderated our consumption and changed our diet (particularly by eating less meat). Furthermore, as Green points out, 'So long as 25 per cent of the food produced in the country is lost in harvesting, processing and domestic garbage, it is not even necessary to consider such extreme measures when greater efficiency here offers such potential.' It is thus quite apparent that those who argue that the destruction of wildlife habitats is in part a consequence of urban land-take are looking for a scapegoat to justify the reclamation of marginal lands.

The Uncontrolled Water Industry: Supply and Drainage

Most people have no idea where their water comes from and who is responsible for regulating its use and providing it to homes and industries. Yet our water industry spends some £1,800 million a year. It is a highly capital-intensive industry (with a capital/revenue ratio of 0·57 compared with gas at 0·25 and general manufacturing at 0·05) and it has a great influence on the ecological and industrial life of Britain. The industry provides some of the best examples of resource mismanagement and, in common with the industries controlling energy and road transport, it is bent on expanding supply regardless of real needs. Already an average 19 per cent of all rain that runs off British soil ends up in 'storage', with the figure being as high as 36 per cent in the Thames region.

New reservoir schemes are invariably controversial and nobody ever wants them on their own doorstep. Ground water abstraction schemes can be equally unpopular when they dry up lowland streams. As with nuclear power stations, sites for new reservoirs are difficult to find. As a rule they are generally built in remote upland areas where there is the most rain and where the sparse population is likely to mount the least effective resistance. There is thus a tendency for reservoir (and power station) builders to try to get as much capacity into a single site as possible; big (as far as they are concerned) is beautiful.

Water in Britain is very cheap and five tonnes of drinking water can be bought for £1 sterling. The average household bill in 1978/9 was only £38 for a year. We do, however, waste water on a massive scale. The ever-expanding water industry provides a classic example of over-capacity and many economists have now joined with environmentalists in arguing for more water conservation, and higher prices to discourage waste. There have also been calls for a stop in the wasteful procedure of supplying all industrial users with expensively purified water which is clean enough to drink.

The Engineers' 'Getafix'

The water engineers who are in charge of the industry are often disarmingly honest about the way in which the industry puts career prospects of its engineers and employees in front of all other considerations. In their comprehensive and authoritative work, *Water Planning in Britain* (on which much of what follows is based), D. J. Parker and E. C. Penning-Rowsell begin their discussion of water planning thus: 'There is no doubt that the professional composition both of the policy making and executive institutions and most of the advisory and research agencies is unbalanced in favour of those with engineering backgrounds.' Engineers 'prefer to see water planning primarily as a technical exercise. This is a view based on positivist thinking which emphasizes data and facts above values and interpretation and consequently sees decision-making as rational if founded mainly on politically neutral data-gathering rather than on genuine political debate.' The two geographers criticize the engineers for 'narrowness of approach' and a rigid adherence to established procedure, 'even where these do not produce the best solutions for specific problems'. Despite the vigorous shake-up involved in successive reorganizations of the industry since 1945, Parker and Penning-Rowsell find that there has been a 'tendency for engineers to continue in senior executive posts from one administration to the next'. It is these engineers who dominate Britain's Regional Water Authorities, and they are trained to solve water-supply problems by building new reservoirs rather than by conserving our existing water resources.

The engineers employ 'supply-fix' forecasting which involves extrapolating past trends of consumption to suggest future shortages. The past trends in consumption are a reflection of the past increases in capacity, increases which have been provided in *advance* of demand. Today's reservoirs were planned between twelve and fifteen years ago on the assumption that we were going to need them. Such 'supply-fix' forecasting is increasingly criticized, but diehards like the Southern Water Authority refuse even to look at demand–

supply forecasting. This latter system assumes that consumption of water will fall if the cost rises (elasticity of demand), while supply-fix requires that it should not. Evidence from Europe and America, and for that matter common sense, supports the demand–supply system of forecasting. (Lovins, in his book *Soft Energy Paths*, notes that it was when American electricity utility companies discovered 'elasticity of demand' for their product that they dramatically reduced the forecasts for future demand.)

Existing purpose-built supply reservoirs cover over 22,500 ha of land in the UK, the most notably useless being Rutland Water in the East Midlands and Kielder in Northumberland. Completed in 1981, Kielder is one of our biggest reservoirs, covering 1,086 ha and holding 4·1 billion litres of water. It cost the Northumberland Water Authority £170 million but demand for water in Northumberland, rather than following the trend towards doubling before the end of the century as the Authority forecast, has dropped since the project began, largely as a result of the industrial recession. Rutland Water (1,500 ha) features a Nature Reserve and is popular with sailing clubs. However, not one drop has been used by the Anglian Water Authority which completed it in 1970 at a cost of £35 million. Not only have these two white elephants consumed over 2,000 ha of land; they have resulted in the eviction of many families who lived in and in some cases farmed the areas.

Until it was disbanded in 1979, the small Water Planning Unit carried out research on demand forecasting. This job is now left in the hands of the Regional Water Authorities in England and Wales (nine English, one Welsh) and the nine Regional Councils in Scotland, which have water-planning functions, along with the three Island Councils. Their functions include water supply (which is also taken on by twenty-eight water companies in limited areas), sewage disposal and treatment, pollution control, recreational planning, fisheries administration, drainage and 'water conservation'.

The State Water Authorities: Poachers or Gamekeepers?

Before Water Authorities were established, following the 1973 Water Act, 1,393 sewerage departments of local authorities carried out the 'dirty' functions of disposing and treating effluent, while twenty-nine river authorities carried out the 'clean' water function of monitoring pollution. One hundred and fifty-seven statutory water-supply undertakings provided water to consumers.

In England and Wales the Water Authorities now have both the clean and dirty functions. Furthermore they are responsible for both setting pollution standards and ensuring that they are met. This means that they monitor the discharges from their own works as well as those from others. They are in the curious position of being able to take themselves to court for failing to comply with pollution standards. It comes as no surprise that the Authorities are frequently criticized for not upholding pollution standards. (In Scotland, with the exception of the Island Councils, which have full water responsibilities, the Regional Councils have responsibility for sewage treatment and the River Purification Boards fulfil the role of ensuring that pollution standards are met.)

Water Pollution

In May 1978 the journalist Jeremy Bugler blew the whistle in *Vole* magazine on what he called 'an exercise that amounts to one of the most astonishing acts of public deception in recent years'. He explained that 'Under the pretext of what Denis Howell, Environment Minister of State, calls "the further improvement of water quality" the pollution standards for *thousands* of factories and sewage works are in the process of being *lowered*.' Water Authorities and the Department of the Environment had panicked because Part I I of the 1974 Control of Pollution Act was due to come into force, thus enabling private individuals or groups to prosecute people or organizations polluting rivers by exceeding 'consents' on discharges. Consents place conditions on the quantity, volume and type of effluent which can be discharged; they are set by Water Authorities and River Purification Boards. The Water Authorities, quite correctly, feared that they themselves were the major polluters and that prosecutions from angling clubs, conservationists, farmers and others would soon follow the enforcement of Part I I of the Act.

Through the National Water Council (NWC) the Authorities embarked on a programme of 'relaxing' consent conditions. They downgraded 'objectives' for river quality, thus allowing themselves to increase pollution while claiming, along with the Secretary of State for the Environment, that more pollution standards were being met than ever before. They got away with it, and as Parker and Penning-Rowsell note, the NWC even takes the view that industrial dischargers should not be prosecuted if only 'occasional samples' exceed consent condition. 'The review of consents,' say the two geographers,

appears to be a softening of the goals and objectives set out in the Control of Pollution Act 1974. There appears to be no mechanism for appeal against revised consents, no sound basis for setting quality objectives other than existing use which may be constrained by pollution levels, no timetable for the conversion of short-term consent conditions into permanent conditions ...

Many environmentalists place great faith in careful public monitoring of standards and registers of information on river quality which must, by law, be published by Water Authorities and River Purification Boards. The problem is that facts which discharging industries consider to be commercial secrets are not made public. According to Roger Gomm, writing in the environmental journal *Ecos*, 'even if this did not impede public scrutiny, the Act would forbid the Water Authority to make details of water samples publicly available'. However, all this is academic, as the government has still not fully implemented the relevant Part II of the Act. Under the 1961 Rivers (Control of Pollution) Act there is nothing to prevent private parties from collecting and publishing data on river pollution but there is no provision under the Act for private individuals or groups to prosecute polluters, something which can only be done under common law (in other words by precedent).

Early in 1982 the NWC reported that since 1970 the overall length of grossly polluted rivers was down by 50 per cent but recent public expenditure on sewage works had also dropped by 50 per cent. In the event of an upsurge in industrial production the works may become overwhelmed as they take industrial as well as domestic waste. Indeed, since 1976 46 km of rivers have regressed from the cleaner category to the grossly polluted, reversing the trend of the last twenty years which brought the salmon back up the Thames and other rivers. Run-off from farms, particularly in the west and north-west, is now becoming an increasingly serious problem, with sheep-dip chemicals, silage and factory farm wastes polluting 1,300 km of previously unpolluted rivers. In all it is estimated that 1,034 km of 'grossly polluted' and 2,220 km of 'poor' rivers remain and these will probably get dirtier, especially if, as seems likely, the government refuses to implement the crucial Part II of the Control of Pollution Act.

One particular pollutant which may threaten water coming through your tap deserves special mention. This comes in the form of nitrates, 50–60 per cent of which comes from the run-off of agricultural fertilizers. Nitrates can be conveniently classed with the 'time-bomb' substances. Measurements indicate that nitrate run-off takes twenty to thirty years to get into abstracted ground water, which suggests that the doubled use of nitrogenous fertilizers on our farms in the 1960s has yet to make its presence felt in the water coming through our taps. According to Parker and Penning-Rowsell, nitrate levels in drinking water in Worksop exceeded the World Health Organization's accepted level for 'a number of years' and a survey in 1970 revealed that sixty out of 173 tested drinking water sources exceeded the recommended maximum levels. High-concentration nitrate water contains nitrites which can cause methaemoglobinaema and are implicated as a cause of bowel cancers.

The Water Bureaucrats

The system whereby Water Authorities are judge, jury, policeman and frequently criminal, coupled with the secrecy surrounding pollution data, raises the question of public accountability. Much water planning is 'bottom-up' rather than 'top-down' and higher echelons within Authorities react to recommendations from the people lower down the ladder. These people are almost always the engineers. This makes the job of the Authority members all the more important as only they can ensure that the public interest is reflected by balanced policy.

The members of Water Authorities and River Purification Boards are a mixture of people chosen by the Secretary of State for the Environment (who chooses, among others, the chairman), district and county councils and the Agriculture Ministries. Local representatives are in a majority but they are, according to Parker and Penning-Rowsell, 'encouraged not to think of themselves as delegates from the electorate but as members of the Water Authority'. Consequently they tend to further the interests of the Authority, as an institution, rather than those of the general public. The

Authorities are thus not under democratic control. As with other quangos (including those involved with conservation) the Secretary of State takes the advice of non-elected civil servants in his choice of members.

The NWC is the only central water-planning unit, but Parliament exercises little, if any, control over its affairs. The Council has a small budget and advisory role, encouraging cooperation between the different Water Authorities. The council membership includes all the Authority chairmen and it is supposed to give a 'general, national view' and not just reflect the opinions and policies of the water industry. Writing in the *Municipal Journal* in 1975, M. Greenfield posed the familiar question: is the Council a watchdog or a lapdog? We give him the last word on the issue on accountability:

> Among these twenty-one advisers and consulters are three former Tory ministers . . . a merchant banker, a farmer and a chartered surveyor, four company directors and a major landowner. Of the nineteen men, six went to Eton; three were Guards and one in the Hussars; two have been office holders in the Country Landowners' Association and one is a master of foxhounds. The Council's knowledge of water and its ways is not called into question but some might hesitate before endorsing its claims that it expresses a general, national view.

Drainage

It is significant that some members of Water Authorities are appointed by MAFF. Land drainage controversies have probably attracted even more attention than the scandal over pollution consent conditions. Land drainage legislation was consolidated in the 1976 Land Drainage Act. MAFF plays a central role in the complicated system which is designed to prevent flooding and bring more land into intensive agricultural production (see also p. 26). Land drainage is carried out by a number of authorities and organizations: district and county councils, regional and local land drainage committees of Water Authorities and the infamous Internal Drainage Boards (IDBs).[3]

Water Authority local drainage committees come under the umbrella of a Regional Land Drainage Committee (RLDC). The RLDC has powers to supervise all drainage matters except finance, which remains in the hands of MAFF. Within the RLDC's area the IDBs can exercise considerable autonomy in carrying out works on non-main rivers (an arbitrary distinction which leaves 'main' watercourses under RLDC influence).

Field drainage, the purpose of which is to lower the water table beneath agricultural land, is generally undertaken by landowners who have secured Ministry of Agriculture grant aid, which averages 55 per cent of cost but can be as high as 85 per cent. 'The successful operation of field drains,' explains hydrologist Ted Hollis, 'requires a low water level in surrounding ditches and streams. It often stimulates or follows arterial drainage schemes which improve the flow characteristics of watercourses by straightening, deepening, smoothing and enlarging them.'

The costs to wildlife and landscape are well known (see pp. 102–6). One consequence which is not so widely appreciated is that this 'improvement' of drains and rivers increases the rate of run-off and size of flood peaks, and as many large areas of washlands have been reclaimed and embanked it increases the risk of downstream flooding. Increased flooding in low-lying areas then encourages demands from farmers and others for more intensive drainage in such locations.

Drying out the landscape necessitates pumped drainage schemes in some very low-lying areas like the East Anglian Fens and the Somerset Levels. The 273 IDBs are among the groups which are heavily involved in these schemes. They have been described by Chris Hall, the former Director of the Council for the Preservation of Rural England, as 'a classic example of a private gravy train subsidized from public funds, hallowed by statute and institutionalized by a complacent bureaucracy'. Let us look at them.

IDBs preside over extensive areas of land, particularly in Yorkshire, Kent, East Anglia and Somerset. Members are chosen from among local landowners and occupiers, almost invariably farmers. By 1981 the row over the activities of IDBs reached the House of Lords. Lord Buxton pointed to the farmer-based membership of IDBs and the problems it causes:

In the good old days there was no problem with drainage boards. It was then sensible to have the local farmers and people who owned the land on the local drainage boards. It also made reasonable sense that the clerks of the boards were often their solicitors. But times have changed ... machines can do work in a morning which used to take 20 men a week or a month.

Buxton pointed out that IDBs are not subject to anyone's authority and are not even required to get permission from land-owners before starting drainage works:

The first an owner may know about it is when he wakes up and sees a JCB digging away at his meadows or dykes ... I understand that when grant is applied for, the application goes from the Ministry's regional engineer to the Ministry. I believe that one individual in the Ministry can then authorize grants up to £1·5 million without further ado ...

Both RLDC and IDB drainage schemes must be subjected to a Ministry of Agriculture cost-benefit analysis. Despite Section 11 of the Countryside Act, which places a duty on MAFF to pay 'due regard and attention to the desirability of conserving flora and fauna', schemes are rarely refused grant aid. 'A serious aspect,' commented Buxton, 'is that IDBs and the Ministry decline to expose their figures, calculations and assessments.' In the case of Amberley Wildbrooks, a 365-acre wet-meadow complex along Sussex's River Arun threatened by a joint IDB/RLDC drainage scheme in 1978, determined opposition from local conservation groups forced the minister to hold a public inquiry. The drainage case was defeated (although it is worth noting that the NCC and the Sussex Trust for Nature Conservation had originally reached a compromise solution with the Southern Water Authority). Buxton said he couldn't understand why IDBs and MAFF wouldn't release figures. He may have had his tongue in cheek; the Amberley PI showed that when they are forced to give figures the economic case for drainage is often a poor one.

Continuing his attack on IDBs (the cost of whose operations is rising at a rate of around 25 per cent a year), Lord Buxton pointed out that they are the only independent rating authorities in Britain. We pay our rates to them without any chance of our views being represented democratically. They are, said Buxton, 'a sort of Monte Carlo or Vatican within the realm'. *New Scientist* reported that in one IDB area 98 per cent of the land was agricultural yet agri-cultural rate-payers paid only 7 per cent of the drainage rates, the rest coming from the pockets of urban rate-payers. 'In another IDB area,' Buxton told the Upper House, 'the average rate per acre for agricultural land is 23 pence, and for non-agricultural property (wait for it, my Lords) is £165·91.'

Other members of the Lords joined the attack on IDBs. Lord

Onslow pointed to the effect of pouring public money into IDBs on land prices: 'The present gross margin for unimproved grazing marsh ... is £67 per acre.' After drainage it rises to between £800 and £1,700, 'increases solely due to public money'. Onslow then raised one of the most controversial drainage issues involving an IDB: 'The Happisburgh to Winterton IDB drained Horsey Mere (a Norfolk Naturalists' Trust Nature Reserve) by deep dyking. This released sulphuric acid and ferric hydroxide into the stream, killing and choking aquatic life. The Smallburgh IDB entered Hickling Broad without notifying its owner, the Norfolk Naturalists' Trust ...' The same IDB had committed the same offence at Martham Broad, an SSSI of international importance to wildfowl, just a few months before. The Broads Authority (whose responsibility is to try to save the Broads) proved that the IDB was responsible for the release of sulphuric acid and ferric hydroxide from the sediments, but the Anglian Water Authority declined to take action against the illegality of the IDB activities.

It is thus quite apparent that Water Authorities, the National Water Council and the IDBs can in no way be considered accountable to the public. Lord Melchett has called for open elections for IDB members or at least proportional representation among ratepayers. Despite heated public debate, followed by the government promise to 'look at it again', nothing is likely to change and Lord Buxton's criticism of IDBs will remain valid for some time:

> As I stated at the beginning, it was all very fine in the old days. The boards are sort of self-perpetuating clubs – very good clubs, and I am sure they are dedicated to their work, both the members and the managements. Of the 214 boards, 11 clerks run 101 of them, and one man is clerk to 32 boards. That is no criticism; it is simply describing the general background. The whole scene is, frankly, supremely undemocratic, but really no harm ever came of it in the past. It was all fine until the new technology and engineering came along, and until substantial Government grants became available. That has revolutionized everything; the situation is no longer tolerable.

The Uncontrolled Forestry Industry

Commercial forestry is one of the most controversial land-uses. At first sight it seems curious that trees, such an important element in the natural landscape, should be at the centre of a dispute between conservationists and other land-users, particularly when one remembers that Britain is one of the most naked countries in Europe, with only 8 per cent forest cover. Environmental opposition is directed towards the methods, objectives and techniques of forestry rather than towards the planting of trees.

In most European countries forestry is based on the exploitation of indigenous natural resources. In contrast, our forestry is based almost entirely on the use of non-native species. The traditional species of the woodman – native oak, elm, lime, hornbeam, cherry, service tree and others – are no longer part of the modern forester's estate. Indeed great acreages of these species are raised from the ground to make way for fast-growing softwoods. Sitka and Norway spruce, lodgepole and Corsican pine, Chilean beech and other introductions are now the mainstay of modern forestry.

The tradition of forestry, as opposed to woodmanship, has been to collect rapid-growing species from wet and mild climates similar to our own (for example Vancouver Island in Canada) and to apply plantation techniques similar to those used in the last century when rubber plantations were established in Malaya and the Far East. Eighteenth- and nineteenth-century naturalists placed great faith in 'naturalizing' (that is acclimatizing) foreign species to our climate and 'improving' our flora and fauna with introductions. Although there is no justification for opposing the use of foreign or 'exotic' species on the grounds that they don't belong here (where would we be without our essential cereal crops which came from the Near East?), there are aesthetic and ecological costs of blanket afforestation with exotic species.

The forest estate is dominated by one tree, the Sitka spruce, an import not from the Atlantic climes of Vancouver but from the drier continental and Arctic climate of Alaska. Unfortunately it has failed to 'naturalize' and foresters now fear that very little of it will prove commercially profitable. The mistake in choosing this species was made long ago when the Forestry Commission, established just after the First World War, was in its infancy. Today's foresters, however, must share the blame with their predecessors for the insensitivity to landscape and wildlife that still characterizes forestry policy.

The Forestry Commission was established in 1919 in response to the belief that Britain would be at a strategic disadvantage were there to be another war in which wood demand exceeded supply. The Commission based its policies on the 1918 Ackland Report which called for 200,000 acres to be afforested within ten years and a further 1,777,000 in the following eighty. In fact by 1939 the Commission had established 230 forests of 655,000 acres. Some 373,000 acres of existing woodland were clear-felled and another 151,000 'devastated', according to Edlin in *Trees, Woods and Man*, because the Commission's woods were too immature to meet Second World War needs. (Ironically, the devastation was mostly of ancient woodlands and for many it was the last time they were coppiced!) Even before the Commission had set out to meet its objectives, the economic and strategic role of wood declined in favour of metals, and the military justification for forestry expansion waned. Nevertheless, once established, the Commission continued to expand its activities and it has amended its justification to suit the prevailing needs of the time. Timber is by nature a long-term crop and the changes in justification for expansion have not been significantly reflected in changing forestry practices.

Before we look at the Commission's activities it is worth giving some basic figures for the industry. The Commission's own estates account for over 40 per cent of Britain under trees. We import 91 per cent of our softwood requirements, 63 per cent of our hardwood needs and each year we have to meet an import bill of around £2,750 million. On the surface, at least, the Commission's activities appear to be of minimal importance in terms of the economy.

The Commission has been nothing if not opportunist, even arguing in the interwar years that it should take responsibility for nature conservation. In recent years it has acquired a bad reputation for making exaggerated claims on its role in import-saving, its importance for rural employment and its provision of recreation facilities. Like the agricultural lobby, the foresters have inevitably developed close links with academic establishments such as the forestry departments at the universities of Bangor, Oxford and Reading. The academics help to promote the interests of forestry and they are very useful when the forestry lobby needs 'objective' facts to argue the case for further expansion within government and the civil service.

The Commission has two roles: first, as 'forestry enterprise', it raises, manages and sells its own timber from an estate of 1·3 million ha; second, as 'forestry authority', it regulates the activities of Britain's 3,700 private foresters and organizations, guiding their activities through law and financial inducements.

Tax and Economics

As practised today, private forestry is the domain of large, rich land-owners. Substantial financial concessions are available through generous tax-relief. At the time of writing a forestry owner could opt for one of three tax schedules (A, B or C). By switching from one to another at the right time forestry owners can start by paying no tax at all, as they set management costs of estates against profits (even high-income foresters can recover up to 60 per cent tax); then at the thinning and felling stages changing to Schedule B relieves children or other inheritors of a great deal of tax as a purely notional assessment of 'sustained income' is made. The Treasury estimated that this tax avoidance cost the tax-payer £10 million a year (over £2,700 per forester on average) at 1972 prices.

In March 1981 the tax advantages for foresters came to the attention of a Parliamentary Committee of Public Accounts, the watchdog over public finance. The Committee noted that government departments, including the Inland Revenue, suggested that forestry syndicates were systematically exploiting the public purse for their own benefit and to the detriment of the rest of us:

> The syndicates might have a score or more members and they moved in as soon as woodlands had been felled and needed replanting. They remained in occupation only for the comparatively short period while expenses were heavy and resulted in losses which they could set against income from other sources. As soon as income began to rise from thinnings and exceeded the expenses they disposed of their interests ... to a pension fund or insurance company as a long term investment free of any charge to tax beyond nominal assessment ...

These activities began in the 1960s but are now responsible for nearly a quarter of all private-sector planting. In tones which are unusually acid for a Parliamentary Committee, the PCPA concludes:

> If the Government consider that additional forestry subsidies are necessary for policy reasons ... they should be granted openly through votes subject to parliamentary control rather than left to the fortuitous consequence of the exploitation of a tax loophole which depends more on personal circumstances ... than on forestry merits.

Yet again we have another good example of the 'gravy train', with public money, through tax concessions coupled with direct grant aid, being creamed off by a small number of landowners. Recent government measures introduced in the Wildlife and Countryside Act are also likely to decrease rather than increase public constraints on private forestry. In a report on the implementation of the *World Conservation Strategy* in Britain, Professor Timothy O'Riordan of the University of East Anglia explained how the gravy train operates for foresters:

> The Economic Forestry Group estimate that a landowner subject to tax at 50 per cent investing in upland afforestation of 100 ha need only pay 41 per cent of a total outlay of £72,550 over 10 years yet enjoy a net asset worth £50,000 excluding the value of the land. Should part of his investment go into agriculture, he would be eligible for grant and subsidy on livestock purchase and management.

Landowners with mature broad-leaved woodlands are thus encouraged to convert them into coniferous plantations and even in National Parks such practices are only under minimal constraint. Forestry Commission estimates have for some years suggested that as much as 33 per cent of future plantations will come from such conversions. Forestry, like agriculture, is subject to no planning controls.

In 1972 a study by the Treasury concluded that the forestry industry was a net drain on national assets. As Leeds University economist J. K. Bowers remarked, 'it is a testament to the power of the forestry lobby that the study was followed by a government policy statement which only called for a 10 per cent reduction on existing Forestry Commission targets'.

Writing in 1982 in the journal *Ecos*, Bowers developed the principal economic critique of the Commission's activities. Noting that the Treasury study had concluded that there were no good strategic reasons, either commercial or otherwise, for new afforestation, and that present planting regimes failed to produce 'a social rate of return', Bowers argued that new planting in the uplands 'compares unfavourably with hill farming it replaces in economic resources and in Exchequer costs per acre'. This is quite an indictment, as he acknowledges that hill farming itself 'produces a negligible or even negative social return' and relies heavily on government subsidies. As far as the balance of payment benefit is concerned the Treasury noted that there is 'no value in import saving'. Even when import-saving was boosted to a hypothetical 20 per cent forestry was still found to be a net drain on tax-payers' pockets.

Despite this, the 1977 Forestry Commission report, *Wood Production Outlook*, concluded that a large expansion of forestry, at a rate of 36,000 ha per year, would be a 'prudent investment', and in 1978 Reading University's Centre for Agricultural Strategy (CAS) called for an even greater expansion in its report *Strategy for the UK Forest Industry*. The CAS study recommended a massive increase in planting to cover the largest area of land thought technically feasible, increasing the forest estate at a rate of 60,000 ha per year.

To boost the weak economic case for forestry expansion its supporters also argue that it is worthwhile on the grounds of employment and import-saving. Cost-benefit studies value labour at less than the actual wages paid to workers, on the assumption that the government, as paymaster, would otherwise have to cough up dole money if workers were unemployed. However, even if labour costs are written off altogether forestry fails to appear a good way in which to create jobs. According to the Treasury study, 'forestry creates slightly more local employment [than farming] but does so at a higher cost per job in resource and Exchequer terms'.

Rather than expanding forestry in the uplands, many conservationists support the unconventional view that new forests should be established on the more fertile soils of the lowlands. Here wheat and barley, much of it grown for animal feed, is effectively supported by subsidies up to 150 per cent, inflating both the value of the land and the farmers' profits. Opposition to this proposal can be expected from both lowland arable farmers and the owners of large private estates, the beneficiaries of the present push to afforest the uplands with conifers.

Forestry's Impact on Conservation and Amenity

Quite apart from doubts about the foresters' use of public money, there is great concern for the way in which forestry affects wildlife and landscape. The Ramblers' Association has led the attack by amenity groups on the visual and aesthetic impact of forestry. In particular, concern has been directed towards the intrusion of coniferous plantations in the Cambrian Mountains, the Pennines, the National Parks and parts of upland Scotland. The Association points out that of 268,000 ha considered plantable in the North West England Forest Conservancy some 167,000 ha would be planted if the CAS plan was carried out, and much of this would have to be in the Lake District and Yorkshire Dales National Parks.

Criticisms of the dark green blocks of conifers on the sweeping moorlands have not gone unnoticed by the Forestry Commission, and in recent years it has employed well-known landscape consultants like Dame Sylvia Crowe to improve its planting patterns. The Commission is now using screens of deciduous species like beech (though often the Chilean *Nothofagus*), oak and the deciduous but non-native European or Japanese larch around its large conifer belts. Experiments with selective systems and mixed plantings are also underway, but conservationists are not convinced of the Commission's good intentions, particularly in the National Parks. Of all the woodland in England and Wales, the Commission manages 34 per cent (more in Scotland), two-thirds of which is in National Parks. In the Parks it is expanding its holdings (at the rate of 8 per cent in 1979/80) and the potential for conflict is increasing.

The Commission places some emphasis on its role in providing often high-quality recreation facilities for tourists and day-trippers. Critics, however, claim that such facilities are in short supply and that their intense use is a reflection of their shortage rather than a vindication of forest policy. We should point out that some conservation groups would take the Commission's side on this issue. Few, though, would go along with the Commission's claims that commercial forestry and wildlife conservation are wholly compatible.

The number of bird species to be found in young plantations increases dramatically for a few years after planting and rises slowly as the trees mature. But plantations are never left to become old enough to achieve the necessary structural diversity to attract as many species as one finds in natural woodland, and forestry on the hills has the effect of replacing birds like dunlin, golden plover and greenshank with common woodland and farmland species. Birds of prey, so often the victims of upland forestry, may benefit from the abundance of small mammals like the short-tailed vole in young plantations with long grass. But by the time the plantation is twenty years old the animals and birds of prey will disappear. For a few species like chaffinch and firecrest mature plantations are fine, but for most they are a dead loss.

In recent years wildlife has caused some problems for foresters, who now face the worrying prospect of having to increase the use of pesticides as mature plantations acquire more and more new pests. In the last few summers the pine beauty moth, a species formerly thought to be confined to native Scots pine, has started to feed on the commercially planted lodgepole pine, an introduction from America. The new pest finds forest plantations very much to its liking and as the speed of evolutionary adaption to a new tree species largely depends on the generation turnover (with insects breeding hundreds or thousands of times within the lifetime of one tree) the prospects of keeping a step ahead of the pest are very poor. We are thus likely to see an increase in pesticide use in the forests.

In a recent statement on modern forestry, Keith Kirby, NCC's deputy chief woodland scientist, noted that of 3,700,000 ha (the forest estate projected by CAS) a mere 30,000 ha will be ancient woodland (about 0·8 per cent). Even if no timber at all were produced from these woods – something which is not envisaged – it would still only represent a long-term loss of under 1 per cent of potential production. Yet the Commission argues that 'it is difficult to isolate the total revenue foregone in the interests of conservation but it is certainly considerable'.

Kirby is one of a growing number of people who argue that ancient woodlands should produce timber in the ways of old woodmanship. There is no doubt that forestry techniques now forsaken by the Commission but still widespread in countries like France could be of great benefit both to rural employment and to landscape and wildlife conservation. In spring 1982 the government made its long-awaited response to the House of Lords Select Committee on Science and Technology. The government response ran to a mere five pages and took the combined resources of the Forestry Commission and the Agriculture Ministries fourteen months to produce. The Lords' report, which ran to over 400 pages, had called for the conservation of all ancient woodlands by renewing traditional management, by appointing a Forestry Commission Chief Scientist to oversee research, and by establishing community woodlands. The Lords Committee argued strongly against merely creating another committee. The government's response was blandly to dismiss or ignore every proposal and to set up a Forestry Research Coordinating Committee run by the Forestry Commission. At its first meeting in spring 1982, no NCC officers were present, and observers feared that the Commission intended to bolster its own 'wildlife research' wing to carry out research aimed primarily at justifying its present policies. Research into the problems created by forestry as a land-use, for example in terms of its hydrological and ecological impacts, has been completely ignored.

Only a few months after the 1981 Wildlife and Countryside Act came into force, the NCC undertook to pay about £100,000 a year just to prevent three Scottish estates from converting the rare remnants of native Caledonian pine forests to commercial conifer plantations. Thus the landowners, merely by declaring an intention to destroy these irreplaceable sites, were being given compensation which comes from public funds. With a budget of only £10 million it is clear that the Conservancy cannot afford to pay such sums to protect our ancient forests. It is a curious irony that a Conservative government, the proclaimed enemy of public waste, initiated a system through which landowners are paid tax-payers' money for doing, in the most literal sense, absolutely nothing.

Three
Planning:
A Much-Abused
System

Ideals and Shortcomings

It is a basic assumption of democracy that conflicts can be resolved in the interests of the whole community rather than in favour of a few individuals or small groups. Governments are elected to carry out the will of the people. If the electorate dislikes the Conservative Party or the Labour Party it can replace them at the ballot box with the Social Democrats or the All Night Party.

Aristotle and the ancient Greeks would have been appalled by any community whose size and population precluded a face-to-face encounter between its enfranchised citizens. Certainly the likelihood of democracy working decreases with an increase in the size (and, many would say, the power) of the state. Many would also argue that the more centralized a government becomes the less likely is true democracy to flourish. Obviously, we cannot discuss the problems of democracy as they exist in Britain, but we must make two important points about the decision-making process which are of vital interest to conservation and land-use.

First, elected members, whether of Parliament or local planning authorities, almost always see environmental concerns as a low priority. The manifestos of political parties and the careers of MPs depend on tempting the electorate with a programme of induce-ments. The major issues of concern relate to material welfare: in-dustrial jobs, housing and so forth. Concern with the long-term exploitation of resources and the 'quality of life' do not find expres-sion within our present political system and take a back seat despite their obvious importance for future generations (the Ecology Party might claim to be the odd man out here but in Britain it has attracted little support compared to its counterparts in Germany and France). The fickleness of today's leading politicians as far as environmentalists are concerned was exemplified by Mrs Thatcher's decision in 1979 to ignore environmental issues as she was advised that they didn't attract votes.

Equally vital in influencing political decisions are the non-elected officials of central and local government, the civil servants and planning officers. Though theoretically responsible to elected M Ps and local authority members, they can feed information to elected representatives in such a way as to ensure that political decisions represent what *they* want. Tony Benn has argued that there is a 'state within a state', and increasingly politicians from both Left and Right concur with his belief that the 'top bureaucracy in Whitehall is now so powerful as really to threaten at certain key points Ministerial control, Ministerial accountability to Parliament, and Ministerial accountability through Parliament to the electors'.

In the course of the last chapter we have shown that a range of different land-uses, and activities which affect land-use, are guided by small numbers of people and interest groups who are often not acting in the interests of the whole community. In this chapter we look at the planning system, the ostensible purpose of which is to resolve land-use conflict between different individuals, groups and sectors of society in such a way as to ensure 'the greatest good for the greatest number'. Our brief survey concentrates on the short-comings and failures of the planning system. In some instances the legislation itself has proved inadequate. An obvious example concerns the exemption of farming and forestry activities from any form of democratic planning control. In other cases the legislation itself is adequate but some of its provisions are either ignored or abused. For example, the Planning Acts empower ministers to set up Public Inquiries (PIs) to help resolve major conflicts and canvass public opinion. Sadly, as we show later, the PI system has been so seriously abused by government departments that its credibility has been seriously undermined. The planning system, in so far as it extends beyond the built environment into the countryside, can be seen as an official palliative to the evident inequity consequent on less than 1 per cent of the population owning land in Britain.

The Ground Rules

According to Sir Desmond Heap, an authority on planning law, 'Planning at its best, if it is to be effective, comes very near to being a sort of benevolent despotism. At its worst it could, of course, develop into an objectionable dictatorship.' It seems a poor choice but Sir Desmond's jaundiced view reflects the traditional right-wing belief that planning 'interferes' with people's rights, in this case to develop property. Since the 1932 Town and Country Planning Act was passed the avowed aim of the planning system has been to regulate development in the best interests of the community. However, since the Conservative Party came to power in 1979 Michael Heseltine and his successors in the Department of the Environment (DoE) have conducted an official campaign which undermines the whole purpose of the planning system. In the most comprehensive critique available at the time of writing of the DoE's onslaught on planning law, the Council for the Protection of Rural England (CPRE) wrote in its *Planning – Friend or Foe?*:

Over the past two years, the Government has taken a series of steps which are progressively emasculating the British planning system. This is being done in the name of 'promptness', 'efficiency' and the removal of procedural obstacles over new development. These are extremely limited objectives for a planning system. In the crude form in which they have been introduced, they also run contrary to the purpose and vision of planning which has developed over the past fifty years.

The CPRE points out that planning regulations have been altered to favour developers, and redefinitions of planning are being mooted which would discard the emphasis on 'control' and 'guidance', which have for so long been the tenets of planning decision-making. Furthermore, the role of local authorities is being undermined in favour of greater centralization, and the planning profession, unsure of either its future role or its present purpose, is in a state of demoralization.

There is now a large body of legislation which influences rural planning. Apart from the Planning Acts, which are primarily concerned with the built environment, a series of Acts have been introduced since the last war which are central to the practice of conservation. The 1949 National Parks and Access to the Countryside Act paved the way for the formation of the forerunners of the NCC and the Countryside Commission of England and Wales. It also established important conservation designations: National Parks, Areas of Outstanding Natural Beauty, National Nature Reserves and SSIs (see Appendix 3). In the late 1960s two Countryside Acts, one for England and Wales and another for Scotland, were passed. Most recently the 1981 Wildlife and Countryside Act attempted to pull together all the previous conservation legislation. In addition the statutory bodies with interests in the countryside (such as MAFF, the Forestry Commission, Water Authorities, etc.) have been required to pay 'due regard and attention to the desirability of conserving flora and fauna' when exercising their responsibilities. As it happens these bodies have done their best to ignore this weak exhortation, but it remains on the statute books all the same.

Local Government Organization

1974 saw the greatest upheaval in local government administration since the formation of the county councils in 1888. The 1972 Local Government Act gave rise in England and Wales to fifty-three county councils, including six metropolitan counties (Greater Manchester, Merseyside, South Yorkshire, Tyne and Wear, West Midlands and West Yorkshire), and 369 district councils. This split-level administration takes slightly different shape in Scotland where six regional councils fulfil a slightly broader role than county councils below the border. There are thus two planning authorities for each square metre of Britain except in National Parks. In England and Wales planning responsibilities in the Parks are exercised by one authority rather than two. The Peak District and Lake District National Parks have their own Special Planning Boards while the remainder come under committees appointed by the relevant county councils and the Secretary of State for the Environment.

The top tier of the planning cake belongs to the Department of the Environment in England, the Welsh Office in Wales and the Scottish Development Department in Scotland. These Departments are responsible for instigating new legislation and for making sure that local authorities implement the law as it is intended. Three men, the Secretaries of State for these Departments, have the last word in all matters of policy relating to the exercise of planning law in Britain.

The powers of local planning authorities are laid down by the Town and Country Planning Acts and in the stream of circulars and regulations which emanate from central government. It is in this latter category that the Conservatives' new changes are ordered.

The authorities are given the responsibility for controlling development, which is defined as building, engineering and mining operations, and changes in the use of buildings and land. All those seeking
to develop must apply to the relevant local authority for planning
permission (see below). Although agriculture and forestry activities
are exempt from planning controls, farmers and foresters wishing
to construct buildings over a certain size must seek planning permission.

Local Authority Plans

The complexity of resource-use in Britain means that forward
planning is essential, whether it be in the field of mineral extraction, energy-use or water supply.

County councils, metropolitan boroughs and their Scottish
counterparts have a responsibility for compiling structure plans.
These are intended to give broad strategic policies for such factors
as employment, housing, mineral extraction and conservation. The
more detailed plans are left to the local authorities which, until
recently, had a statutory responsibility to prepare local plans. However, in a recent circular from the DoE rural district councils have
been told that local plans will not be needed if little change is
expected in the future. This planning vacuum will, according to
the CPRE, introduce unplanned-for change and favour the
developer.

Structure plans have a life-span of about twenty years and each
lays down constraints to development and broad policies for the
activities mentioned above. They require the approval of the
Secretary of State. Local plans, only seventy-four of which had been
adopted by 1981, with nearly 300 district councils lacking any such
plans, do not require the approval of the Secretary of State unless
he specifically decides to vet them.

Although local authorities have a statutory duty to encourage
public participation during the formulation of their policies, few
members of the public have the specialized knowledge which enables
them to understand the complexity of the planning process and thus
the significance of the proposals put forward in structure and local
plans. The number of private individuals who make representations
at the public participation stage is pitifully few; indeed most people
are unaware that they can do so. However, conservation organiza-

tions, both those with statutory duties like the NCC and the Countryside Commissions and voluntary bodies like the RSPB, the CPRE and Friends of the Earth (FoE), scrutinize plans closely and attempt to ensure that their interests are protected.

Incidentally, if you are now thinking of participating in the process you will have to wait for the next round of structure plans in the 1990s: most counties and regions have had their plans approved by the Secretaries of State. These plans are important as they set the context within which development proposals are considered by planning authorities. They vary greatly from county to county in terms of their thoroughness, usefulness and intelligibility (planners being inordinately fond of jargon). Unfortunately, most counties have felt bound to accept the market forecasts of industries such as those involved in mineral extraction, not least because other data are often not available. Needless to say, it is in the interests of these industries to exaggerate future demand (see pp. 31–2, for example, on how water industries do this).

Some counties have acquired much better reputations than others for environmental conservation. For example, Dorset and Grampian are often considered to be particularly enlightened, while others like the Highland Region and Kent are considered less so. Areas suffering from unemployment and loss of population are likely to view many conservation constraints as a nuisance on the grounds that they deter potential developers from even considering the area.

These plans are important but they lack clout as they have no influence over farming and forestry. Furthermore, Mr Heseltine's attack on the planning system compounds the trend whereby central government is eroding local democracy and determining local affairs. Water planning is in the hands of engineers (although in Scotland water-supply functions do fall to Regional and Island Councils), while energy and major transport planning are beyond local authority control.

Applying for Planning Permission

Whether you wish to add a garage to your house or build an oil refinery you must apply for planning permission. The developer must lodge an application with the local planning authority; it will probably be in 'outline' if he wishes to develop land which he doesn't own, but wants to gauge the probable reaction of the planners before buying land. The district authority will pass the proposal on to the county authority if it falls within the county council's responsibilities. The authority must give publicity to planning applications through the press and site notices in all cases involving 'bad neighbours'. Bad neighbours include developments like public lavatories, knackers' yards, mineral extraction schemes, casinos, pin-ball parlours, Turkish baths, cemeteries and zoos. The authority must consider any representations made in *writing* within twenty-one days of the application being publicized.

The planning authority can treat the application in three ways. It can grant unconditional permission; it can grant permission subject to stated conditions; it can refuse permission. Applicants can appeal against the decisions of planning authorities to the Secretary of State. For the year 1977 over 11,000 appeals were lodged in England and Wales and the Conservative relaxation of development control is apparently encouraging more developers who have been refused planning permission to appeal. According to the CPRE, 'Where local planning restraint policies conflict with developments proposed in the new climate, they are being increasingly tested by developers on appeal to the Secretary of State. The volume of decisions being overturned on appeal suggests that local planning priorities are being increasingly eroded.'

Public Inquiries and the Technological Imperative

In cases where there is significant opposition, either from a local authority, other government departments, or the public, to issues of importance, government ministers may order PIs to be held. The nature of the development proposal determines which minister is responsible. The minister in charge of the Department of Transport will institute PIs into road schemes; the Energy Minister tackles, for example, nuclear power station inquiries; the Minister for Agriculture will be the key person if the proposal relies on MAFF grant aid (see p. 38 on Amberley Wildbrooks drainage proposals); and of course it is the Environment Minister who deals with inquiries into issues covered by the Planning Acts. Government ministers do, however, have the power to refuse to hold PIs regardless of what the general public or anybody else thinks. It now falls upon us to consider in some detail the way in which the PI system has failed in Britain. And it is here that we discuss a factor of crucial importance to an understanding of how the agriculture, forestry, water, energy and transport industries promote their activities regardless of the needs of the community and outside any true system of democratic control: 'the technological imperative'.

When a minister orders a PI to be convened he does so to gather as much information as possible about the pros and cons of a proposed development. He appoints an *inspector*, or in Scotland a *reporter*, whose task it is to compile a report and recommend to the minister whether or not the proposed development should be granted permission. In some case (see p. 38, Amberley Wildbrooks) the inspector will recommend whether or not development should be grant-aided by a government department.

PIs are held in the locality of the proposed development. The developer puts his case first and is followed by the objectors, who may include local authorities, other government departments and private groups or individuals. Examination and cross-examination are carried out, generally by counsel hired by the main protagonists. At the end of the inquiry the last word is given to the developer. The inspector asks questions whenever he wishes and after the inquiry he compiles his report for the minister.

Although the PI is not a judicial proceeding, both objectors and developers are keen to 'win' in the sense of persuading the inspector that they have the strongest case. In fact one of the more obvious problems with the system is that objectors increasingly view PIs as debating forums where the merits of proposed developments can be assessed in a semi-judicial manner, while ministers see them as a means of gathering information prior to making a decision (or, at least, making public their decision).

PIs vary from brief one-day affairs dealing with minor issues such as the closure of footpaths or the re-routing of a village bypass to massive events running for many months and costing the tax-payer millions of pounds. Major PIs concern projects such as the building of nuclear power stations, the construction of airports, motorways and reservoirs, and the establishment of oil refineries, petrochemical plants and mining operations. They are costly not only for the tax-payer but also the developer (often a government department, financed through public taxes) and for the objectors, generally the most penurious of the participants. The majority of the PIs are concerned with the activities mentioned above and it is only in rare instances that forestry or agricultural schemes are seen in the role of the developer at inquiries. For that reason much of what follows relates to transport and other inquiries.

There have been many criticisms of the PI system, and here we briefly discuss those which are of particular importance and should be borne in mind by anyone attending an inquiry. In many cases objections to a proposed development will be multi-pronged: damage to landscape, wildlife and amenity; nuisance to local residents; loss of agricultural land, etc. Objectors will often try to undermine the economic case presented by developers, and the developers will invariably point to the advantages of their schemes (if any) for local employment and the economy. At major inquiries great play is made of something called the 'national interest'. Conservationists may say that the conservation of an estuary threatened by an oil refinery is in the 'national interest' because the site is considered of such importance. Likewise an oil company may say that its plan to build a refinery should proceed as it is in the 'national interest' for the economy. As a general rule the 'national interest' is seen as overriding the 'local interest'.

Fears over the PI system's waning credibility were succinctly put in 1981 by Chris Hall, a past director of the CPRE and now the editor of the sober and respectable *Countryman* magazine. Interviewed for *Ecos* he had the following to say:

Objectors are feeling increasingly impotent as government seeks to foreclose public discussion on such matters as official forecasts and background policies. I fear that the projected nuclear power programme will strain the inquiry system to breaking point: then there are two ways a government can go. It can either accept that that is the end of the programme which it is trying to push through the inquiry system *or* it can try to abbreviate or by-pass it. I believe it is more likely to do the latter than the former. There will then be the danger that groups of individuals believing that there is no opportunity to be given a fair hearing will resort to semi-violent, physical opposition and civil disobedience.

In recent years it has been evident that with some major government-inspired development proposals the PI system has been used as a public relations charade. John Adams, an established expert in transport planning at University College, London and a *bête noire* of the Department of Transport, describes the purpose of inquiries as follows: 'Most inquiries are held not because politicians and civil servants responsible for the relevant controversy do not know their own minds, but to provide support for policies and decisions that have already been made.' Why, asks Adams, should the Department of Transport (DoT) ever hold an *independent* inquiry into anything? The answer, he believes, is that it never does, except through miscalculation or indifference.[1]

The infamous *Peeler Memorandum* – an official circular intended only for the eyes of senior civil servants in the DoT – was leaked to the *Guardian* in 1978. It confirmed what anti-motorway campaigners had maintained for years. The *Memorandum* concerned the question of an upper limit to lorry weights and it made it clear that any inquiry into the issue would be purely 'presentational': its main purpose would be to assuage public fears about increasing lorry weights.[2] 'At the end of the day,' says the *Memorandum*, 'recommendations would be made by impartial people of repute who have carefully weighed and sifted the evidence and have come to, one hopes, a sensible conclusion in line with the Department's view.'

Both Adams and Hall believe that with minor issues the PI system probably works in the sense that inspectors do act impartially and honour the purported *independence* of inquiries. Indeed Adams suggests that the Secretary of State might welcome decisions that go against civil servants' proposals on small issues such as the question of route alignment 'in order to foster the inquiry system's image of independence'. He notes that the original Ministerial Inquiry had its name changed to Public Inquiry, a change which implies a greater degree of independence.

During the last decade PIs into proposed motorways have been interrupted by sporadic outbursts of dissent and disruption from the public and this has been countered by some fairly harsh and uncouth behaviour by inquiry stewards who, it has transpired, are usually in the pay of the DoT.[3] The breakdown of discipline which led to a temporary halt of the Archway inquiry into the proposal by the DoT to build an urban clearway through a residential district in north London occurred, according to Adams, 'because respect for the fairness and impartiality of the inquiry procedure collapsed'.

At the opening of the Archway inquiry in September 1976 John Tyme read out a statement on behalf of 600 objectors. Tyme was already well known for his contributions to inquiries around the country. He began his statement by denouncing both the inspector and the proceedings. He told Mr James Vernon that 'the authority you have been granted to preside over [the inquiry] is itself improper in that it derives from a wholly corrupt process of government'. The word 'corrupt' is important here as it is central to the critique of the DoT put forward by Tyme in his book *Motorways versus Democracy*. His criticisms are worth considering as their significance extends beyond the official manipulation of inquiries to the wider role of government departments and civil servants in formulating official policy (which cannot be challenged at PIs).

We have shown that the people in this country who determine the policies of the water, agricultural and forestry industries are committed to promoting the growth in supply of their products. The same could be said for the energy industry: rather than exploit ambient sources of energy – the sun, wind and waves – and in preference to introducing radical energy conservation programmes, the Department of Energy continues to promote electric power stations which deliver three-quarters of their energy to the atmosphere in the form of waste heat. There is no doubt that we could dramatically decrease our energy consumption if we concentrated on very simple conservation measures. Similarly the Ministry of Agriculture demands further increases in agricultural productivity at the rate of $2\frac{1}{2}$ per cent a year despite the fact that we are members of the EEC, whose countries are collectively self-sufficient in every temperate food product. The water industry is obsessed with supply-fix forecasting and expands its activities in line with what it wishes to give us, not with what we need now or in the future. Thus all these activities are placing unnecessary demands on land.

John Tyme has argued that the influence of the industrial/financial lobby on government decision-making 'constitutes a corruption of government and thus a major threat to democracy'. This unseemly influence is just part of the *technological imperative*, which Tyme has characterized by its six component parts.

Tyme interprets the technological imperative in terms of the road transport industry, but here we have broadened it to include some of the other industries discussed in this book. The first component is the technology itself: for example, nuclear power, water-supply reservoirs, motorways, agricultural production. Second comes an industrial/financial complex whose role it is to carry out research and development (such as British Nuclear Fuels Ltd, Forestry Commission Research and Development Department), and to build, sell and use the technological hardware (for example for farming, Massey-Ferguson producing machines, ICI manufacturing fertilizers and pesticides, the farmers using the hardware). The third component is a lobby whose specific function is to ensure that decisions are made in its favour in central and local government, for instance by recruiting MPs and planning officers to its cause (for example for the farming lobby, the CLA and the NFU).[4] The fourth component of the technological imperative is an 'interest section' within the relevant government ministry or department, 'the personnel of which have close connections with the industry and whose role is to cooperate with the lobby to help ensure that favourable decisions are in fact made' (that these exist is clear from our discussions of MAFF and the DoE). The fifth component is a body of expertise in the form of scientists and engineers, whose careers depend on the industry (obvious examples include MAFF's advisory service, Water Authority engineers, and scientific research divisions tied to government ministries). Tyme's final component is a brain-washing machine geared to establishing 'economic truths' in the interest of the imperative (for example the industry of the north-east would have been seriously undermined without Kielder Reservoir – false; demand for energy will rise – only if we continue to waste it; upland forestry helps our balance of payments deficit – false; we will 'freeze in the dark' without nuclear power – untrue).[5]

In describing Tyme's six components of the technological imperative we have given a few examples of the organizations and groups implicated in its practice. The reader will be able to think of many more. Tyme points out that one of the main objectives of the imperative, and thus of the vested interests, is to ensure that the law and the system works in their interest. If Tyme is right, and the evidence suggests that he is, then it is difficult to see how more rational resource policies will arise in the near future. It is, as Tyme suggests, the object of the technological imperative to expand at its own rate and escape any form of control.

Now we must come back to the problems which beset PIs. Leaving aside the technological imperative and the use of inquiries for presentational purposes, the dice are loaded against objectors in major PIs. The lack of impartiality of inspectors is not just confined to inquiries involving the DoT. The Windscale Inquiry into the construction of a nuclear fuel reprocessing plant was a celebrated case of political rather than rational determinism. Many objectors have claimed that the report of the inspector, Mr Justice Parker, actually distorted and misrepresented their evidence in a deliberate manner. Witnesses who claim to have been seriously misrepresented include energy experts Walt Patterson, Dr Brian Wynne, Professor Joseph Rotblat and Gerald Leach, as well as Dr Alice Stewart, a leading epidemiologist studying radiation and cancer. On the evidence Parker was far from impartial.

Major PIs often involve government departments which can draw their expenses from public coffers. At Windscale it was the Central Electricity Generating Board; at Archway it was the DoT; at the Vale of Belvoir it was the National Coal Board. Even when a developer is a private company its ability to finance its case is invariably much greater than that of the objectors. Objectors have to pay barristers exorbitant sums of money to defend their interests and even if they 'win' the case by proving a development undesirable they cannot claim legal aid. Friends of the Earth's unsuccessful bid to stop Windscale expansion cost them over £100,000.

The developer often starts from a position of strength as he generally does not have to make his arguments clear until the PI is convened. The developer is under no obligation to tell either the public or the local planning authority anything other than that he wishes to use a certain site for a particular purpose (except in cases where the minister requires him to produce a written statement). The objecting planning authority, on the other hand, must make a statement outlining its objections twenty-eight days before the inquiry begins.

Robin Grove-White, Director of the CPRE, has pointed out that objectors, to have any real chance of success, 'must seek to undermine the economic certitudes which are the developers' real strength'. In some instances objectors have successfully achieved this aim. However it is far from easy to counter developers' economic arguments when criticism of government policy is held to be beyond the reference of an inquiry. Determination of much government policy, whether it be for agricultural expansion, energy use or transport planning, is carried out by members of the civil service who are, if Tyme is right, the lynch-pin of the technological imperative.

Four
The Faltering
Conservation
Movement

In Chapter 2 we discussed why the farming, forestry and water industries are causing problems for Britain's wildlife and landscape. In Chapter 5 we shall look in detail at the species and habitats which have suffered most. But first we examine the approaches that conservationists have taken to counter such threats.

Such approaches are as various as the groups which comprise the conservation movement. The belief that the environmental lobby is a unified and coherent collection of organizations and individuals is quite mistaken, and there is considerable conflict between many of them. The movement can be conveniently split into two camps – which we term the Old Guard and the New Wave – and in the first part of this chapter we look at their different approaches to conservation. (This survey of the movement mentions many groups, and the reader is referred to Appendices 3 and 4 for information concerning their aims and achievements.)

Conservationists are often branded as elitists who care little for the economic welfare of those areas in which they are most active – often where rural deprivation and high unemployment compound the problems of declining public services – and we look at the NCC's role in promoting this elitist image by posing the question: 'Who is state conservation for?' Finally we discuss the ineffectiveness of government conservation agencies and consider how they came to be so toothless.

The Old Guard

The history of the nature conservation movement in this country has its roots in the organized study of natural history. Not surprisingly Victorian and Edwardian naturalists saw no conflict between their pursuit of natural history as a hobby and a life spent working in industries which destroyed or damaged the very objects of their study. To these early naturalists fauna and flora were generally seen as existing quite independently from man, and questions of what was scientifically interesting (for example, rare or exotic species) dominated the minds of these forerunners of the modern ecologist. Ethical considerations of what man was doing to his environment seldom influenced the activities of the naturalist although the second half of the nineteenth century saw sporadic lobbying for legislation to protect a minority of threatened creatures.

The pioneer conservationists were closely wedded to scientific investigation and the Old Guard has clung to the respectability of scientific doctrine with extraordinary tenacity. Falling in behind the science of the times conservationists found themselves searching for a rationale which could reconcile the environmental disadvantages of economic 'progress' with their own aspirations for nature conservation. Justifying conservation as a 'science' meant that any reference to their motivation stemming from romantic notions of a love of nature or landscape was swept under the carpet.

The strong reliance on science has dominated the activities of the government's NCC. The Conservancy was founded under the 1949 National Parks and Access to the Countryside Act and under the Act its future activities were seen as being guided by a 'scientific rationale'. The Conservancy could not say that places were important for historical, ethical or aesthetic reasons.

Even today our traditional and long-established voluntary conservation bodies like the RSPB and the forty-two County Naturalists' Trusts are still pursuing their objectives within the framework set by the Nature Conservancy, as it then was, whose faith rested on the optimistic belief that science and technology will always bale us out of our troubles. But there is a clear contradiction here, as conservationists' demands are seldom met by major industries. In their fruitless search for a consensus with the industrialists our science-based conservation bodies have been compromised to such an extent that even a minor concession is held up by the conservationists as the paradigm of a success story. Max Nicholson and Bob Boote, two long-serving chairmen of the Conservancy in the 1960s and 1970s, were both influential optimists who believed that the captains of industry would eventually come round to view things in a conservationist way. 'It can be said with some confidence,' wrote

Nicholson in 1970, 'that the 1970s will mark the first moment during man's tenure of this earth when the nature of conduct of his steward-ship will be continuously under critical scientific scrutiny, not too far separated from the seats of power and from the enforcement of accountability.' But as things turned out, and as this book shows, the environment has received as much, if not more, of a battering during the last ten years as it did in the previous decade.

The traditional nature conservation approach to agricultural and industrial development often attempts to explain the continuing problems between ecologists and engineers, between the environ-mental lobby and industry, as a result of the lack of communication between the two groups and the shortage of 'hard facts' which will convince industrialists and land-users of the errors of their ways. The establishment of Environmental Data Services (ENDS) by Max Nicholson in 1978 was the most explicit attempt by a conser-vationist to bridge the perceived communication gap. ENDS is now under the direction of John Elkington, whose book *The Ecology of Tomorrow's World: Industry's Environment* is the most comprehensive review of attempts at ecological 'technofix' in British industry. The assumption, or presumption, that there are technical solutions to environmental problems is central to the technofix philosophy.

In short, the traditional approach of the Old Guard to environ-mental problems, through its reliance on science and thus scientific or technical solutions to these problems, makes no direct challenge of the basic economic assumptions which presently determine our industrial development. To the New Wave environmentalists, the subject of the next pages, the nature conservationists who fail to address themselves to broader environmental concerns are, to use a popular analogy, merely rearranging the chairs on the deck of the *Titanic*.

The New Wave Environmentalists

Unlike the proponents of traditional science-based conservation, many people remain unconvinced that the captains of industry and the farmers and foresters will moderate their environmentally destructive activities. These people – the New Wave environ-mentalists – believe that our entire political and economic system is in urgent need of a thorough overhaul.

Professor Timothy O'Riordan once wrote of the environmentalists' view that 'The dominant ideology of capitalism in all its forms is to protect the structure of power, to promote progress and economic growth and above all to maintain control of the total order of things. Environmental *reformists* [our italics] are shooting with pea-shooters at this particular beast: whatever they come up with is transformed to reassert the status and power of those in control.' Hence the New Wave environmentalists seek radical change, unlike the Old Guard who see themselves as reformists. Many environmentalists claim to transcend traditional political alignments: 'We're neither to the left nor right, but out in front', as one German eco-slogan runs.

The present economic order, according to the New Wave, is guided by an imperative which demands the greatest possible returns from investment and the most cost-effective (in the short term) exploitation of resources. The quicker we pump oil from under the North Sea, the greater the returns per unit of time. The faster we chop down the Amazon forests, the greater the profits for the pulp mills.

Even our yardsticks for measuring success pander to the economic myopia which sees all achievements on the scale of immediate material profit. Our politicians tell us that British agriculture is the most efficient in Europe. In terms of productivity per man that is true. But the costs in terms of energy are ignored as is the industry's appalling employment record (see p. 20). A similar story can be told for numerous other industries.

Environmentalism [says O'Riordan] challenges certain features of almost every aspect of the so-called western democratic (capitalist) culture – its motives, its aspirations, its institutions, its performances, and some of its achievements. It seeks a reformulation of national income accounts in favour of some kind of measure of economic and social well-being; it aims to substitute a love of humanity, companionship, a concern for posterity, and the joy of natural experiences for the persistent and widespread exploitation of people and land, the desire for monetary reward, materialism, and striving for status; it hopes to alter institutional forms and procedures by replacing corporate hegemony, bureaucratic discretion, and routinization with radical proposals for human-scale cooperative enterprises, and for consultation and participation.

The reforms, remarks O'Riordan, will not come easily. That is an understatement, but we quote him at such length as this is as close to a definition of environmentalism as one can hope to find.

In the space of a few pages we cannot hope to do justice to the philosophy of environmentalism, and it already has many champions. Below we trace the thoughts of some of the most influential.

In his book *Small is Beautiful: A Study of Economics as if People Mattered*, E. F. Schumacher pointed to the present alienation of man from nature. 'Modern man,' he wrote, 'does not experience himself as part of nature but as an outside force destined to dominate and conquer it. He even talks of a battle with nature, forgetting that if he ever won the battle he would find himself on the losing side.' One of the aims of the environmentalist is to promote an attitude which recognizes nature not as an economic resource to be plundered at will, but as an integral and almost sacred part of his own existence. It is not surprising that many attribute the Western world's preoccupation with 'fighting' nature to the commands of God in Genesis: man was told to 'subdue' the earth and God's message to Adam after the Fall can be interpreted as a mandate to exploit the earth without limit. Indeed James Watt, President Reagan's Secretary of the Interior, is a born-again Christian who has, in his self-appointed capacity as God's spokesman, decided to wage a battle with astonishing vigour against all the environmental safeguards adopted in American legislation over the past decade.

But quibbling with a religious parable is not going to get anyone very far and some environmentalists have looked elsewhere to find examples where postlapsarian man has treated the earth and nature with the respect now so lacking in our own society. They have found that the American Indian, among others, does not measure his achievements, nor assess the resources on which he depends, in the cold terms of Gross National Product.[1] Replying to a letter from the US President (who had stated his desire to buy land 'owned' by the Duvanish tribe) Chief Seathl replied:

How can you buy or sell the sky – the warmth of the land? The idea is strange to us. Yet we do not own the freshness of the air or the sparkle on the water. How can you buy them from us? ... Every part of the Earth is sacred to my people. Every shining pine needle, every sandy shore, every mist in the dark woods, every humming insect is holy in the memory and experience of my people.

To the environmentalist the philosophy of the American Indian does not call for a return to the land in the most literal sense. What it does do, however, is affirm that the natural resources of the world are

– or should be – common resources in which we all have an interest. Further, nature should not be seen as an enemy to be subjugated but as something to which we should attribute the same degree of sanctity as we do (or should do) to human life.

But the search for spiritual ties with nature does not provide a critique of our present industrial behaviour. A group of eminent industrialists, the Club of Rome, published a book in 1972 entitled the *Limits to Growth*. Its message was simple: man was in the process of consuming energy and resources at such a rate that he would himself perish (he already is doing so in large numbers) and unless he recognizes that the finite resources on which he depends are indeed finite, civilization 'as we know it' will come to an abrupt and tragic halt.

Schumacher criticizes conventional economic theory on the grounds that to believe that the problems of production have been solved is just an illusion, as it fails to 'distinguish between income and capital where this distinction matters most ... namely, the irreplaceable capital which man has not made, but simply found, and without which he can do nothing'. This irreplaceable capital compromises natural resources, from fossil fuels to minerals and the gene pools of tropical forests.[2]

There are signs that even the most conservative nature conservationists are beginning to acknowledge the environmentalists' compelling critique of our present industrial behaviour, even if they are shy of their solutions. We now find the conservative CPRE playing an active role in pointing out the fallacies of official energy projections. It is convinced by the environmentalist argument that energy conservation obviates the need for any further generating capacity. More surprising, perhaps, is the gaggle of even more conservative conservation groups – for example, the Royal Society for Nature Conservation, the World Wildlife Fund and the Council for Environment Conservation – behind efforts to help put the World Conservation Strategy into practice in Britain (see p. 124). The Strategy is an ambitious attempt to reform, if not revolutionize, the world economic order. At a Conference of the British Association of Nature Conservationists on the World Conservation Strategy in December 1981 Lord Melchett declared that 'the rapturous welcome given by governments to the WCS suggests they either haven't read it or that they don't understand its implications'. The same could probably be said for the Old Guard nature conservationists.

The traditional nature conservationist will look at mercury seeping into a stream or a farmer chopping down an ancient woodland and he will say: 'The pollution must be stopped and the farmer should leave the wood.' The environmentalist will ask: 'Why is the river being polluted? Why is the wood coming down?' For his answer he will look to the fundamental assumptions made by those who guide industrial and agricultural development. His challenge goes far beyond the individuals who turn the tap on and wield the chainsaw.

State Conservation: Who Is It For?

The charge of elitism is commonly levelled at conservationists; there is no doubt that it has sometimes been justified and it cannot be ignored. The sociologist Howard Newby is one of many people who have pointed out that the upper- and middle-class domination of the environmental movement raises the important question of political equity. 'Does the political mobilization of environmentalists,' he asks, 'accentuate the already existing disparities between the favoured environments of the powerful and wealthy and the degraded environments of the deprived?' There is no straight answer to this. Evidence suggests that in urban areas more affluent protesters to road schemes have successfully resisted plans which have later been foisted on those living in more deprived areas nearby. However, where conflicts take place away from centres of population between different land-uses the actions of environmental groups seldom result in direct detrimental impact on Newby's 'deprived'.

In any case, whatever the answer to Newby's question, the environmentalists cannot be blamed for accentuating existing disparities between the affluent and the less fortunate. The interests of any pressure group, whether it is the Ramblers' Association or the CLA, are inevitably sectarian, though those most capable of influencing the planning process and political decision-making will be those who by virtue of their prosperity, social connections and education understand how to play the system. It is worth noting that a survey of environmental groups in Bath revealed that members of the apparently conservative CPRE have the strongest distrust of government, probably because they have the greatest experience of it!

An unfortunate consequence of many of the battles fought

between conservationists and developers is that the debate has often been polarized into one of jobs and prosperity versus preservation, as though the two sides are necessarily incompatible. Conservationists are accused of mourning the past and being anti-progress, while developers are sometimes wrongly cast as the wanton destroyers of the 'national heritage'. Without doubt one of the factors which has contributed towards this typecasting of the conservationists has been the preoccupation of the government conservation agency, the NCC, with scientific justifications of what it says and does. We have pointed out that the science-bias was inherited by the NCC from earlier conservationists and sanctified by the Parliamentary Act under which it was established. The 1949 National Parks and Access to the Countryside Act institutionalized the split between scientific conservation and aesthetic and amenity conservation by creating a separate NCC and National Parks Commission. So let us look now at the influence of science-based conservation.

The celebrated controversy during the 1960s over whether or not a dam should be built at Cow Green in Upper Teesdale highlighted the apparently elitist stance which has frequently been taken by conservationists when opposing developments. By 1960 ICI employed 10 per cent of the Teesside work force and news that the company wished to expand its operations in 1964 was greeted enthusiastically in an area which has long suffered from unemployment. ICI needed more water than the Regional Water Authority could then provide in order to establish and operate a new plant. The Water Authority identified possible sites for a new dam and found that the ideal and most 'cost-effective' was at Cow Green on the edge of Moorhouse National Nature Reserve.

Preliminary meetings between representatives of ICI and the Conservancy's Director-General, Max Nicholson, suggested that the Conservancy (it was still the Nature Conservancy, the NCC's forerunner) would not oppose the Cow Green development. However, following work by its Chief Scientist, Dr Derek Ratcliffe, the Conservancy performed a swift about-turn. Dr Ratcliffe discovered that the combination of sugar limestone and acid peat soils supported a unique relict Arctic-Alpine flora and before long the pages of *The Times* carried letters from botanists around the world pleading that this 'internationally important conservation site' be saved. During the following months there was bitter conflict between the conservationists and local and national politicians who supported the reservoir case. One side emphasized the need for jobs while the other championed the site's 'scientific importance'.

I C I put a Private Bill before Parliament and eventually won its case. The conservation cause was embodied in a blocking motion which was narrowly defeated by 112 votes to eighty-two, a split which did not reflect party lines. In his excellent account of the Cow Green affair Roy Gregory suggested that 'it was emotion and sentiment, rather than cool open-minded appraisal of the issues involved, that dictated the attitudes of most M Ps'. In the Upper House Lord Walgrave argued, somewhat melodramatically, that 'if we feel that there is no case here then we should be honest about it and repeal conservation legislation and abandon the whole idea'. Ted Leadbetter, M P for Hartlepool, took the opposite view. 'In this region the primary thing at this stage is unemployment,' he said. 'It is important to stress the point that in my region we cannot evaluate beauty and scientific interest of flora until we have the social conditions for all those who live there to enjoy it' (we should mention that conservationists did not say there should be no reservoir; they wanted it elsewhere).

It is tempting to take the Cow Green débâcle as a moral lesson for elitist conservationists, getting their come-uppance for ignoring the needs of industry and the problems of unemployment. Indeed this view has been seized on by detractors of the environmental movement in an attempt to discredit the basic arguments in favour of conservation. Nevertheless it is singularly naive.

The Conservancy argued in terms of 'scientific importance' at Cow Green because that was what it perceived its job to be, and in an era when government still sought 'scientific solutions' there was general support for the idea that things should be conserved for science. The weakness of the argument in this case became obvious when it was realized that few scientists actively *used* Cow Green. It is easy to decry the scientists, who by definition were taking a narrow view, but at that time no other conservation groups raised their voice in support of conserving the site for reasons other than the scientific ones promoted by the Conservancy. Nor did I C I suggest that if the site were conserved for 'people' rather than for 'scientists' it *would* have opted for a more expensive reservoir scheme elsewhere.

It was undoubtedly unwise to rely so much on the power of the argument that the value of an ecological community to science was so great, but the Conservancy was not making a moral judgement: elitism crept in *de facto* rather than by intent. It is a measure of how much support conservation has today that the real scientific value of genetic resources is now widely perceived, accepted and used as a prime reason for conservation. Perhaps we now have a more mature view of 'science', seeing its possible role as a benefit to society rather than as an academic pursuit for a minority.

Nevertheless the Conservancy's attitude towards the unscientific laity has scarcely been enlightened. Even before it was established, Charles Elton, the father of modern ecology and later an NCC member, warned against the possibility of a 'new feudal aristocracy' of scientists establishing Nature Reserves for their own purposes. His warning went unheeded and for many years the Conservancy's main preoccupation when setting up reserves was to keep the public out or at least limit access to a minimum. Such an attitude can only be partly attributed to the ambiguous remit set out for the Conservancy under the 1949 Act. It was very much one law for the scientists and another for everyone else. Dr Bryn Green, formerly NCC Regional Officer for South-East England, recently berated conservationists for 'their constipated attitude towards public access'. He claimed that 'the continued promotion of nature conservation as a scientific activity is responsible for much of this negative attitude'.

In the 1960s conservationists were worried by what Michael Dower called the 'Fourth Wave': the great insurge of town-dwellers to the countryside following post-war affluence and the rise in car ownership. Conservationists drew on circumstantial ecological evidence to suggest that 'public pressure' posed a serious threat to wildlife. Nature Reserves were surrounded by signs which would have done credit to the Ministry of Defence: 'Keep Out', 'Trespassers will be Prosecuted', etc. Naturally, this reduced the contact between the Conservancy and the public, to the detriment of both, and sometimes led to deep and justifiable resentment. It also aggravated the access-conscious and landscape conservation groups, further emphasizing the split which government had institutionalized by creating separate agencies to deal with wildlife and landscape.

So, were the conservationists' fears about 'public pressure' justified? Certainly no one could deny that large numbers of visitors had worn down the top of Helvellyn in the Lake District, scarred the fragile soils of Snowdon and Cairngorm and caused localized problems of erosion on sand dunes and heaths. The scientists in the research branch of the Conservancy, which became the Institute of Terrestrial Ecology in 1973, soon established a large volume of esoteric literature on the problems of public pressure. Sadly, their efforts had missed the point. The RSPB and the National Trust, both of whom were forced to come to terms with the public use of their reserves and estates (they depend heavily on visitors and paying members), have established that the fears of the public swamping the countryside have been misplaced and counter-productive. The erosion of soil following vegetation destruction may be a very local problem in some areas, but astute management and the provision of footpaths and nature trails help to channel people away from particularly sensitive areas. Indeed if anyone among the countryside visitors causes real problems it is the fanatical fringe of ornithologists who 'twitch' their way round the country in their quest to tick off as many species as possible in one year (see p. 104), and the RSPB now has an internal working group looking at the problem. An exhaustive eighteen-month study of the effects of recreation and tourism (financed in 1978/9 by the NCC but still unpublished at the time of writing) showed that the public cause few problems for our wildlife, particularly when seen in relation to agricultural and other threats.

It is sad that the apocryphal fear of the 'Fourth Wave' served to divorce the government's conservation agency from the public on whose support it ultimately depends. When in 1979 the NCC found that its budget had been drastically cut there was no public outcry as so few people had heard of this self-effacing and almost secretive organization. It has been the voluntary bodies like the RSPB, the National Trust and the County Naturalists' Trusts who have done the most to canvass public support for wildlife conservation.

The idea that conservation bodies cannot welcome the public on to their holdings at the same time as maintaining some sanctuaries where man doesn't tread is nonsense. Indeed the knowledge that there are some places where nature alone reigns still exercises a powerful fascination over many people. There is thus widespread willingness to tolerate or even encourage some restrictions on access to sensitive parts of Nature Reserves and National Parks. But that is a very different thing from locking the gates and leaving the keys with the scientists.

The Government's Toothless Watchdogs

The state's conservation agencies – the NCC and the two Country-side Commissions – are often referred to as 'toothless watchdogs'. The two most obvious reasons for their lack of bite is that they have no effective legislative powers to curb activities which are destroying or damaging the countryside and have to do their work on derisory budgets. For 1981/2 the NCC's budget was £10 million; the combined budget of the two Commissions was £12 million. Put another way, the state nature conservation effort receives a budget for a year's work which is equivalent to about double the expected annual running costs of London's new Barbican Arts Centre, or one Mars Bar per year for everyone in Britain. The projected £8,000 million which the Conservative government intends to spend on the Trident nuclear missile system is the equivalent to eight centuries of state conservation at present prices. However, there is another reason why the NCC and the Commissions are toothless, and this is the subject of this section. The members of the ruling Council and national committees of the NCC are loath to challenge activities such as farming and forestry. Close inspection shows that many of the members have vested interests in the very activities which are often incompatible with nature conservation.

Members of the Council and its three Advisory Committees – one each for England, Scotland and Wales – are chosen by the Secretary of State for the Environment. Their business is to determine NCC policy and oversee the running of the organization. Between 1953 and 1966 Max Nicholson, the charismatic Director-General of the Conservancy, used the Council primarily to rubber-stamp decisions taken by himself and his officers. When in 1973 the Nature Conservancy was abolished and its research functions split off to form the Institute of Terrestrial Ecology, leaving the rest of the organization as the NCC, many members of staff and observers saw it as a move by the civil servants to bring conservationists back into line. Nicholson's ferocious criticisms of the civil service, expressed most notably in his book *The System*, had failed to keep the Conservancy out of its hands. He had never had much time for the classics-educated generalists, ignorant of both science and industry, who presided over Whitehall. Nicholson's powerful machine, funded through science research sources rather than the civil service, was broken up and brought within the control of Whitehall. In 1974 Sir David Serpell, a senior civil servant formerly with MAFF, was appointed Chairman; he introduced a new doctrine which advocated greater public use of reserves but he also increased the secrecy surrounding Council policy meetings to the extent where the NCC's own officers were often left out in the cold. (Limited circulation of Council papers was restarted several years later.)

In the following years the NCC slid into decline. Staff morale plummeted while the voluntary bodies like the RSPB grew in strength and became increasingly dissatisfied with the NCC's inability to deal with the ever-more destructive forces of agriculture and forestry. The NCC failed to confront forestry and agriculture: the three Cs of Consensus, Compromise and Cooperation were the order of the day. This was the formula championed by the Countryside Review Committee (CRC), an anonymous group of civil servants set up by the government in 1974 to investigate all aspects of rural land-use. However it was quite apparent that the efforts of conservation bodies to pursue policies in cooperation with farming and forestry interests had failed. As Malcolm MacEwen pointed out at the Conference of the Council for National Parks in 1979, 'to make the achievement of consensus the primary aim of policy is to sacrifice the weaker interest to the stronger, and the long-term interest to short-term expediency. Those who own and control the land and the resources then become the real policy makers.'

The Council of the NCC should have taken a key part in explaining that the three Cs formula was not working. However they did not and they continued throughout the 1970s to promote the CRC philosophy. Ironically Reg Hookaway, former Director of the Countryside Commission and widely regarded as the inspirer of the insipid CRC paper on *Conservation and the Countryside Heritage*, wrote in the *Sunday Times* that 'everything we have achieved in protecting the environment has been by dint of fighting the combined opposition of vested interests'. These are fine words but a brief examination of the achievements of the Commission, Hookaway's own organization, shows that it has been as eager as the NCC to avoid confrontation with landowning interests. Throughout the 1970s the people invited by the Secretary of State on to the Council and Committees of the NCC gave the impression of a short-list for a country landowners' *Who's Who*. In theory more direct control, with power wrested away from the scientists, should have made the NCC more responsive to public views about wildlife and the countryside. Indeed in the summer of 1981 an opinion poll published by the *Daily Telegraph* revealed that increased rural conservation was ranked only second to curing unemployment in the public mind. There is no doubt that the NCC and the Countryside Commissions are still led by people who in no way reflect this public interest.

When at Easter 1980 Sir Ralph Verney was appointed the new Chairman of the NCC, it seemed to many conservationists that their worst fears had been realized. Sir Ralph had a long record of opposition to conservation arguments and though nobody doubted his integrity and knowledge of countryside matters his appointment seemed ill-judged. Sir Ralph's case is worth considering in detail, not just for the dilemma in which he found himself, but for the way in which his appointment personified the friction between the government's countryside interests and the demands of the environmental movement.

Sir Ralph's track record did not impress conservationists, many of whom recalled his attitude about where the Third London Airport should be sited. He had opposed the choice of Cublington way back in the 1960s. In view of the fact that the site was close to his north Buckinghamshire estate this was not surprising. But not only did he oppose the Cublington site, he actually advocated that the airport should be put at Maplin, an internationally important wildfowl site. At that time Sir Ralph was a member of the England Advisory Committee of the Conservancy and it was only after protracted wrangling that the Conservancy officers managed to maintain their right to oppose the choice of Maplin as the airport site.

In 1971 Malcolm MacEwen wrote after hearing Sir Ralph address the National Parks Conference that he

laid so much stress on the priority to be given to the production of food, the needs of the hill farmer, the production of timber and the extraction of minerals, that I was left wondering whether the National Parks enjoyed, in his eyes, any special protection at all. He was opposed to any form of additional control over farming and forestry echoing the Scott Committee in saying that 'the farmer seeks not to destroy the landscape, but to enhance it'.

On his appointment to the NCC in 1980 many people wondered how Sir Ralph could jump out of one camp, that of the country landowners (he was a past president of the CLA), into another whose main protagonists were, and are, to be found within the land-owning lobby.

Not long after Sir Ralph's appointment a report in the *Sunday Times* revealed that for some years he had successfully resisted the designation of Sheephouse Wood on his family estate as an SSSI. Without SSSI designation it was feared by NCC officers that Sheephouse Wood might meet the same fate as nearby Charndon Wood, which has now been almost totally destroyed by excavations of the London Brick Company. Sheephouse Wood is a fine deciduous woodland and harbours the rare black hair-streak butterfly. A former NCC scientist, now working elsewhere, recalls that 'We were not even allowed into those woods to do a survey.' It appeared to be a classic case of private interests conflicting with conservation.

In *The Times* of 2 April 1970, at the time of the Cublington debate, Sir Ralph was reported as calling for a fight 'against tyranny in its various forms', and he pledged himself 'to the inalienable rights of the little man in his home, unharassed by the tyranny of public interest in whatever guise'. Time and again, the public interest in conservation places (or should place) limits and restrictions on the profiteering activities of private landowners. How, one wonders, can Sir Ralph, the outspoken protagonist of public interest, comfortably adapt to championing the public interest in his role as the Chairman of a public body? The 'little men' Sir Ralph refers to are, of course, the beneficiaries of the theft of the commons which we discussed in Chapter 1.

Sir Ralph's discomfort, caught between the two roles of private landowner and enforcer of the public interest, was shared by other NCC Council and Committee members. (Sir Ralph, incidentally, was still a Forestry Commissioner when appointed NCC Chairman; he carried out planting of conifers in Sheephouse Wood during the 1970s and was still seeking government grant aid for this purpose in the early 1980s.) Close inspection of the constitution of the NCC Council at the time of his appointment shows that other members also had strong vested interests in the forestry business.

Dr Jean Balfour, Chairman of the Countryside Commission for Scotland during the controversy over its National Scenic Areas Project (see p. 205), was a Fellow of the Institute of Forestry, President of the Royal Scottish Forestry Society and a large absentee landlady in Sutherland. Lord Dulverton was a member of the

Home-Grown Timber Advisory Committee, former President of the Timber Growers' Organization, and a large landowner. And so the list continues. Links between the Forestry Commission, private forestry and the NCC were strong if not incestuous.

We have taken this forestry example to show the cause and effect of such appointments to the Council and Advisory Committees of the NCC. During the late 1970s NCC threatened to produce a policy review document on forestry to follow in the footsteps of its commendable if over-cautious *Conservation and Agriculture* (1977). In the early stages of the review (it is thought that over twenty drafts were written) senior scientists recommended to their Council that it should press for the introduction of planning controls over forestry operations. Not surprisingly the Council rejected the suggestion and none other than Dr Balfour set about rewriting the statement (which never appeared). At a 1981 meeting held to discuss the implementation of the Wildlife and Countryside Act, Sir Ralph told representatives of conservation groups that he had shelved plans for a written policy statement on forestry, preferring to emphasize 'cooperation' with professional forestry interests. Policy statements on water drainage and habitat conservation have similarly been dropped.

We could have told a similar story for the Countryside Commissions. As the public has no access to the civil service and ministerial communications about the choice of individuals for the conservation agencies' ruling bodies, we have no clear proof that members are chosen deliberately to ensure that our watchdogs remain toothless. It does, however, seem very much that way.

Five

Habitat Destruction

So far this book has been primarily concerned with the politics of conservation and land-use. Now we must look at the effects which the activities we discussed in the preceding chapter – in particular, farming and forestry – are having on our flora and fauna. It would take a whole series of books to detail all the plants and animals which are on the decline or have already disappeared from our landscape. The best we can do here is to give some indication of the losses of our major habitats and some of their plants and animals over the last few decades.

Where figures exist for rates of decline we give them, and for each habitat we give a brief description of its main characteristics and an explanation of why it is under threat. The accompanying maps highlight the plight of some of our most endangered species and habitats. We have arranged the habitats into five groups. We give the most thorough treatment to deciduous woodlands, and indeed they have claim to the greatest attention. Woodland occupies a place in our culture, our landscape and our literature unrivalled by any other habitat. The destruction of so much of our woodland over the past fifty years is one of the saddest aspects of the rape of the land. The section on woodlands is followed by one on grasslands, and this by a discussion of heaths, mountains and moors. We then look at the watery habitats; here we include lakes and streams, bogs and mires, and fens. Finally we take the diverse group of habitats which fringe our shores: estuaries, saltmarshes, sand dunes, cliffs and rocky shores, shingle beaches, and the open sea. Where we have felt it will be helpful we have given brief case studies of specific sites and species.

Woodlands

Until recently it was widely believed that the natural forest cover of Britain was a fairly dense oak forest, with other trees present only in small numbers where it was too wet or too chalky for oak to flourish. It was also thought that nothing of our original forest cover – the wildwood – survived.

It was known that many copses had been planted up for game by the Victorians but only a few places, like Wistman's Wood on Dartmoor, were considered to be anything like 'natural'. Subsequent investigations showed that Wistman's, like other upland woods straddling mountainsides or high in sheltered hanging valleys, was of comparatively recent origin. Foresters pointed out that great, ancient-looking trees such as the king oak of Moccas Park in Herefordshire or the huge cedar of Lebanon at Fountains Abbey were often only a few hundred and not thousands of years old (though the Perthshire Fortingall Yew is now known to be 1,500 years old), and the planting of some was even recorded in estate records. From this the foresters concluded, and conservationists mostly agreed, that as woods were not *natural*, there was no *a priori* argument for not 'improving' them. Faster-growing imports could replace native trees, and if there was nothing intrinsically valuable about a wood one might as well replace one lot of trees by another. Anyone who believed that twentieth-century woods were anything like the natural forest of the distant past was regarded by foresters and naturalists as hopelessly romantic.

Fortunately, studies in historical ecology have jolted conservationists awake. Studies of pollen preserved in layers of peat have shown that around 3000 BC the natural wooded cover of the 'postglacial' forest was not uniform but richly varied. The Scottish Highlands were dominated by pine and birch. In northern England, much of Wales and western Ireland, oak and hazel were the commonest trees. Across a great area of the south of England, small-leaved lime was the commonest tree. In Pembrokeshire, Cornwall and the rest of Ireland, hazel and elm dominated the landscape.

A closer look at contemporary woods revealed strong regional similarities to the ancient forest. People soon began to wonder if many existing woods could be direct descendants of the primeval wildwood. The historical ecologist Oliver Rackham discovered several kinds of elm woods, sweet chestnut woods (an early introduc-

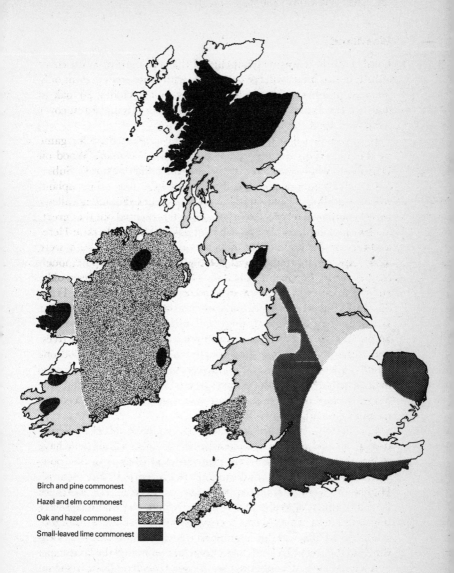

Birch and pine commonest

Hazel and elm commonest

Oak and hazel commonest

Small-leaved lime commonest

Map 2 The commonest tree species in Britain 5,000 years ago (after Rackham, 1976). This map represents a simplified version of what is known of Britain's natural woodland, around 5,000 years ago (*c.* 3000 years BC by radiocarbon dating). Most of the information is derived from layers of pollen preserved in peat bogs. Shortly after this time, elm became much less common, although it is not known exactly why.

tion), maple woods, alder woods and many more. He unearthed a hitherto unknown group of lime woods in Suffolk and others were found in Lincolnshire, Derbyshire, Essex and Norfolk. Botanists everywhere began a dramatic revision of their ideas, and the current predominance of oak in many woodlands is now attributed in large measure to its utility as a timber tree. Quite simply it has been greatly encouraged, while other trees which were also valued, such as the wild service (much commoner in medieval times than today), were used but, for reasons we do not understand, not replaced or allowed to regenerate.

Ecologists have also produced convincing evidence to show that certain plant species (such as yellow archangel, herb paris, dog's mercury and, in East Anglia, even the bluebell) are good indicator species of ancient woodland (woodland which documentary evidence confirms was present in medieval times). As almost all our planted woods originated after 1700 it is most probable that ancient woodlands have a very long history, going back substantially further than medieval times. In other regions, where other climates and soils prevail, there are other good biological indicators of ancient woodland. Around London, for example, wild service tree, wood millet, coral root and bilberry seem reliable, while in the Cotswolds meadow saffron and angular solomon's seal can be used. Certain lichens are also indicators of ancient forest continuity.

Deer parks were among the earliest enclosures and have long been signs of rank and privilege. There were a few hare parks, but deer were highly valued as an easily kept source of fresh meat for the winter months, and for centuries royal dispensation was required to keep, let alone hunt them. Although they have lost most of their flowers from centuries of intense grazing, deer parks have some very ancient trees. They provide a habitat which was once common enough in the wildwood but which has not often survived the intensive if sporadic utilization of ancient woodlands for timber. This habitat consists of large, standing, 'over-mature' (an unpleasant forestry term) trees. Such trees provide living, dead and dying wood in all stages from new shoots to crumbly cubes of dry rot falling through to a hollow central trunk. These trees are in what ecologists term advanced stages of 'retrenchment': growth on poor soils or repeated pollarding (cutting the upper branches, reducing the tree to a boll or single trunk) extends this period, and hence longevity.

In entomological terms the insects of these trees are the 'dead wood fauna', and make up a complicated interdependent community of beetles and others which exploit every stage of timber, dead and alive. Many such beetles are restricted to just a handful of sites (Windsor Great Park, Epping Forest, Sherwood Forest, parts of the New Forest and Moccas Park are nationally important) and, as at Moccas Park, even to just a single tree. The precarious lifeline that this handful of venerable trees provides to their inhabitants, survivors of the wildwood, is matched by the powerful feeling of immense antiquity that they convey to any visitor. Here is a description of the oaks in Moccas by the Victorian diarist Francis Kilvert:

> I fear those grey old men of Moccas, those grey, gnarled, low-browed, knock-kneed, bowed, bent, huge, strange, long-armed, deformed, hunchbacked, misshapen oak men that stand waiting and watching century after century ... such tales to tell, as when they whisper them to each other in the midsummer nights, make the ... aspens shiver and the long ears of hares and rabbits stand on end. No human hand set those oaks. They are 'the trees which the Lord hath planted'. They look as if they had been at the beginning and making of the world, and they will probably see its end.

Little of Britain's ecological heritage can have been so concentrated and distilled as in these old trees. Surely here, if anywhere, is a good case for planning controls to ensure their survival, and the essential ecological continuity that enables their passengers to survive. Replacing them with cultivars from a tree nursery will iron out their wrinkles, the variety and ecological niches and microhabitats; letting them grow unpollarded, as now happens in places such as Richmond Park, will hasten their death; planting around them with vigorous young trees, as happened at one Northamptonshire park, also kills them. Only careful conservation management will save them and one of our most irreplaceable natural assets.

Written evidence from sources such as the old *Coucher Book of Ely* reveals that the boundaries of many ancient woodlands have not changed for hundreds, perhaps thousands of years. A good number of case histories appear in Oliver Rackham's classic little book *Trees and Woodlands in the British Landscape*. Charcoal remains, and other physical sources of evidence, show a history of continuity back to Roman times. But the most astonishing evidence of all comes from the discovery of 'corduroy roads', Neolithic and Bronze Age trackways buried and preserved in peat in areas such as the Somerset Levels. Radiocarbon dating puts one from that area at almost 6,000

years old. The wood from which they were constructed includes
millions of small logs of uniform, carefully used and selected size.
Rackham argues that such wood could never be found in the wildwood, unless it was coppiced. Thus the known beginnings of traditional woodland management can be put at around 4000 BC. The
trackways themselves are remarkable feats of workmanship, built
of oak logs with poles of ash, lime, hazel, alder and holly, each with
a particular structural role, and joined with birch pegs.

There is good reason to believe that woodland management
changed little for the next forty centuries or more. 'For the 1,000
year period between the end of the Roman occupation and the
beginnings of the Renaissance,' wrote Richard Mabey in *The
Flowering of Britain*, 'the people of Britain lived in a state of extreme
seclusion. A relative absence of unsettling new ideas, and a deep-
rooted connection between community and place ... helped rein-
force the intense relationship with nature that is one of the most
conspicuous features of early medieval culture.' To early British,
Celtic, Viking, Roman and Anglo-Saxon woodland lore and
culture were added the practices of the Normans, and the resulting
woodland-based economy is recorded in the Domesday Book of
1086. In these isolated centuries there was plenty of time to develop
the special uses and industries that employed every scrap of wood,
timber, bark and foliage from the woodlands, to find the medicinal
value of every herb and discover the ways of every bird and animal.
In fact life depended on it. Oak was used for timber; elm for anything which needed to stand water (elm water-pipes are probably
still carrying some mains water under city streets today); ash to 'give'
in tool handles; and the extra-hard hornbeam, known formerly as
'hardebeme', for cutting a screw thread. Maple was valued for
turnery, dogwood (a shrub of calcareous soils) was good only for
'dogs' or meat-skewers, and when wool was first spun by machine,
the spindle bush proved useful. Hazel was used for rods in hurdles for
'dead-hedges' before many fields were permanently enclosed, and
in wattle walls, which were stronger and more waterproof than
modern sand and lime rendering. Hazel was also a 'quick' tree,
with 'lively' supernatural powers.

Various barks were valued for tanning, and waterproof alderwood
was used for making clogs. In Wales there is still the occasional
Coed Clocsau – clogs wood. Beech came from the Chiltern woods
for 'bodging' into chairs, as did cherry, which was used in furniture

and carving. Lime was used in shields and later its fibres were employed as 'bast' for string or rope. Willows were used in basketry, hats and eventually cricket bats. In parts of Scotland, where clearances removed almost all woodlands, the rowan or mountain ash – a tree which was reputed to drive away evil spirits – was used for almost everything.

Right up to the twentieth century, the wildlife that relied on woods – leaf moulds, plants, insects, fungi, and animals – all survived in a deep peace. True woodland inhabitants are expert at marking time. Now confined to a few Cotswold beech woods, the red helleborine can retreat underground to live in confinement and controlled parasitism with a fungus for two decades or more, until conditions are right for flowering again. In this way it can await the outcome of a protracted death-struggle between two giant forest trees until, for a season or two, the canopy opens above. Caper spurge and downy woundwort have similar vanishing abilities. Primroses in Haley Wood, Cambridgeshire, flowered continuously for eighteen months when a neglected coppice was cut in 1955, so pleased were they to see the light. But there are things these plants cannot stand or escape from. One, of course, is woodland clearance: conversion to modern agriculture. And another is the draining, spraying, ploughing and smothering that conversion to conifer cropping involves.

Between 1947 and 1980, 50 per cent of our ancient woodland was lost. Most was converted to conifers, the rest mainly to arable. Between 1951 and 1981 the destruction of ancient woodland in East Anglia was greater than it had been in the previous 300 years. The area of ancient woodland in a county like Lincolnshire has now shrunk to a perilous 0·48 per cent of the land surface and Cambridge-shire has only 0·63 per cent, yet felling continues. Over half the ancient woodlands that were present in Lincolnshire in 1920 have now been converted to commercial plantation forestry. One of those lost was the famous lime wood in which the artist the Reverend Keble-Martin drew the lime for his *Concise Flora* in the 1930s. The destruction is widely grant-aided by the MAFF and the Forestry Commission.

The losses are countrywide. The Metropolitan District of Wake-field in Yorkshire lost just under a quarter of its woodland cover – almost all to agriculture – in the seventeen years prior to 1978. The borders of Scotland lost a staggering 80 per cent of their deci-

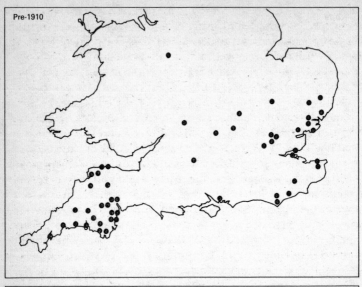

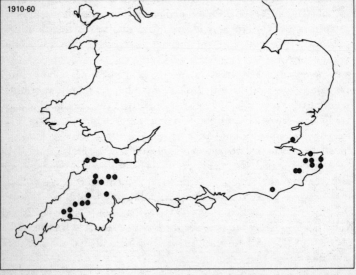

Map 3 The decline of the heath fritillary butterfly (compiled from data kindly provided by Dr Jeremy Thomas, Institute of Terrestrial Ecology). The heath fritillary is one of a number of British butterflies threatened with extinction through habitat destruction. It requires specific woodland management to breed successfully and its decline parallels the loss of ancient coppice woodland.

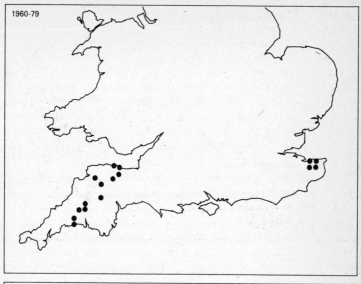

1960-79

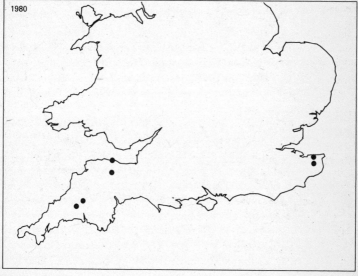

1980

duous woodland between 1950 and 1980, as did Kincardine, while Fife lost a third. Devon, one of our most wooded and attractive counties, lost 20 per cent of its woodland in just two decades up to 1972 and more has gone since. Of the particularly fine woodlands of Hertfordshire, rich in flora and with an unusual abundance of the locally distributed hornbeam, 56 per cent of the woodland has been eliminated since 1850. In Cambridgeshire, which is the least wooded English county, 17 per cent of the woodland was lost in only thirty-five years. The fate of our hedgerows has already been touched on (see p. 23): 140,000 miles have been lost since 1945 and destruction continues at the rate of 2,000 miles a year.

The victims of this destruction are many. Even where the woodland is converted to conifers or to hardwood plantation forestry (such as the Chilean beech) the loss is complete. The very reasons why species are good 'indicators' mitigate against their being able to re-colonize secondary (new) woodland or withstand such changes.

For example the heath fritillary, which despite its name is a woodland butterfly, requires young coppice where its food plant, cow wheat, grows (it may also need plantains). Although its exact habitat requirements are not known it seems incapable of spreading from one wood to another across open ground. The heath fritillary was known from fifty sites in fourteen counties before 1910, then declined to twenty-seven sites by 1960 (after a period when many woods fell into neglect as traditional skills died out), sixteen in the period 1960–79 as habitat destruction took hold, and today it is confined to just six widely separated sites. These are the woods at Blean, near Canterbury, and a handful of sites in Wessex. The heath fritillary cannot escape its ancient woodlands; it is locked into a lifestyle which was made in the wildwood but which can only survive with traditional management. It looks a good candidate for extinction. Indeed the chequered skipper, another butterfly, became extinct in its traditional Northamptonshire woods in 1976 (although another small population has turned up in Scotland). Dr Jeremy Thomas of the Institute for Terrestrial Ecology at Furzebrook feels that the extinction of another butterfly, the high brown fritillary, is 'not unlikely' in the near future. It is, he comments, 'another butterfly about which we know almost nothing although it is declining fast'. The high brown is an attractive woodland species which lays its eggs on dog violet.

Plant indicators spread equally slowly and stand little chance of reaching suitable new habitat even where it exists. Dog's mercury creeps along at 10–30 cm a year, depending on soil conditions. Its seed may be carried by ants, but quite how far, nobody knows. Ox-lip has been observed spreading into some secondary woodland from the ancient Cambridgeshire Haley Wood at the relatively rapid pace of 4 ft a year. But such species cannot cross unwooded modern pastures or arable land.

Whatever foresters may claim, plantations are no replacement for ancient woods. There is no way, in this case, that 'nature can adapt'. Old woodland species are specialists that need the lineal descendants of the wildwood to survive. The purple emperor, our largest and most spectacular butterfly, is now reduced to a handful of secret old oak forest locations with high canopy in southern England. The black hair-streak, restricted to woodland with thickets of blackthorn, is now found in just thirty sites.

The red helleborine, the ghost orchid, the wild gladiolus (now found only in the remotest glades of the New Forest), the shrub mezereon (whose pink flowers can only be seen in the wild at a few limestone dale and gorge sites), and the elegant soldier orchid are a few woodland plants that received the protection of Parliament under the 1975 Conservation of Wild Creatures and Wild Plants Act. It is an offence to take any part of them, cut them or uproot them, but their habitat has no effective legal protection.

The ghost orchid epitomizes the plight of real woodland plants. It is a saprophyte: without chlorophyll it cannot manufacture food of its own by using sunlight and the atmosphere. Instead it digests food directly from the deep leaf litter in which it lives. The plant was first found in 1854 by Victorian botanists in damp oak woods in Herefordshire and Shropshire. They collected its bulbous root and weird pale pink and orange neck and flower, transporting it to gardens where it soon died. It was not seen again in those haunts but the next hundred years brought nine sightings from the Chiltern beech woods. The plant grows slowly and may flower only once in twenty years after a damp spring. Even then it is unpredictable, appearing in any one of the summer months.

Case Study: Bedford Purlieus: What Would Be Lost If It Went

Bedford Purlieus, a fragment of Northamptonshire's Rockingham Forest, is an ancient woodland of 440 acres of probably unparalleled richness. A total of 462 species of plants have been found (excluding thirty-four mosses, a minimum of 309 different sorts of fungi and, in a wood that is poor for them, thirty-five lichens). Its diversity owes something to its ten different soil types, from glacial sands to chalky boulder clay, older cornbrash, Bisworth clay and several limestones, giving a wide variety of soil chemistry.

A map of 1589 refers to 'ancient boundaries' while a perambulation (meaning a walk using landmarks as boundaries) defined it as early as 1299. It was probably among the 'old walls and wild woods' referred to in the tenth century when St Athewold rebuilt the nearby monastery of Medehamstede (now Peterborough). We know a great deal about Bedford Purlieus as it has been subject to the research of a team of historical ecologists centred at Monks Wood Experimental Station, but there is no reason to suppose that it is not broadly typical of many ancient woodlands. Let us therefore look in some detail at what the loss of such a wood can mean.

The wood was certainly being managed for both pannage (acorns) and grazing in 1212 and on a coppice basis in 1457 when hedges were also being plashed to keep out browsing beasts. One Nicholas Thorogood was taken to task in the Manorial Rolls of 1599 for grazing horses, cattle and sheep in the wood, as well as for letting sett-gatherers (hedge-planters) into the wood without permission to collect young bushes, fell and remove forty loads of thorns, old maples, sallows and hazels, and cut down 'two great crab trees, one servis tree [wild service], two ashes and divers old sallows'. In 1639 the wood was 'disafforested' (meaning not that it was cut down, but that it was removed from the deer forest of Rockingham) and gained the status of 'free warren' or purlieu wood, hence its name.

From 1640 to 1870 a rotation of roughly eighteen years was used for coppice, allowing the tree stumps or 'stools' to regrow after cutting, and many species of plants such as the bristle scirpus and the rare caper spurge benefited from the small-scale disturbances that track-making, the digging of saw-pits, uprooting of trees, coppicing and clearing of undergrowth created. It is a mistake to think that such management will threaten rare species today as they have been able to survive centuries of such cutting and churning. In the nineteenth century, the wood was very private property and payments were made for catching 'nutters' (people gathering nuts).

Historian Phyllida Rixton records that in 1912 the *Peterborough Advertiser* carried a remarkable article which noted:

only half a century ago it [Bedford Purlieus] was an enormous forest covering about a thousand acres of land and today it is only about half that area ... men are still living in the villages of Wansford, Kingscliffe, Nassington and all around that were employed as foresters, woodsmen and oakers ... others are still living that helped grub up nearly half that thousand acres of forest and make it into farmlands ... If the Duke of Bedford who ordered the clearance could have forseen how much cheaper wheat would have become, it is very probable that the old Purlieus would never have been interfered with, for they yielded a good harvest of timber and underwood every year ... and a large number of woodsmen were constantly employed.

Two old men related their story to the paper:

We got £10 an acre for grubbing – getting up the roots and undergrowth. In an acre there would not be very many of these great trees – oaks, ashes, elms and lime ... Some of the great trees were so large that it was impossible for men to climb up them with the rope (to direct their fall) ... One of the woodmen would fasten this (a noose, at the end of a rope thrown high in the tree) around his waist and clasping the rope over his head with his hands would be drawn up into the boughs by the other end of the rope ... When grubbing around these roots we would come up with strange things which had made their homes under the trees. In the first place we should dig up whole colonies of newts which had made their nests there. Snakes, too, in abundance would be found curled up in cavities lined with leaves. Occasionally we should unearth hedgehogs in this way, but not often; we generally found them outside the wood in hedgerows. A few dormice too we should find, but not many.

While engaged in the Purlieus, continues the report, they would be 'surrounded with swarms of foxes and [red] squirrels and in the early morning and evening the air would be filled with the hooting of owls ...'.

The diversity of wildlife has persisted, in part at least, up to the present day. Seventy-one bird species were recorded between 1961 and 1969, of which forty-nine were known to breed in the wood, including the long-eared owl. Although it is set in an intensive agricultural area and the sparrowhawk has only been recorded once in recent years, a decline in the use of pesticides (see p. 25) might bring it back, together perhaps with the similar but larger and more secretive goshawk. Eight earthworms, eighteen snail species, nine harvestmen (nearly half the number of British species), six different woodlice, five species of ants, thirty-nine butterflies, 275 of the larger moths and 507 species of beetles and a variety of bugs and bees have been found in the wood. Some came to light over a period of decades but most were found in a concentrated survey lasting only a couple of days. A single visit by a beetle enthusiast raised the number of species known to be present by thirty-four, so the animals are certainly under-estimated.

Yet despite its richness Bedford Purlieus only just escaped complete destruction for ironstone extraction by the British Steel Corporation in 1964. Conifers, however, have also been extensively planted in some areas by the Forestry Commission. Today the NCC is trying to persuade the Commission of its views on management and the wood is a Grade 1 SSSI (of international importance). However, while the British Steel Corporation holds the mineral rights (to valuable industrial sands as well as ironstone) the woods will never be entirely safe.

Grasslands

The heyday of British grasslands came during the late seventeenth and eighteenth centuries. They were then extensive but unimproved. At that time, drainage of the fens and areas like Romney Marsh was still adding to pasture, as was the gradual erosion of woodland. For centuries sheep had become steadily more important in the medieval economy and the wool industry remained our key manufacturing industry until the Industrial Revolution.

Land had also been passing in and out of arable and grassland use for centuries. Sheep walks stretching hundreds of miles across the country often occupied land which had been cultivated with primitive ploughs during Neolithic times. Later they had been abandoned, only to be revived as arable during the Roman period. Once the Romans left they reverted to pasture. The land stayed under grass until the medieval population grew large enough to demand more crops. But then the Black Death killed so many people that in the fourteenth century extensive sheep-grazing returned and was to last until the twentieth century. In the valleys, cattle-grazing reflected similar influences.

It was about the turn of the eighteenth century, as the Agrarian Revolution really caught hold, that the grassland communities first began to succumb to the ecologically impoverishing effect of agricultural improvement. Downland was extensively enclosed and much was ploughed up to provide root crops for winter feed. Grasslands were resown with clover, and the process accelerated over the next 200 years. The last great bustard, a bird of the wide open grasslands, was shot in Norfolk in 1838, becoming extinct at the same time as the rural wool industry went into decline and its habitat contracted. During the Second World War, great areas of downland were ploughed up (see p. 27) and the era of slow agricultural change gave way to the technochemical era of farming. Within a few decades, characteristic grassland birds such as the corncrake were reduced by over 80 per cent (today it is extinct over most of its mainland former range and is confined to the Hebrides).

Grassland plants and animals originated in many natural habitats. Moles are common in grassland but are really woodland animals, where their runs may last not just for one but for many generations. One of the plants fought over at Cow Green (see p. 69) included the tiny Teesdale sandwort which is a relict of the Ice Age tundra that has only managed to survive there because the very crumbly Upper Teesdale Limestone will not support trees. The celebrated chalk downland flora derives from sea cliffs, the tops of ant hills, forest glades, sand dunes, river banks and other diverse habitats. But while many species can survive elsewhere – unlike many true woodland species – old grasslands are like ancient woods in that they are places with a unique history of human use and natural opportunism. The grassland tapestry has grown richer as each character has found a niche, settled and multiplied. As with woods, age has added diversity.

Man's agricultural methods were tolerable so long as they were slow, based largely on natural species and conducted without synthetic chemicals. Before the age of freight transport and the seed merchant, local seed had to be used. Seed from haylofts was employed to revert fallow or arable into pasture. Before herbicides, the seed bank (the buried population of viable seed) was not much altered from the days of the wildwood.

The beautiful blue pasque flower is an indicator of very old chalk or limestone grassland. It produces abundant seed but the seedlings have leaves only 0·2 cm long after two years' growth. So it seems unlikely that its opportunities for active spread would be very frequent. And such species are slow to recolonize disturbed land. Porton Down, for example, was ploughed for wheat for thirty years from 1830 and is now our second largest remaining fragment of chalk downland. But probably because of that disturbance it has few of the rarer chalk grassland flowers. It seems that the agricultural improvements of the nineteenth century were already enough to prevent its full recovery. Nowadays old grasslands are remote islands in seas of barley and rye grass, and natural recovery following destruction would be quite impossible.

Grazing by sheep (whose teeth cut) and cattle (whose tongues pull up mouthfuls) has different effects, as do the grazing methods of other animals. But in general grazing suppresses taller grasses in favour of herbs with underground corms, rhizomes or tubers (such as orchids), or basal rosettes, leaves pressed to the soil. In addition, highly alkaline soils derived from chalk or limestone are poor in nitrate and phosphate, so the more demanding species are at a further disadvantage. Grazing depletes the nutrient levels (as does hay-cutting) still further. This changes the balance of competition, resulting in a high diversity of attractive flowering plants and associated insects. Similar tricks of soil chemistry occur on serpentine soils (rich in magnesium, chromium and nickel), resulting in many kinds of small flowers, and in light calcareous sands as in the Brecks of East Anglia.

If grazing stops, everything changes. At first, many species flower in a profusion that had been suppressed by grazing. This happened with maiden pink in the Brecks and pasque flowers on the chalk once myxomatosis virus killed off local rabbits. But these species are soon overtopped by others (pasque flower, for example, can't flower in vegetation over 20 cm high). Yet increased structural diversity allows more species of invertebrates such as spiders and butterflies to occur. The rare Lulworth skipper butterfly has benefited from reduced sheep-grazing on the Dorset army ranges in recent years. The species has reached a population of over a million on just one hillside of its food plant, chalk false-broome grass, but as it is just about the only population it is still vulnerable. In a couple of seasons it could crash to just hundreds, as indeed the adonis blue has done in the same area. This species requires a turf of very short grass. It needs temperatures over 9°C to breed, which is only provided by the closest cropped chalk sward in the south. It is now so rare that it could be exterminated by collectors.

Ground-nesting birds are also highly sensitive to management. Grasshopper warblers churr away in the longest grass, and the old flood meadow system practised in areas such as Oxford's Otmoor, where winter alluvium acted as a natural fertilizer, gave nest sites for snipe and others, and a hunting ground for barn owls. One such site that is now safeguarded as a National Nature Reserve is Cricklade North Meadow, in Wiltshire. It is still managed in the traditional way. In winter it is flooded by the rivers Churn and Thames, and on Lammas Day (12 August) it becomes common grazing until 12 February. A hay crop is then grown and sold in lots, like coppice, in July. Cricklade is still a stronghold of the snake's-head fritillary as a result.

On acid soils, over rocks such as granite or slate, intensive grazing reduces diversity, leaving a poor sward dominated by unpalatable species such as the wiry mat grass, *Nardus*. Centuries of rain and grazing have leached away nutrients or carried them off on the hoof, denuding the soil of chemical bases such as calcium. In such circumstances the addition of nutrients in small amounts can increase diversity, and the presence of hard rush or golden saxifrage shows up base-rich wet flushes among impoverished grasslands. But fertilizer will upset some specialist species, and while nitrates are easily leached, concentrations of phosphate, which is relatively immobile in the soil, are likely to build up.

In 1980, a survey of sixty-one of Oxfordshire's 249 remaining flood meadows, a particularly rich habitat, revealed that twelve (one-fifth) had been destroyed in just two years. Most had been drained and ploughed up. The plight of the fritillary (see p. 9) is shared by other plants and animals of these ancient alluvial meadows. Curlew, yellow wagtail, redshank, corncrake and even black-tailed godwits used to nest in such meadows before the hay was cut. Modern methods remove their cover, and modern grass mixtures contain only one or two species and support very few insects. As the Friends of the Earth note in *Paradise Lost*, twenty-four species of butterfly are known to occur on old pastures in southern England, but not one on chemically treated grass fields.

The losses are countrywide. In the new county of Avon 50 per cent of the unimproved meadows were destroyed in the ten years leading up to 1980, and 67 per cent of Devon's rough grassland was lost in the twenty-year period up to 1972. A fifth of the Hampshire chalk downland was destroyed between 1966 and 1980, and 17·5 per cent of that on the Isle of Wight. At least half of the ancient grassland in Lincolnshire has been lost in the last thirty years. The list of casualties in the one-way war goes mournfully on.

Several of our most endangered butterflies are among the victims.

The adonis blue is reduced to under seventy individual sites, and this number is halving every twelve years or so. Its extinction can be expected before the year 2000. Its habitat is chalk grassland. The glanville fritillary is down to just twelve small colonies on the Isle of Wight, though it used to occur on the mainland (its habitat is grassland and scrub), and the silver spotted skipper, another chalk grassland butterfly, has only thirty known populations. After the heath fritillary, it is probably our most endangered species.

Particular mention should be made here of the fate of the large blue butterfly which became extinct in 1979. It is a prime example of a species which has disappeared as a result of the loss of its habitat. The extinction of the large blue had been predicted fifty years earlier but no serious study of its ecology was launched until 1972, when it was already far too late to save it. The species had a specialized life cycle that made it highly dependent on undisturbed habitat. It laid its eggs on thyme flowers, upon which the young caterpillars fed. But the older larvae mimicked those of one species of small red ant and were carried into an ant nest where for the next nine months they would feed on ant grubs. To breed continuously and successfully at a site, conditions therefore had to be right for the thyme (which could be overtopped by other species if the grazing was too light), for the ants (the desirable species was outcompeted by another if grazing levels dropped) and for the mating and feeding of the adult butterfly itself. Moreover, high mortalities occurred among larvae if there were not enough ant nests, and crowding took place. In addition, thyme had to be growing within the small foraging area of a caterpillar around each ant nest.

Collectors had always hunted the large blue but the main threat was total habitat destruction, mainly through ploughing up of old grassland. So it was that ninety known sites had declined to thirty in the 1950s – in the Cotswolds, Somerset, Devon, and Cornwall – then to only four by the mid-1960s. These were lost in 1967, 1971, 1973 and 1979. Ecologists had feared such an inescapable decline because the sites were too small and too isolated from one another for an exchange of populations to take place, thus making the species vulnerable to a series of adverse events. Sadly, the full ecological requirements were not understood until only one colony remained, and despite final despairing efforts at semi-captive breeding, the last of twenty-two large blues laid a few sterile eggs in the summer of 1979 and the species vanished from the British countryside.

Case Study: Wendlebury Meads

On one remarkable farm, Starveall Farm on Oxfordshire's Wendlebury Meads, several strands of the story of grasslands come together. It is said to be the most intact medieval pasture in Britain, and is recognized as of international importance for conservation (a Grade 1 SSSI).

Probably the last farm hacked from the wildwood in the area, Starveall was enclosed by Act of Parliament rather late, in 1801. In 1979 ecologist Mary Scruby made a detailed study of the site. She found that several of the nine fields had not been ploughed since 1801, and probably not for many hundreds of years before that. One had probably never been ploughed. In all, 148 species of herbs, mosses and grasses were found in the sward, at densities of up to forty-five per square metre (in Furze Ley, the oldest field), with even a respectable thirty per square metre in a field ploughed only forty years ago. Despite various agricultural rotations in the last 170 years, involving beans, wheat and so on, the pasture has always recovered to a richness equalling chalk downland. The main reasons seem to be that in winter cattle were fed from ricks carrying hay cut from the fields on the farm, so the seed cycle was unbroken. The fields were also never reseeded and in nearly all parts fertilizer was never used. Lime and basic slag were only applied once or twice in odd places. Recolonization was always possible from surrounding fields. Herbicides were completely unknown.

Each of the fields is different, and while ninety-six species occur in the richest one, that is still just a fraction of the total. The farm must be preserved intact as each part is distinct. National rarities abound: the very scarce green-winged orchid is abundant, as are devil's bit scabious and greater burnet. Fourteen tree and shrub species occur in the hedgerows, including the almost extinct wild pear, as well as spindle. The fields undulate in complicated mixtures of dry ridges and damp furrows, each of which has a different ecological community.

But in August 1980, despite SSSI designation, some twenty-nine acres were ploughed up by a local farmer, tired of waiting for a NCC grant. An extraordinary deep black soil was revealed beneath the turf, torn like a huge green carpet. The farmer anticipated that it would take two or three years to 'plough in' the ridge and furrows. Ragged robin, yellow meadow vetchling, orchis, cowslip, carnation

sedge and hayrattle hung upside down, green for a long time before
wilting on the uprooted turves. At high summer the next year, a
uniform cereal crop stood in their place. It seemed almost un-
naturally green and vigorous. 'Field 3' of the ecological study had
entered the world of chemical farming.

Farms of the Wendlebury type were once ordinary, not international rarities. (Parsonage Down in Wiltshire is perhaps its only
chalk downland equivalent.) Some species were once so widespread
that they had over fifty common names. After agricultural improvement, probably less than twenty species could survive at Wendlebury.

Heaths, Mountains and Moorlands

Heaths, almost without exception, were once covered by forest.
Having been cleared for agricultural purposes they proved too
infertile to sustain real pasture or arable crops. Within the category
of heaths, however, there is much variation.

The archetypal heaths are the lowland, dry heaths of southern
England. These areas, dominated by gorse and the low shrubby
Erica heathers, are very rich in insects. The insects attract birds such
as the nightjar – a nocturnal moth-hunter – and the hobby, a small
falcon. All six of Britain's reptiles – smooth snake, adder, grass snake,
sand lizard and common lizard and slow worm – can be found on
some southern heaths, though each has specialist feeding and habitat
preferences. Specialist invertebrates include a range of hunting and
potter wasps, and the spectacular black, white and scarlet spider,
Eresus niger, only recently rediscovered in Dorset.

Other sorts of heaths are less distinctive. In wet areas, for example,
many 'bog species' will grow on heaths. Cotton grass, sphagnum
moss, the insectivorous sun-dew and bog asphodel can be found in
damp pools only inches away from purple heather which favours
dry soil. Extensive wet zones occur in shallow depressions on strongly
'podsolized' heaths. Here, nutrients and chemicals such as iron salts
are leached down into the soil forming an impermeable layer or
'pan', thus trapping water above.

Another type of heath is lichen heath, where the low vegetation is
dominated by ground-living lichens such as *Cetraria* species and the
bluish grey *Cladonia* (reindeer moss) species. Similarly, the mountain
moss *Rhacomitrium*, which covers boulder screes on some high

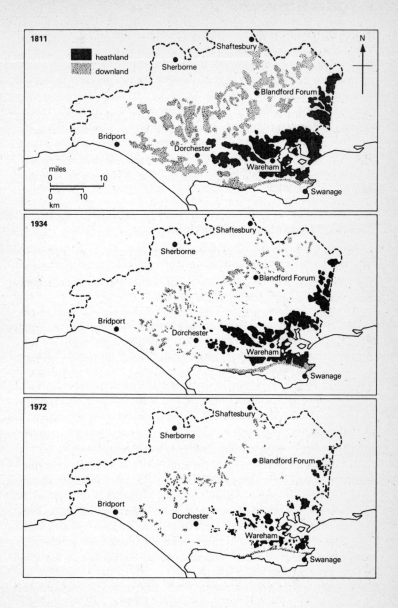

Map 4 Dorset heath and downs: vanishing habitat (redrawn from Fuller, *Bird Habitats in Britain*, Poyser, 1982)

plateaus, has given its name to *Rhacomitrium* heath. 'Upland heath', on the other hand, normally refers to short rough grassland with substantial amounts of moss, as well as plants such as bilberry. Unlike moorland, such vegetation normally forms on mineral as opposed to peaty soils.

Many of our heaths are disappearing fast, the upland ones being rapidly afforested, and those in the lowlands being reclaimed for agriculture with the liberal use of chemical fertilizers. As a result, many lowland heath species are under threat and some species like the smooth snake face the prospect of extinction in the near future. The rates of lowland heath loss have been particularly dramatic. Twenty per cent of the heaths in Hampshire and the Isle of Wight were destroyed in fourteen years, 75 per cent have gone from Dorset over the last fifty years, and in Fife 76 per cent have been lost since the mid-1950s. Of the upland heaths, 90 per cent were lost from Dumfries and Galloway in the same period. And in the Brecks of Suffolk and Norfolk, a massive 70 per cent of the former characteristic heath has now been improved, mostly for cereal cropping.

Britain is a relatively mountainous country and among our most important conservation sites are ranges such as the Cairngorms, Snowdon, Ben Eighe, Ben Nevis and Helvellyn. The Highlands and Islands was the only area of Britain identified as of global significance in the World Conservation Strategy in 1980.

Much of the vast Caledonian pine forest, which once swathed the middle of Scotland, survived until the sixteenth and seventeenth centuries, thousands of years after most of the lowlands had been converted to intimate but tamer countryside. Fragments still remain in forests such as the Black Wood of Rannoch, Rothiemurchus and Glen Affric. They are still an impressive sight, although pressures for conversion to plantation forestry and over-grazing by red deer are ever-present threats. Some of their inhabitants, however, are doing well. A recent survey suggests that the polecat has increased its range in Britain almost three-fold since 1963, though the less adaptable pine marten is declining. Flowers are few in these great forests though the beauty of plants such as the chickweed wintergreen makes up for the lack of species. In the pine forests species such as the crossbill, crested tit and pine beauty moth are pine specialists, each exploiting the dominant tree for food.

When grazing and browsing are not limiting factors, heather

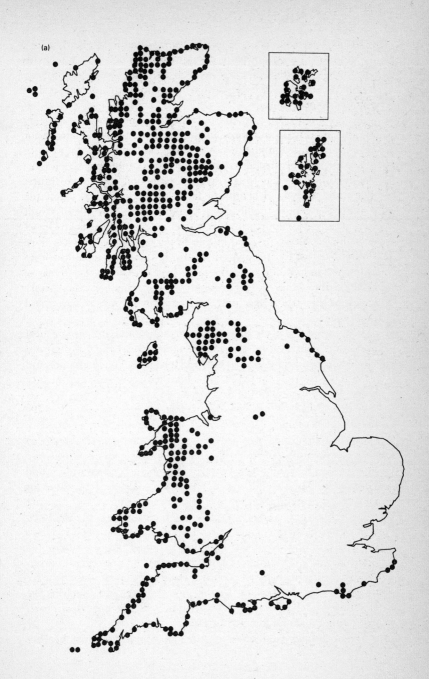

(a)

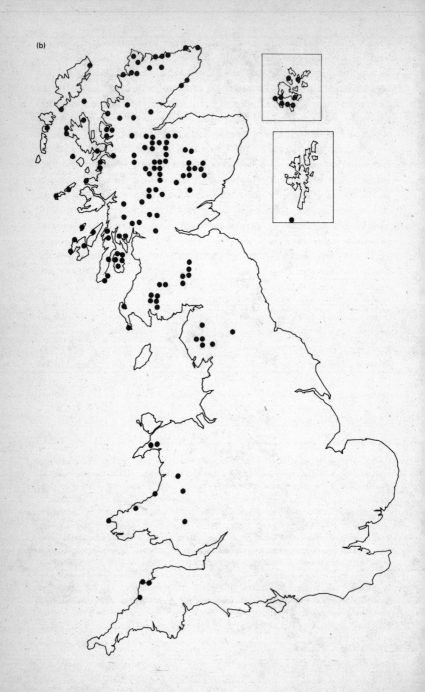

grows into great bushes, birch and juniper grow among the pines, and bilberry carpets the ground. Black grouse (or black cock) live around the upper limits of the forest, while the huge capercaillie (reintroduced after a short period of extinction in Britain) live in dense pine thickets. Wild cats are still more frequent than a casual visitor would realize, and the golden eagle has now moved as far south as England and recolonized the Lake District.

Although great areas on the lower hills are still managed by muir-burning for sheep, and for red grouse by patchwork heather-burning, some rich moorlands like those on the Berwyn Mountains in Wales still exist. Here, sadly, afforestation threatens the moors and if blanket planting does occur the local bearberry and unique abundance of birds of prey (including hen harrier, merlin and peregrine) will be eliminated.

The high mountains themselves have very characteristic species. Birds like the meadow pipit, the wheatear and golden plover are confined to the intermediate slopes, while the tops, especially on our highest range, the near-Arctic Cairngorms, are left to a hardy few. These include the ptarmigan, the peregrine, the raven, the dotterel and, of course, the golden eagle.

Most mountain species are threatened, endangered or at risk in Britain. Several, such as the blue heath, are confined to only one or two sites and are being trampled out of existence by unwitting walkers. The Snowdon lily is in a similarly serious plight. The latest ski-lift developments in the Cairngorms have led to an outcry because it is feared that an influx of people will not just disturb the

Map 5 The peregrine population of Britain: effects of persecution and pesticides (redrawn from D. Ratcliffe, *The Peregrine*, Poyser, 1980). Map (a) shows the 'natural' distribution of the peregrine falcon in the British Isles, based on breeding records from 1900 to 1955 (although prior to 1900 the peregrine also bred on cliffs in Norfolk, at more sites in the Peak District and elsewhere). Map (b), based on consistently occupied territories from 1961 to 1971, shows the distribution of the peregrine following persecution by pigeon fanciers, but more importantly, after the introduction of persistent organochlorine farm chemicals. These chemicals, such as DDT and dieldrin, caused a huge decline in birds of prey and the peregrine especially, in the late 1950s and early 1960s, mainly through thinning and consequent breakage of egg shells. Although the peregrine is now recovering in some north and westerly areas it is not spreading back into former haunts where agriculture is now intensive. The taking of young birds for falconry is a new and growing threat (one gang stole the young from forty eyries in the summer of 1982 alone), as is the spread of conifer forestry.

mountain birds but also start serious erosion of the delicate mountain soils. There are few statistics to chart these dangers but for the moorland's part, 7 per cent was destroyed in only six years (mostly under afforestation) in Powys and a third of the SSSIs in Northumberland, many of them uplands, were damaged or destroyed in fifteen years.

The Freshwater Habitats

Lakes, Rivers and Ponds

Freshwater habitats are as variable as anything the dry land has to offer. They are also under great threat.

Be they streams, lakes, ponds, rivers or marshes, freshwaters vary from being very poor to very rich in nutrients. Closely connected with their 'nutrient status' is the hard/soft (alkaline/acid) property of water. Nutrient-enriched water is known as *eutrophic* and nutrient-poor water as *oligotrophic*, the nutrients being primarily nitrates and phosphates. In between are the *mesotrophic* waters, and some scientists recognize peculiar sorts such as *dystrophic* waters which may be high in dissolved metals or suspended particles of peat but low in other nutrients (and often in oxygen).

The ecology of freshwaters depends very largely on these physical factors (together with the slope, hence the pace of moving waters). Thus, for example, the miniature freshwater lobster, the crayfish, is found only in hard (alkaline) streams, lakes or rivers, where there is enough calcium for it to manufacture its shell. But should that river become polluted by sewage, which contains a great deal of phosphate and nitrate, oxygen levels may become too low or the water too turbid for the crayfish to prosper. The same applies to many other freshwater invertebrates, and trout fishermen are well aware of the sensitivity of their quarry to pollution. Kenneth Mellanby gives a classic account of the consequences of sewage pollution in his book *Pesticides and Pollution*. High dissolved or suspended nutrient levels encourage growth of algae and bacteria, as well as causing chemical reactions to occur which take dissolved oxygen from the water. The increased growth of algae and bacteria also uses up oxygen, especially at night, when the products of respiration (carbon dioxide) outweigh those of photosynthesis (oxygen), which comes to a stop in the absence of sunlight. This may favour a whole new set of organisms which prosper in anaerobic conditions, such as sulphur-reducing bacteria and others which produce methane, along with blood-worms and eels, the only fish to survive in the blackest days of the Thames.

It has long been feared that the Norfolk Broads are suffering from pollution. The nutrients bound up in the silt on the beds of the lakes have been churned up by motorboats and sewage has oozed in from surrounding villages and been discharged from boats. This has led to the elimination of many plants and animals. Where a broad has been physically cut off and undeveloped – land-locked – this has not occurred. A similar problem has been encountered at Llangorse Lake in South Wales in the Brecons National Park, which is much used for recreation, and which has a sewage system which is often over-loaded by summer visitors. The same phenomenon applies in the species-rich ditches of the Yare Marshes in Norfolk.

Other nutrient sources include factories (for example a chicken processing factory appears to have been one major source of phosphate on the Broads) and sea-gulls which roost on lakes. Their droppings, together with any disease they may introduce, have been a cause of concern to many Water Authorities as the gulls often use reservoirs (for example those in the Thames Valley, west of London) as dormitories.

Lakes and ponds are usually in the slow process of filling up with silt. They are therefore rather more susceptible to lasting damage from pollution than rivers, though the slower reaches of rivers are inevitably less capable of flushing away pollutants than fast-flowing upland streams. Canals are similar in this respect to long thin lakes. Sewage treatment aims to reduce the nutrient, pathogens and solids load to certain levels and the two standard but rather crude measures of pollution are known as COD and BOD (meaning chemical and biological oxygen demand – the amount of oxygen a volume of effluent absorbs in coming into equilibrium with the clean water, through the action of chemicals and bacteria). Neither measurement reflects the concentration of dangerous pollutants such as heavy metals (for example lead, cadmium, etc.), or stable chemicals such as synthetic hormones, pesticides and food additives. Indeed, many pollutants are not even measured.

Because pollution tends to be most extreme in slow-moving lowland water courses (like, for example, the Trent) and because most chalk and limestone rocks which give rise to hard waters are also found in the lowland zone, the rarest sort of freshwater ecosystems are now the oligotrophic hardwater ones: the nutrient-poor streams, rivers and lakes on chalk or limestone. This is particularly sad as these probably supported the richest flora and fauna.

Outright destruction of ponds and lakes – for example by land infill from the 17 million tons of refuse dumped each year – has eliminated many species from the countryside. The common frog is now more often seen in suburban ponds than on farms. It has been reduced to less than one-hundredth of its 1947 population in some parts of East Anglia. Twenty-two aquatic plants are now classified as rare while twenty-eight are heading that way. Four out of our forty-one dragonflies are now extinct. The NCC noted in 1981 that only three broads remained unpolluted and one was under imminent threat of nutrient-enrichment from a pump drainage scheme. Only one major river in England and Wales, the Wye, remains unpolluted. Thirty-five per cent of the ponds in Worcestershire were lost, mostly through agricultural 'tidying-up', in the fifty-five years up to 1971. And in Nottinghamshire it was worse: 90 per cent lost in the twenty-five years up to 1980. The natterjack toad, which breeds only in shallow pools in the lee of sand dunes, has lost over 80 per cent of its habitat this century.

While gravel pits destroyed many marshlands and fine old meadows they proved a boon for some birds and, coinciding with a decline in shooting, they played a role in bringing the great-crested grebe back from the brink of extinction, but now even these modern refuges are increasingly disturbed. Angling clubs proliferate and Water Authorities spend large sums on the promotion of fisheries. Angling is a major cause of disturbance to both breeding and wintering wildfowl, and the increasing trend for using aerosol herbicides is another threat.

Bird-watchers too cause some disturbance to breeding birds, although they rarely use boats and are present in fewer numbers than anglers. Studies on Home Counties lakes showed that even common species such as coot, mallard, little grebe and various warblers increased markedly when coarse fishing was banned during their breeding season. In the Highlands, conservationists fear that the slavonian grebe and the red-throated diver are among the birds suffering from disturbance from bird-watchers and boat-fishermen who are reaching their remote breeding lochs in increasing numbers.

Once a very familiar sight on lowland ponds, lakes and rivers, the mute swan has declined over much of England in recent years as a

Map 6 The dwindling otter (redrawn from M. Wood, *Natural World*, 1981, and G. B. Corbet and H. N. Southern, *The Handbook of British Mammals*, Blackwell, 1977). The map on the left shows the known distribution of the otter prior to 1977. Black areas: otters presumed present or common; blank: presumed absent. The map on the right shows the results of a survey carried out between 1977 and 1980. The otter is now extinct over much of Britain and is only represented in some areas by small, endangered and isolated populations. The North Norfolk population, for example, may number only a few individuals, small enough to cause considerable in-breeding. The causes of the decline are thought to be pesticide residues plus habitat destruction. Otters in north-west Scotland where the main surviving population now lives are threatened by oil developments and fish-farming. Black areas: otters common; grey areas: otters present but not common; white areas: otters absent/recently extinct.

result of lead poisoning. The NCC estimates that 250 tons of lead may be introduced into the environment each year in the form of anglers' lead shot. Mute swans, which require grit for their digestion, mistakenly take the lead shot which affects the nervous system. The problem is particularly acute on the Trent, the Avon and the

Thames where between 1973 and 1981 over three-quarters of swan deaths were due to lead poisoning. The NCC reported in 1981 that between 2,700 and 3,500 mute swans die of lead poisoning each year; in some areas the population has been reduced by over 80 per cent in twenty years.

If any one species epitomizes the lost wildlife of rivers it must be the otter. A recent NCC census revealed that the otter is well-nigh extinct in most of Britain. Only 6 per cent of the previously occupied English river sites had any otters left at all, and the main Norfolk population is thought to number just fifteen individuals. For many other species, habitat destruction (river 'improvement' by Water Authorities involving straightening, removal of cover and canalization), poisoning from pesticides and fertilizers, and oil pollution are posing great threats to their survival.

Bogs and Mires

Sphagnum moss or 'bog moss' (a name which covers dozens of species) flourishes in nutrient-poor, permanently waterlogged conditions. Blanket bogs dominated by sphagnum now cover hundreds of square miles of once-forested hillsides on the Pennines, in Wales and in Scotland. No one is quite sure how they originated, although a climatic shift bringing increased rainfall may have been an important factor. It is feared that the remnants of the Scottish pine forests are threatened by this today, as moist cushiony carpets of sphagnum are extending over the forest floor in many places as our climate becomes wetter. Trees find it difficult to establish in sphagnum and are prone to wind-blow when they do. But man is also implicated. It seems most likely that he hurried the process along by forest clearance, perhaps using fire and following up with grazing, at a time when the mosses were poised to spread. Trees are powerful agents in drying soils out (by evapotranspiration through their foliage) and removal of forest cover, even for a short period, might produce a sudden and irreversible increase in waterlogging.

Under such conditions, few microbes or invertebrates can prosper and there is little oxygen available. Plant and animal remains do not rot at all quickly, and build up into layers of peat, in this case mostly sphagnum peat. On sloping hillsides there is a continuous process of sloughing off as the peat breaks up under its own weight and slips off downhill (forming the characteristic scars known as 'peat hags').

The depth of peat is thus determined by a balance between production and erosion.

On gentler slopes, the conditions are even more waterlogged. Here pools and hummocks may be formed, with each species of sphagnum occupying a particular place in the microtopography. Other species such as the cotton grasses may become abundant. Where the land is drier, the vegetation merges into heather moorland.

In deep peat almost all water movement is downwards. Without deep-rooted plants and in the absence of soil invertebrates, there is effectively no nutrient cycling and all the nutrients available to plants come in with rainwater. In natural conditions there is very little available in this way, and peat bogs are very nutrient-poor habitats. Not surprisingly the peatland pools and margins harbour plants such as the sun-dew, and the bladderworts and butterworts, which can trap insects on sticky hairs, on glands on leaves or in underwater vegetable equivalents of lobster pots. Insects provide a valuable source of nutrients. Some animals do manage to make a living in such places, including rare spiders with specialized ways of life, and in summer waders such as the dunlin, golden plover and curlew may breed in bogs. Pollution by sulphur-dioxide and other substances causing acid rain has made many bogs too acid even for sphagnum and has killed many bogs on the Pennines. The few truly intact ones include Borth Bog and Tregaron Bog in west Wales.

Where land is flat or in wide valleys, a valley bog (such as Tregaron) or raised bog (such as Borth) can develop. In their centres they are very acid, while towards the periphery species such as the beautiful shrub bog myrtle can grow, and carr conditions may develop with small wet woods formed by willow, sallow or alder. Other species found in bogs include the purple moor grass, bog asphodel, bog violet and the little bog orchid.

In glaciated areas, 'kettle-holes' were formed when large rocks or blocks of ice were temporarily forced into soft ground. In the right conditions, the resulting deep holes have gradually filled with sphagnum leaving a central well of dark water, often almost overtopped by floating mats of moss. Trees, usually pines, will grow on the moss but at a certain size they often drop through into the water beneath under their own weight. In Shropshire, Cheshire and Lancashire these places are known as meres (a term also applied to more open lakes), mosses and mires.

In lowland areas, pollution and nutrient-enrichment from fertilizer in dust and rain have both taken their toll of mires and bogs, but direct destruction for agricultural use has been most significant. Most are ploughed up and drained, eventually going under arable crops, perhaps after the peat is removed and sold off. In Lancashire, 99·5 per cent of the lowland bogs have now been reclaimed, while in mere-rich Shropshire, of 600 prime wildlife sites identified in a county-wide survey, nineteen were lost in only eighteen months in 1980/81.

Fens

The initiation of fens rather than acid raised bogs depends on lower rainfall and higher evaporation, but they produce peat in essentially the same way as bogs do. Waterlogging inhibits the breakdown of dead plant and animal material. The essential difference is that fens are base-rich (alkaline) and tend to be nutrient-rich as well, so they support quite different species. In fact fens are much richer in species than bogs. They have formed in river valleys where alkaline waters, from chalk or limestone, run on to impermeable clays or silts.

The most characteristic plants – although there are very many distinct communities – include the sedges and *Phragmites*, the tall Norfolk reed. As the alkaline peat builds up fens naturally begin a gradual process of drying out, and species such as marsh willowherb, hemp agrimony and yellow flag appear alongside specialities such as the fen violet and fen orchid. The final stage in this 'ecological succession' comes when trees colonize the fen. Alders, sallows and willows may be followed by oak, dogwood and ash. Streams and rivers which cut into such established banks of peat produce open water which attracts duck, fish and invertebrates in great profusion.

NCC Chief Scientist Chris Newbould has provided a fine description in *Conservation and Agriculture* of what a great fen area was like, based on Whittlesey Mere, which was finally drained in 1852:

In the early nineteenth century the Oxford clay scarp of southern Huntingdonshire was heavily wooded and some of these woods merged into the vast reed beds of Whittlesey Mere. In the summer, bittern would boom, marsh harriers would be seen silently quartering the ground, while buzzards and red kites, both woodland species, would circle in the rising warm air currents along the scarp. Sparrowhawk and hobby, nesting in woodland, would prey upon the tits and warblers nesting in the reeds or, in the case of the hobby, the rich invertebrate fauna which must have existed. Wildfowl – gadwall, mallard, teal, pintail, shoveler, tufted duck and pochard – were also abundant; indeed Ramsey, a market town on the edge of the mere, was famous for the sale of wildfowl ... Most of the birds have now disappeared from this area. A number of wetland butterflies and moths are now also extinct (namely the large copper and swallowtail butterflies) with the exception of the rosy marsh moth rediscovered in Wales and the swallowtail butterfly confined to the broads.

As Newbould notes, drainage schemes from Roman times onwards finally led to 'a flat, hedgeless, almost treeless but highly fertile farmland ...' In the peat fens (some are silt-based) the soil itself has proved fragile. It oxidizes readily and is blown away. Thus the already low-lying fens have 'shrunk' and are now many feet below sea-level. Fenland fertility is legendary (the fens are said to produce more food than the whole of Wales), but it is based on a diminishing resource, the soil itself.

The landscape of the fens is utterly flat and strangely wild. Deep dykes (ditches) and the straightened watercourses of rivers criss-cross the flat black fields. Wildfowl are still abundant in winter. The water-birds are particularly appreciative of the embanked Washes of the Great Ouse, built as flood-alleviation schemes and now harbouring several Natural Reserves. They also drop in on the few preserved real fens – such as Wicken Fen and Woodwalton Fen – where management depends on pumping water up and into the Nature Reserve from surrounding 'shrunken' fields. A winter bird-watching trip will usually reveal short-eared owls, bewicks and whooper swans, wigeon in hundreds or thousands, and perhaps pink-footed geese together with teal, mallard and other ducks. Similar areas include the Somerset Levels, the Pevensey Levels, Amberley Wildbrooks, Derwent Ings, Nene Valley and Romney Marsh.

At Woodwalton Fen raised bog conditions occur alongside true fen (as the build-up of peat rises above the alkaline groundwater) and mosses, liverworts, ling, bell-heather, cross-leaved heath, bilberry, crowberry and the surface-creeping cranberry occur. The water-soldier is one of a number of increasingly rare water-plants which can still be found in the few fenland reserves. Like the stonewort, the water-soldier accumulates a coating of calcium salts on the stem. This makes it sink to the bottom but it recovers each spring, sending out small shoots or 'turions' which carry the rosette of serrated leaves and three-petalled white flower to the surface.

At the National Trust's Wicken Fen traditional cutting of the sedge meadows continues and a close inspection of the summer sedge-stacks reveals such specialists as the marsh pea (not unlike a sweet pea) and yellow loose-strife, along with a great number of sedges, milk parsley and wild angelica. Brandy bottle (the yellow water lily) and sixteen different species of true pond-weeds (the *Potomagetons*) with floating leaves are characteristic of the remaining open waters.

The Norfolk Broads still boast substantial tracts of fen. The exact nature of each depends strongly on the water course and geology which feed and surround it. All are medieval peat cuttings and are slowly but surely being recolonized by a similar succession of plants which first produced the peat. This succession goes right through from floating aquatic plants such as the starwort, to woodlands of alder with a dense undergrowth of tussock sedge. Reed warblers, sedge warblers and, in recent years, Cetti's and Savi's warblers have exploited the range of fen and marsh conditions, together with water rails and crakes, though these are rarely seen. Larger lakes and reed beds can support bitterns, which feed on frogs and other aquatic animals, marsh harriers and, in the Broads, coypu.

Fens and allied habitats are amongst the most dynamic of all natural environments. This makes them especially difficult to conserve. To conserve their plant and animal communities effectively, large areas must be protected. Unfortunately this is not the case in practice. In the fens themselves, for example, well under 1 per cent of the original area survives in anything like a damp, let alone a natural, condition.

Each community has its extreme specialists, and plants and animals are strongly interdependent. The fenland historian H. Godwin notes, for example, that, gathering dust in a museum, there is a single specimen of an obscure insect known as *Trichoptilus paladum*, once found at Wicken Fen, which can only live on the sticky hairs of the sun-dew plant, which ensnare all other species. Today it is unknown in the fens. Much better known was the swallowtail butterfly, an elegant black, yellow, blue and purple creature dependent on the tall umbellifer, milk parsley. It became extinct at Wicken Fen in 1949 and attempts at reintroduction have failed. Luckily, another closely guarded colony lives on in Norfolk. The large copper butterfly, which fed on the great water dock, became extinct early in this century. These losses are directly attributable to a shrinking area of suitable habitat. The fenland Nature Reserves are an object lesson of what is likely to happen with other habitats such as woodland and grassland: they are now simply too small and isolated to support many of their characteristic species.

The bittern, once common, has now been reduced to a population of 100 birds, and wetland plants are under ever-increasing pressure, not just from direct habitat destruction but also from pollution, both agricultural and industrial. Indeed twenty-seven or more are threatened and likely to become extinct over the next decade.

Many fenland species were lost long ago. Remains of the elk and the auroch (wild cattle) have been found in fen peat in East Anglia, as have those of the beaver, which could be reintroduced. The spoon-bill and the crane, which survived until the end of the sixteenth century in Yorkshire, might one day recolonize Britain unaided, but the extent of habitat suitable for them continues to decline. Street Heath SSSI, for example, a Grade 1 site in the Somerset Levels, was dug up for peat in 1981.

The Coastlands

Estuaries and Saltmarshes

Instead of serving the permanent private interests of a few land-owners, the shifting sands of estuaries, creeping saltings and treacherous creeks have for centuries remained a largely un-regulated preserve of small fishermen, bait-diggers and cockle-gatherers, of smugglers and wildfowlers. In the past the elements conspired to keep the estuaries and saltmarshes one of our last commons. Now engineers, ambitious planners and land-hungry farming cartels would like to tame, confine and smother our estuaries. Barrages, tidal energy schemes, 'reclamation', power stations and chemical complexes may well destroy many of our remaining estuaries.

Ecologically estuaries make up in production what they lack in diversity. Few species can withstand their demanding conditions of shifting sand and silt, extremes of temperature and fluctuating salinity. But those that do may occur in great densities. Estuaries are living evidence of Woody Allen's contention that nature 'is a huge restaurant with everything eating everything else'.

A single square metre of estuarine sand and silt can harbour up to 2,000 cockles or 60,000 shrimp-like *Corophium*. High tides sometimes strand vast harvests of algae or tiny floating snails (*Hydrobia*) which feed off the surface film of single-celled algae which forms in the warm summer months. These in turn are the food of wading birds like the redshank, which nests on the saltmarsh that fringes most estuaries. Each wading bird, visitor or resident, has its own gourmet preference for food. It is determined mainly by bill-length. For example the long bill of the curlew (12 cm) can reach down into the burrows of lugworms or even the largest bivalve mollusc, *Mya*. Dunlin and knot, which gather in vast flocks at the height of the winter, have bills only 3–4 cm long, so they hunt food nearer the surface. Avocets sift food from the surface waters with their upturned bill. Sanderling have very short bills and feed on the sandiest banks and shores, running in and out between the waves. Long-legged godwits can wade in deeper waters while snipe, with equally long bills but short legs, restrict themselves to marshy fringes and shallow pools.

The bivalves (mollusc shellfish) which these birds prey upon are also discrete feeders. The elegant baltic tellin and the cockle select particular parts of the sand and mud banks and feed by filtering out food of different types and sizes. The way that they seem to 'avoid' competing with each other is the product of millions of years of co-evolution. They sieve silt which, in an estuary like the Wash, bears a heavy load of organic detritus from agricultural lowlands. Rivers like the Dyfi, which runs down to Cardigan Bay from Snowdonia, are poorer in nutrients and support fewer waders in winter. But the Dyfi is clean and pure and boasts otters, salmon and, in summer, Manx shearwaters which come to take small fish around the estuary's mouth.

Winter brings about 1,400,000 wading birds to Britain: knot, dunlin, grey plover, golden plover, bar-tailed godwits and others. In spring and autumn migrant waders stop off in our estuaries on their way to or from the high Arctic breeding grounds, which means that the estuaries are a magnet for bird-watchers. However, it is the huge winter gatherings that make our estuaries of international importance for conservation. Of the thirty estuaries in Europe and North America which hold populations of 20,000 waders or more, half are in Britain. Morecambe Bay, for example, holds up to 235,000 birds in winter. Other important sites are the estuaries of the Thames and Medway, Wash, Ribble, Solent, Solway and Cromarty. All, however, are under threat.

It is important for us to remember that these are the *only* places where wildfowl and wading birds can go. Their future depends on these wintering grounds even more than it does on their much larger tundra breeding grounds in the Arctic. The dark-bellied brent goose, for example, is a threatened species which depends almost entirely on British estuaries for its survival. Agricultural encroachment on the banks of estuaries has enabled bird-watchers to get close to the flocks and disturb them, while at the same time the areas of suitable feeding grounds where the food plant eel-grass (*Zostera*) grows have been reduced over the years. The brents have taken to feeding on farmland as a result where, together with pink-footed geese, they have upset farmers, who have put pressure on the MAFF for a shooting programme. Now, at considerable expense, the taxpayer is providing farmers with Section 15 grants via the NCC to provide grass for the geese in winter. Further 'reclamation' of estuaries will make matters worse.

Saltmarshes are an integral part of estuaries, although they may also develop on other sheltered coasts. The uniform-looking saltmarsh vegetation is surprisingly rich in plants. There are marked successions of species depending on height above low tide, the degree of sand or silt, and the geographic location of the marsh. Glasswort (*Salicornia*) flourishes in bare mud, while on the edge of the creeks which dissect the saltings, shaggy drapes of the grey sea purslane may be found. Here also is the sea aster and higher still are acres of grasses, short creeping flowers and taller sea lavender. At the top of the saltmarsh a freshwater marsh of rushes and Norfolk reed may develop if agriculture does not push right down to the sea. Saltmarshes have their own characteristic fauna which includes large numbers of grazing ducks and geese in winter, together with strandline specialists like the snow bunting and the shore lark, which come to feed on the seeds of salting plants. These in turn attract predators such as the sparrowhawk, peregrine and merlin, together with hen harriers and short-eared owls, which also prey on voles as well as small birds.

The North Kent Marshes have disappeared largely within the lifetimes of those trying to save them. 'On the Isle of Sheppey', remarked one RSPB officer despairingly, 'the NCC has tried to compromise four times in a row and each time we've lost another saltmarsh.' Research by another RSPB officer, Gwyn Williams, has shown that since 1969 the area of rough unimproved grazing marsh in the Thames and Medway estuaries has been reduced from 8,000 ha to 5,500 ha. Conversion of such surrounding land is the precursor to reclaiming the intertidal area of the estuary itself. This has happened in the Wash, where 30,000 ha have been lost for arable farming. The Tees is threatened by more industrial development, and the Cromarty Firth, another area of international wildfowl importance, is threatened by a gas or petrochemical plant which oil companies and the state-owned British Gas have vied with each other to build beside a National Nature Reserve. The Wash and Morecambe Bay are the subject of continuing proposals for reservoirs and barrages. The Severn Estuary Barrage Scheme has been shrouded in secrecy and government obscuration. If built it will destroy no less than seven key wildfowl sites. In early 1982 conservationists were encouraged by the decision of Michael Heseltine, Secretary of State for the Environment, that no more agricultural expansion should occur on the south Lincolnshire coast of the Wash, following a prolonged public inquiry around Gedney Drove End. It remains to be seen how far this will serve as a sustained precedent, and whether it will have any effect on the plans of the Central Electricity Generating Board, the Port of London Authority and other 'statutory undertakers' who have plans that presently threaten sites on the Thames and Medway.

Sand Dunes

At the mouths of many estuaries and along other parts of the coast are complexes of sand dunes. They form one of the most remarkable of all habitats. Plants such as the sea sandwort, tolerant of drought and wind-blasting sand, gain a foothold in the strand line. In the right conditions, wind accumulates sand around them. An embryo sand dune is formed. It is then colonized by plants like sea couch grass and, once the sand builds up above the highest tides, the tough marram grass arrives. This plant is the chief architect of the sand dunes. It has extremely tough leaves which roll in on themselves to conserve moisture, razor-sharp hairs (which help deter grazing) and roots long enough to reach down many metres in search of water.

In their early years dunes are almost sterile. They lack nutrients, especially nitrogen. But microbes around the marram roots soon fix nitrogen, and the group of plants known as the spring annuals arrive. The marram becomes denser and a damper microclimate is established amongst its stems. Mosses such as *Tortula ruraliformis* and the characteristic striped shell snail *Cepaea nemoralis* join it. Gradually a soil is built up. The dunes are now termed 'grey' (with humus) and the components of a full terrestrial ecosystem begin to slot into place. Away from the sea, marram loses its vigour, perhaps owing to the action of nematode worms in the soil, and bushes of elder, bramble, hawthorn and blackthorn may appear. Eventually, if left undisturbed, woodland becomes established.

Dune systems are inherently mobile and during great winter gales they may get up and move. Development in their vicinity is often unwise. At the Sands of Forvie in Aberdeenshire an ancient settlement lies buried under the dunes, and another suffered the same fate at Newborough Warren in Anglesey. A great deal of often wasted effort is put into trying to stabilize dune systems, most often by putting in fences to trap wind-blown sand, sleeper tracks to stop human feet eroding the marram and by planting marram, also designed to stop 'blow-outs' where a gale enlarges an existing gap to much larger proportions. The need to stabilize sand dunes arises as a result of landward encroachment by agriculture, forestry, golf courses and so on.

It is also at the back of the dunes, in 'slacks' where water collects in winter, that the greatest diversity of flowering plants is found. Pyramidal and spotted orchids and unusual plants like wintergreen or grass of parnassus may occur here. If sea buckthorn invades the slacks – as at Gibraltar Point in Lincolnshire – the floristic diversity is reduced, but in open slacks rare animals such as the natterjack toad can also flourish. No specific figures exist to show the threats to our sand-dune ecosystems but, like most coastal habitats, they have suffered great losses in the period immediately before and after the Second World War from uncontrolled building development, and in more recent years about one in ten of our best dune sites has been lost altogether. Quite indirect threats, such as new breakwaters cutting off a supply of sand along the coast, can lead to the destruction of a sand-dune system within a few seasons.

Cliffs and Rocky Shores

The coastline of Britain stretches over 6,000 km. Much of it is cliff and rocky shores; its character depends upon the geology. Orkney's Old Man of Hoy and other magnificent stacks of the northern islands are splinters of Old Red Sandstone. The beautiful Seven Sisters of the rolling chalk on the south coast could hardly provide a greater contrast. In Northumberland, carboniferous coal measures with alternating beds of limestone, sandstone and shale have been eroded to produce a craggy coastline of bays and headlands. The elements of wind and rain help shape the ecology as well as the topography of these habitats.

The distribution of Britain's nesting sea-birds follows that of suitable cliffs and islands. The east coast has only a few stretches of cliff, in Yorkshire, Norfolk, Berwickshire, and Aberdeenshire, marooned among long stretches of soft rock shoreline. But in the west and along the south coast rocky shores and cliffs predominate.

Britain's sea-bird colonies are of international importance. Over a million pairs of guillemot, razorbill, puffin and gannet nest around our shores. Kittiwake, gannet, razorbill and guillemot nest on cliff tops and ledges while puffin, Manx shearwater, storm petrel and the rare Leach's petrel use rock tumbles and old rabbit burrows. Two centuries ago gyr falcon, peregrine, raven, chough and sea eagle were familiar sights to coastal fishermen. Today they are all very rare. The sea eagle is currently the subject of a reintroduction attempt on the Isle of Rhum National Nature Reserve off western Scotland. Sadly, one of these magnificent birds was found, probably poisoned, on Skye in November 1981, and another was found dead in Caithness. Altogether forty sea eagles have been released on Rhum although none has yet survived to reach maturity.

Both rocky shores and cliffs are diverse in form and the life they support. The hard rocks of the south-west peninsula and the Outer Hebrides receive the greatest battering from the Atlantic, while the soft boulder clays of Whitby and Hampshire are crumbling under the relatively mild pressures of the North Sea and the Solent. Neither setting provides much comfort and the environment is a harsh one. Plants in the cliff habitat need resilient constitutions and must be able to withstand high levels of salinity and wind. They have strong roots and are often dwarf versions of their inland cousins. Within the tidal range species must survive twice-daily inundation and desiccation. The presence of rock pools enables species of the lower shore to survive higher up but the greatest richness of species is found in the lower shore itself.

Sheltered shores develop the richest sea-weed floras. Below the orange and black encrusting lichens of the splash zone, a thin line of channel wrack (*Pelvetia*) often marks the high tide. Down towards the low tide line one passes through zones of bladder wracks (*Fucus* species) and the egg wrack (*Ascophyllum*), before reaching the beds of tangle (*Laminaria*) and dabberlocks (*Alaria*). As well as these large brown algae, many beautiful green and red algae are found throughout the shore.

Winkles, top shells and other molluscs graze the sea-weed, and dog whelks track down barnacles and the edible horse mussel, a prey species which is also popular with oyster-catchers and eider ducks. Sea anemones, dahlia anemones, tiny gammerid shrimps, wobbly prawns, quick eels, shore crabs, hermit crabs and numerous fish make the rocky shore pool one of Britain's most colourful habitats.

Birds of the rocky shore are few but include several specialists. The turnstone flicks over pebbles while searching for food such as small shrimps, the purple sandpiper forages in rocks and sea-weeds, and the rock pipit holds a territory on a cliff face. Oyster-catchers specializing on rocky shores apparently have more chisel-like bills than their worm-hunting soft-shore cousins. At night the scavenging gulls are disturbed by visits from foxes, herons or, in Scotland, otters.

Familiar cliff plants include the ancestral stock of the domestic garden cabbage and radish, as well as rarities like the sea stock (now confined to two areas). The short turf grazed by sheep or rabbits on the cliff top provides the ideal habitat for the attractive spring squill and for the much declined chough, which feeds on insect larvae in the short sward.

Gone are the days when mulled auk in ale was a popular northern dish. Harvesting sea-birds and their eggs for food has almost entirely ceased though the colonies of roseate terns are sometimes badly hit by egg-collectors. Sea-weeds are still harvested for fertilizer and alginate chemicals. Winkle-picking is on a similarly small scale. The collecting of specimens for schools and universities causes only local problems at present.

Apart from the potentially serious but still unknown consequences of wave-energy schemes (such as those proposed off the Hebrides), the principal threat to the rocky shores comes from oil pollution. Animals of the shore itself recover remarkably quickly from oil pollution, though the detergents used to disperse oil are actually far more damaging than the oil. The sea-birds, however, are hit hardest. Many dive when they meet oil, only to surface in the middle of a slick. Others home in on the calm of oily seas in rough weather. Oil clogs their feathers and the birds eventually become cold and waterlogged and slowly starve to death. As sea-birds are strongly colonial and nest and feed in flocks, whole colonies may be wiped out by one slick.

When the *Esso Bernica* collided at a jetty at Sullom Voe in the Shetlands in 1978, 105 miles of coastline were polluted. In addition to over 3,500 bird corpses recovered from the shores (a fraction of those killed), over thirty otters were killed by oil, as well as many sheep. Many Scottish conservationists were shocked and angered at the spill, more so because the NCC was very slow to react, and it was left to the initiative of a junior officer to condemn the terminal operators. (In fact Sullom Voe has a large and elaborate monitoring system manned by expert scientists connected with the NCC and largely financed by oil companies. But monitoring does nothing to stop oil pollution.) Oil pollution seems to be worsening despite years of quiet lobbying by the RSPB. January 1978 figures showed the worst death toll on record, with 1,478 oiled dead birds picked up in a survey of 2,241 km of European beaches, while 85,000 corpses were found (a small fraction of the total killed) in just a few months on British beaches in winter 1981.

Shingle Beaches

These range from tiny patches of ephemeral shingle mixed with shell fragments up to giant geomorphological set pieces like Dorset's Chesil Beach. Here, a 29-km shingle beach encloses a lagoon known as the Fleet. Longshore drift of pebbles produces such spits and they are also found at Spurn on the Humber, Orfordness in Suffolk and Dungeness in Kent.

Shore-nesting birds are ever more dependent on such places, as the coastal hinterlands where they once nested have been swallowed up by caravan parks, shanty housing and nuclear power stations. Each bird has its own choice of substrate, so ringed plover, little, common and sandwich terns may all be found nesting on different parts of the same shingle beach system. The little tern is particularly threatened and is now closely guarded at every one of its few coastal nest sites against dog-walking beachcombers, foxes and egg-collectors. There are now under 2,000 pairs left in Britain.

Some of our rarest plants find a stony foothold in the more stable shingle. Purple spurge, for example, is now found only in a few Channel Island sites and on Lundy in the Bristol Channel. On boulder beaches, the oyster-plant is another species under threat.

The Open Sea

Man has traditionally regarded the oceans of the world both as a repository for his rubbish and a limitless source of food. His habit of using the seas as a dustbin for his urban wastes, with the continents leaking oil, sewage and chemicals into the shallow seas, has resulted in serious ecological damage. In addition modern fishery techniques and over-fishing now pose a serious threat to some marine life.

Two-thirds of the world's surface is covered by the oceans which are the last great global commons. Although maritime nations have established territorial rights round their coasts, the seas have yet to be 'enclosed'. However, research since the war has shown that there is vast mineral wealth on the sea-bed and there is little doubt that the nations with the greatest wealth and most advanced technology will soon move in to exploit the sea's resources, to the inevitable detriment of the developing world.

It is in the margins of the oceans, where light filters down as far as the bottom on the inshore continental shelf, and in places where currents bring nutrients up from the depths, that ecological production is greatest. Coastal areas produce many of the chemicals of the world ecosystem in the great submarine forests of kelp (large sea-weeds). These include strange substances such as methyl iodide, which play essential roles in the natural catalysis of atmospheric reactions. Such natural chemical factories are highly sensitive to pollution, and sewage and industrial pollution have similar consequences here as they do in freshwaters (see p. 103). Such pollution is especially serious in semi-enclosed water bodies such as the Mediterranean and the Baltic Sea and, on a smaller scale, in harbours such as Poole.

It was once assumed that nuclear waste dumped deep in ocean abysses would be immobilized in a lifeless, still environment. Recently, however, research has revealed that these areas are geologically active, and there are deep-water ecosystems which are linked to those in surface waters. Many animals make diurnal migrations of hundreds of fathoms up to surface waters, and these creatures and currents could bring pollutants back to the surface.

About 60,000 tons of metal waste are dumped in the North Sea each year, and radio-active materials, most notably the radio-active isotope Caesium-137, enter the sea at Windscale. Data collected by the MAFF show that the concentration of Caesium-137 in the Irish Sea around Windscale increased by a factor of ten between 1973 and 1978, reaching a level some 4,000 times higher than clean water off the south-west Atlantic coast. Even off the east coast of England radio-active Caesium reached forty times the clean-water level by 1978.

During the 1960s, explorers like Jacques Cousteau and Thor Heyerdhal travelled thousands of miles in close contact with the seas and returned to report that oil and rubbish floated on the surface of even the remotest ocean. Today it is worse. Rather than the dramatic break-up of oil tankers, it is the routine washing out of tanks which causes most oil pollution. In the Dutch Waddensea for example, a mere 150 tons of residual fuel oil killed 40,000 sea-birds. Sea-birds have also been affected by synthetic chemicals. Both the persistent organochlorines used by farmers and the polychlorinated biphenyls (PCBs) used in the manufacture of paints, plastics and varnishes, have been found in the eggs of sea-birds. PCBs have turned up in high concentrations in ocean-going sea-birds like the great skua, the fulmar and the kittiwake, and in the eggs of guillemot, razorbill, shag and common tern. It seems very likely that it was PCBs that caused the Irish Sea 'Sea-bird Disaster' of 1969 when between 15,000 and 50,000 were killed. The PCBs accumulate in stored fat but cause severe damage when the fat is metabolized in times of stress, for example during hard weather when birds cannot feed.

Fishing at sea is the hunting arm of the food industry. It is even less efficient in energetic terms than farming (and like agriculture it is overseen by the same two government departments: MAFF in England and Wales and the Department of Agriculture and Fisheries in Scotland).

Two centuries ago the Atlantic salmon was the staple diet for many estate workers in Scotland and was familiar to river folk of the Thames. Years of over-fishing have now elevated the salmon to the status of a delicacy and all the indications are that other once-common fish like the skate, herring and mackerel have gone or will go the same way. Since the last war the fishing industry has provided a sad example of how man abuses communal resources.

The image of the fisherman fighting against the elements in bitter and dangerous seas is no longer so relevant to the modern technologically based fishing industry. Accompanying the expansion of industrial fishing has been the shift towards taking fish for purposes other than providing us with food. In 1940 only 10 per cent of the world's fish catch was diverted away from human mouths. Today over half goes to making oil, fishmeal and fertilizer for those countries which can afford it.

Industrial fishing and the use of fish for non-food purposes has led to many species, formerly considered useless, being cropped at alarming rates. These are often species like sand eel (converted to fishmeal, flour and oil) which are individually small but found in great abundance; their removal is not just a minor affair but can cause wholesale ecological destruction as marine food chains collapse. Figures compiled by the International Council for the Exploitation of the Sea show that during the sixteen years following 1962 the percentage of the catch for capelin rose from 0·1 to 25. In the other direction went herring (33·3 to 6·9 per cent), haddock (5·7 to 3·9 per cent) and cod (24 to 15 per cent). We should also add that modern industrial fishing techniques combined with over-fishing have had serious effects on traditional fishing communities with the smaller low-capitalized fishing fleets suffering at the expense of the larger ones.

Government departments have sadly always reacted too late to over-fishing. Over-fishing of the herring through the 1950s and 1960s eventually led to a four-year moratorium on herring fishing and attention was turned to the mackerel. By 1980 the mackerel constituted around 40 per cent of Britain's edible fish catch but all the signs are that it is now threatened by over-fishing. MAFF now admits that the common skate will soon be extinct in European waters. In fact in the case of the skate the damage had already been done before the Second World War. In 800 trawls by MAFF vessels in the Irish Sea – once the main skate fishing area – between 1971 and 1981 not one skate was taken. There has been a similar decline of the skate in Atlantic waters with a 90 per cent drop in the numbers landed during the decade following 1971. As far as the skate is concerned its life-history made it particularly vulnerable. Unlike herring and cod it lays few eggs each year and the juveniles are too large to avoid the standard mesh size of 80 mm used by fishing fleets.

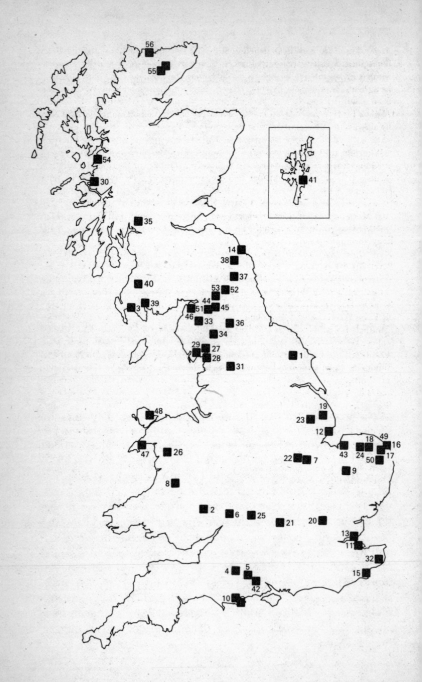

Map 7 Three years in the destruction of Britain's countryside. Sites of national and international conservation importance which were among the 735 in *A Nature Conservation Review* in 1977 but which had been seriously damaged or totally destroyed by agriculture or forestry by 1980. (Based on information collated by W. M. Adams from a written answer to a Parliamentary Question (Mr Munro to Mr Ennals), *Hansard* II, November 1980, 171–2.) These are only a fraction of the places affected by agriculture and forestry during those years.

1. Wintringham Marsh (N. Yorks); 2. Clehonger Meadow (Hereford and Worcester); 3. Kilquockdale Flow (Dumfries and Galloway); 4. Starveall Down and Stony Hill (Wilts); 5. Homington, Oddstock and Coombe Bisset Downs (Wilts); 6. Coombe Hill Canal (Glos); 7. Sibson–Castor Meadows (Cambs); 8. Carn Gafallt Meadows (Powys); 9. Lakenheath Warren, Eriswell High and Low Warren (Suffolk); 10. Hartland Moor and Arne Heaths (Dorset); 11. The Swale (Kent); 12. The Wash Flats and Marshes (Lincs); 13. Leigh Marsh (Essex); 14. Lindisfarne–Ross Links Budle Bay (Northumberland); 15. Romney Marsh (Kent); 16. Hickling Broad and Horsey Mere (Norfolk); 17. Upton Broad (Norfolk); 18. Calthorpe Broad (Norfolk); 19. River Great Fan (Lincs); 20. Wormley Wood–Hoddesdon Park Wood (Herts); 21. Waterperry Wood (Oxon); 22. Bedford Purlieus Group (Cambs); 23. Bardney Forest (Lincs); 24. Foxley Wood (Norfolk); 25. Kings and Bakers Wood (Beds); 26. Coed Maes Yr Helmau (Gwynedd); 27. Whitbarrow and Witherslack Woods (Cumbria); 28. Faves Wood (Lancs); 29. Roudsea Wood (Cumbria); 30. Loch Sunart Woodlands (Strathclyde); 31. Conistone Old Pasture and Baslow Wood (N. Yorks); 32. Alkham Valley Woods (Kent); 33. Finglandrigg Woods (Cumbria); 34. Orton Moss (Cumbria); 35. Coille Ardura (Strathclyde); 36. Upper Teesdale (Durham); 37. Simonside Hills (Northumberland); 38. Kielderhead Moors (Northumberland); 39. Cairnsmoore of Fleet (Dumfries and Galloway); 40. Merrick-Kells (Dumfries and Galloway); 41. Keen of Hamar (Shetland); 42. New Forest Valley Mires (Denny Bog) (Hants); 43. Sandringham Warren (Dersingham Bog) (Norfolk); 44. Cumwhitton Moss (Cumbria); 45. Moorthwaite Moss (Cumbria); 46. Biglands Bog (Cumbria); 47. Cors Geirch (Gwynedd); 48. Cors Erddreiniog (Gwynedd); 49. Bure Marshes (Norfolk); 50. Surlingham Marshes (Norfolk); 51. Glasson Moss (Cumbria); 52. Hummel Knowe Moss (Cumbria/Northumberland); 53. Coom Ring Moss and Seletia Moss (Cumbria/Northumberland); 54. Blar Na Caillich Buidhe (Highland); 55. Forsinard-badanlock Flows (Highland); 56. A 'Mhoine (Highland)

Six

Recipe for a Future

We have argued that the traditional Old Guard nature conservation approach to economic development and the use of resources is both insular and weak. It is no small measure of recent changes in attitude that an organization like the International Union for the Conservation of Nature and Natural Resources (IUCN) has shifted, albeit somewhat tentatively, into the 'environmentalist' camp. In the conclusions of its *World Conservation Strategy* the IUCN states: 'Much habitat destruction and over-exploitation of living resources by individuals, communities and nations in the developing world is a response to relative poverty, caused or exacerbated by a combination of human population growth and inequities within and among nations.'

For the moment the material welfare of the majority of Britons may seem secure but the plight of the 'South' is all too apparent. Hundreds of millions of rural people in developing countries, including 500 million malnourished and 800 million destitute, are being forced to destroy the resources necessary for their survival in an attempt to free themselves from starvation and poverty. The collective debt of the low-income Third World countries is over 300 billion dollars and rising, and about a third of all the money they borrow is used just to pay interest rates on loans. Soil erosion as a result of deforestation and over-grazing is devastating rural land in many areas. As long as the poor are forced into the position where they can do no more than consider the next day's survival the environmental problems will get worse. More tropical forests will come down; more grazing land will be destroyed. Species extinctions will become increasingly rapid.

This book has concerned itself with the problems of wildlife and landscape destruction in Britain, but it is worth mentioning briefly the gravity of the global situation. In 1979 the ecologist Norman Myers estimated that the world's rain forests contained between 2 and 5 million species and that during the next twenty-five years at least 1 million species are doomed to extinction as the forests are cleared. Myers' figures work out at an average extinction rate of 40,000 species per year, or 100 a day. This calculation ignores species losses for the seas, the coral reefs, the temperate forests, the polar regions and the prairies, pampas and steppes.

The *World Conservation Strategy* showed clearly that the problems of conservation, both here and abroad, must be related to problems of economic development. And neither conservation nor development can be considered without reference to equity and justice. It is with this in mind that we look briefly at the challenges which our present profligate use of resources has thrown up. We would be insulting the reader if we now gave a 'blueprint' for the future of rural Britain. We offer no cast-iron solutions to the problems which we have discussed. Rather, we give some thoughts on the changes needed.

Sharing the Commons

We began the book with a discussion of the fate of the common lands in England and Wales, and it is to the theme of the commons that we now return. The historical events which took place when the rich and powerful dispossessed the rural peasantry have provided a contentious parable which has figured prominently in debates on the ownership and control of land and non-renewable resources.

In 1968 the biologist Garrett Hardin argued, in an essay entitled *The Tragedy of the Commons*, that man is incapable of managing non-renewable resources communally as this inevitably leads to their destruction. Using the metaphor of the commons, his argument runs like this: If ten farmers have access to an area of common land which will support 1,000 cows, and if each has 100 cows, the grazing land can theoretically be equitably and lastingly shared between all the farmers (the figures are ours, not Hardin's). However, if one man adds an extra beast his neighbours will not notice, and though the collective returns of the other farmers will be slightly diminished as a result of this addition, the opportunist herdsman will increase his profit. The addition of one cow may not have any serious effect but each commoner, according to the *Tragedy* argument, will think the same way and add an extra cow. The process inevitably continues and the commons soon become overgrazed, thus damaging or destroying the livelihood of all.

Hardin has seized on this parable to assert that the tragedy can only be averted by the authoritarian rule of a managerial elite. His views, not surprisingly, have strong appeal to those attracted by the dictatorial rule of either the Left, the Right or a scientific technocracy. Hardin has argued that giving aid to the poor countries of the world will not only fail to help them, but will actively damage the rich.[1] Aid to developing countries has the effect of encouraging further increases in their population and thus raises future needs and expectations. Resources are therefore consumed at an increasingly fast rate and the rich of the world, who are presently sailing in Hardin's allegorical lifeboat, should do their best to make sure that the poor who wallow in the sea around remain in the sea. If we allow them to clamber aboard (through providing development aid, agricultural fertilizers, medical programmes, etc.) then the lifeboat will sink and we shall all go under.

Many writers have challenged Hardin, and in his book *Environmentalism* Timothy O'Riordan has summarized the three main criticisms of the lifeboat argument. First, the rich nations are not in a position to exercise unilateral power in determining the future of mankind, and our economies are heavily dependent on resources which come from poor countries. Second, Hardin's belief that people are incapable of controlling their breeding when given adequate resources and means goes against the findings of demographic research. In fact withholding aid only exacerbates the situation by widening the gulf between rich and poor. Third, the lifeboat metaphor flounders because of its internal inconsistencies. In O'Riordan's words:

> The care of the commons, by definition, requires a communal effort and the mutual respect of all participating members ... Yet Hardin advocates the deliberate jettisoning of an undetermined number of the present earthly community for the good of 'humanity' (defined, implicitly, as the affluent minority). The ethics of a lifeboat denies the existence of a community and guarantees the persistence of discrimination.

In fact Hardin's argument fits neatly into traditional Malthusian thinking. In 1793 Thomas Malthus published his famous work, *An Essay on the Principle of Population*. Malthus's central proposition was, in the words of the economist J. K. Galbraith, 'the inevitability of mass poverty'. He postulated that human populations tend to increase exponentially (1, 2, 4, 8, 16, 32, etc.) while at best one can hope for an arithmetic increase in food subsistence (1, 2, 3, 4, 5, 6, etc.). As population increases faster than the means of subsistence people will starve; poverty is thus a consequence of overpopulation. Malthus's essay was written in reply to William Godwin's *Enquiry Concerning Political Justice* in which the author championed human equality. Poverty, said Godwin, derives from the unequal distribution of wealth. Malthusian theory, on the contrary, blames nature rather than human institutions.

Judging from the grudging way in which the British government has reacted to the Brandt Report (which advocates a massive programme of aid to developing countries) our political leaders are not unsympathetic to the Hardin philosophy.[2] It is, however, a philosophy based on contempt. Human beings are assumed to be inherently selfish and incapable of regulating their resources through mutual aid and cooperation.

We have not raised Hardin's argument simply to dismiss it. The *Tragedy of the Commons* ethic helps to concentrate our minds on the possible options which face us in the near future. Our first option is to muddle on as we have been doing for some time. We know that we are consuming land, energy, minerals and so on at a rate which cannot continue for long, and we accept (and thus condone) the inequitable distribution of resources within and between nations. This *laissez-faire* attitude assumes that we shall somehow be baled out of our future problems: we must hope, if we adopt this stance, that a 'technofix' will sort out the soil erosion, water pollution, and over-exploitation of animal, plant and fuel resources which result from our present activities. However, the benign hope that things will 'get better' presupposes a degree of faith in our decision-makers that has not been hitherto justified, and the adoption of the *laissez-faire* attitude implies a passive acceptance of the doctrine promoted by Hardin for the simple reason that the likelihood of the rich and powerful monopolizing and appropriating resources increases dramatically the scarcer they become.

The only way in which an affluent minority will be able to control the resources on which we depend will be through coercion and force. The present misuse of resources should not, therefore, be viewed in the simple context of the diminishing physical resources themselves (their ultimate depletion, incidentally, will lead us not back to the caves but to the urban slums), but as a step towards a world in which individual freedom will be denied the majority by a minority who will see it as their task to regulate our behaviour. Whether or not one sees this in terms of the wise protecting scarce resources for the social good of all, or the rich and powerful protecting and consolidating their present wealth and power for their own benefit, depends very much on one's political persuasion. If you have read this far you will probably fall into the second camp.

The Brandt Report and the *World Conservation Strategy* are both agreed that the future prosperity of the Western world can only be assured if the developing South is helped into the lifeboat. Some of Brandt's prescriptions (its members think very much along the lines of Big is Beautiful) may seem wayward, while some of the *Strategy*'s proposals are naive. The naivety lies not in its proposal that all trade barriers to goods from developing countries should be removed, nor in its call for greater financial assistance for the Third World, nor even in its plea for a rapid halt to the arms race. The *Strategy*'s proposals are naive because the IUCN fails to challenge the one factor which underlies the whole problem of resource-use and allocation: the distribution of power. None of its important proposals can be implemented without a thorough shake-up of the power pyramid which dominates politics and land-use.

However, the *Strategy* and the Brandt Report at least represent a reaction against the *laissez-faire* syndrome. But nothing, of course, will happen without the will to change. Events in Europe over the last decade already show that many people, particularly in the environmental and peace movements, are beginning to mount their challenge. An article in the *International Herald Tribune* in November 1981 hinted at the growing disillusion within West Germany, the most affluent of all Western democracies. Its author was reflecting on the enormous protest by the people of Frankfurt against the government plans to replace a great forest on the edge of the city with an airport runway:

There is – and has been for considerable time – something out of kilter here, and it is more than the tailspinning economy, the apparition of both leftist and rightist terrorism, or what some conveniently describe as a new youth rebellion and peace movement. Rather, it is an alienation from the values and precepts to which West German society is reputedly committed, a disillusionment with previously accepted goals, a ground swell of frustration with consumerism, promises of reforms unfulfilled, and economic growth for the sake of growth.

The challenge is against some of the materialistic values of Western society and the way in which power and resources are shared (or not shared).

Environmentalists are realizing in increasing numbers that political leaders and civil servants do not necessarily act for the greatest good of the greatest number. They often have little knowledge of what they are doing to the environment and care even less. The decisions they make are heavily influenced, and some would say controlled, by industrial and financial interests whose main concern is to maintain the *status quo* and their own grip on the power machinery. The challenge of the environmentalist in the 1980s will be a direct challenge to these interests.

The *Tragedy of the Commons* argument is not only abhorrent but deeply pessimistic. Its advocates and disciples, denying man's ability to act in the interests of others, abrogate faith. Fortunately, environmentalists, though they may have lost faith in our political leaders and industrial masters, have not yet lost faith in themselves. Let us now look, in more parochial terms, at how some of the main problems raised in this book might be resolved.

Land Reforms

The most immediate and pressing problems for British nature and landscape conservation are caused by modern farming and forestry activities. But the present plight of the countryside goes deeper than these impacts of technological food and timber production: many rural communities have suffered decades of social decline.

We have identified a number of specific problems. Increased mechanization has led to a rapid decline in the agricultural labour force. The number of farm workers today is about a third of what it was before the last war. Government policy not only favours the replacement of men by machines (see p. 19), it works in favour of the highly capitalized farmer and against the smallholder. Agriculture is a significant consumer of energy (see p. 20); farming consumes between 2 and 4 per cent of our annual fuel budget and food production (processing, packaging and transport) consumes around a further 13 per cent.

Government projections for future agricultural growth completely ignore limiting factors, such as energy shortages, which will come into play before long. They also ignore the need for more rather than fewer jobs in the countryside. The steady stream of men from the land into other industries or on to the lengthening dole queues has had predictable effects: many rural communities have atrophied and their dwindling populations have become increasingly dominated by the aged and the retired. Public services, such as transport, have become increasingly poor, and labour-intensive techniques or farm management have been forsaken with the modern machinery being used to clear hedges, copses, ponds, marshes and heaths.

The claim that Britain is one of the most efficient farming nations in the world is based largely on calculations of productivity per man. It is high time that we thought about replacing and modifying the present system to take account of employment needs, energy limitations and ecological constraints to the development of land. If we are to save the countryside from further devastation there are a number of courses open to us.

The first option open to conservation organizations is to continue buying land for Nature Reserves, as they have been doing for a long time. This, however, is becoming increasingly impracticable; the organizations have few resources and cannot usually compete on the open market with the big agriculturalists. Even the National Trust, with an income approaching £30 million, is increasingly wary of taking on new properties without some guarantees of future financial help to manage them. The escalating price of land has, incidentally, also prevented many young people from setting up in farming.

Second, the government could introduce planning controls over agriculture and forestry operations. This is possibly the option which most conservationists would like to see. There is no reason why the small number of individuals who own and use land should not be subject to constraints which we all accept in towns and villages. There is no chance of the million acres of land identified by the N C C as being worthy of Nature Reserve status being protected unless such controls are introduced. We have pointed out that the present system whereby farmers and foresters are compensated for not altering or destroying S S S Is is ridiculous. As Chris Hall wrote in *Ecos* in 1981:

the farmer takes on his land (whether he buys it, inherits it or rents it) with the moorland, downland, hedges or whatever in position. By removing them he may be able to make the land *more* profitable, but it can hardly be claimed that, if he is not allowed to remove them, he *loses* anything, for loss implies previous possession. If farmers are to be paid for these notional losses then by the same token the ordinary citizen refused planning permission to add a garage to his semi-detached ought to be able to claim compensation for the 'loss' of value to his property.

Hall also suggests that it is more than a question of equity; it is also a question of what society can afford.

However desirable planning controls (they may well be a precursor to the third option we discuss below), there is no reason to believe that they would help revive ailing communities in rural areas. They might protect our wildlife and landscape but they would not get people back on to the land.[3] There is, however, a third option – land reform – which could go a long way towards saving our natural heritage and patching together the social fabric of the countryside.

There are few subjects guaranteed to cause greater disquiet than land reform, particularly when such reform entails the erosion of existing property rights of landowners. This is indeed curious. Looking back through the telescope of time to the days when the commons were appropriated from the community, we might shudder with disgust at the callousness of the acquisitors and the injustice of the theft. Yet we seem wary of undoing the process by introducing a system of ownership which would benefit the whole community rather than just those in whom land is presently vested.

Robert Waller, in his essay *Principles of Land Reform*, points out that there is an alternative to both private and state ownership of land. Those who oppose private ownership of land (including Waller, who claims that 'Title deeds to the ownership of land are records of theft from the community') do not necessarily believe, like the National Union of Agricultural Workers (now part of the Transport and General Workers' Union), that land should be nationalized. There is no reason to think that the state (whose policies, after all, are responsible for encouraging private landowners to act in the way they do) can be trusted with the ownership of land.

Waller's proposals for land reform, involving the introduction of a land tax, are based on those outlined by the American economist Henry George in his book *Progress and Poverty*. Both George's book and Waller's essay should be read in their original form, but here we can give a brief sketch of the reforms they envisaged.

The ownership of land [wrote George], is the great fundamental fact that ultimately determines the social, the political, and consequently the intellectual and moral condition of a people ... Material progress cannot rid us of our dependence upon the land . . . Everywhere, in all times, among all peoples, the possession of land is the base of aristocracy, the foundation of great fortunes, the source of power.

Times, of course, have changed. Industrial depressions, which George attributed to the land monopoly, have little or nothing to do today with who owns and uses land. But much poverty, today as a century ago, stems from the unequal distribution of land and resources. (According to Susan George in her book *How the Other Half Dies*, 'a mere 2·5 per cent of landowners with holdings of more than 100 hectares control nearly three-quarters of all the land in the world – with the top 0·23 per cent controlling over half'.)

The land reform promoted by George involves the introduction of a land tax, or the nationalization of ground rent. The use of the word 'rent' must be clarified here. To quote George:

In the economic sense there is rent where the same person is both owner and user. Where owner and user are thus the same person, whatever part of his income he might obtain by letting the land to another is rent, while the return for his labour and capital is that part of his income which they would yield him did he hire the land instead of owning it.

Private ownership, in its present form, would cease to exist, but the state would not be able to claim ownership. In Waller's own words:

[The land tax] separates natural resources beneath and upon the surface of the land from wealth produced by labour and capital. Land is of no economic value until labour has been applied to it. If a site on which a land tax is paid were owned by the state, then it would have to be leased by the state and when the lease expired the product of all the labour and capital used could be claimed by the state . . . But by separating what nature has created (land and natural resources) from what man has produced (houses, quarries, mines, factories, farms, etc.) we can lay the foundations for a new economic order that safeguards enterprises from being seized by the state without depriving the state of its just share in the communal wealth; for the wealth created on any site is partly the fruit of labour of those who work on it and partly the consequence of the prosperity of the community as a whole. Thus the community has of right a share in the wealth produced on its land. This is secured by a variable land tax related to the value of the site.

The introduction of a land tax has many attractions. Landowners could not be legally dispossessed; they would have to pay the tax or surrender their rights to the land. 'Let the individuals who now hold

[land],' wrote George, 'still retain, if they want to, possession of what they are pleased to call *their* land. Let them continue to call it *their* land. Let them buy and sell, and bequeath and devise it. *It is not necessary to confiscate land; it is only necessary to confiscate rent.*'

Were a land tax to be introduced, land could no longer be subject to speculative hoarding and selling as it is today because, as Waller points out, 'all the benefits flowing from the rising value of land would be clearly reflected in the site valuations and increased common wealth'. The occupier of a site could not leave it idle as he would be unable to pay the rent (unless he was prepared to offload wealth derived from other sources) and land would inevitably become more equitably distributed. The 340 families and institutions which own 65 per cent of the 10 million acres of the Highlands and Islands of Scotland would not be able to pay the land tax unless the land was used more productively. Land would thus only be left idle, and people excluded from working it, when the community wished to reserve it for other purposes: for example for conservation or amenity. In these situations the occupier could be exempted from the land tax.

Before we leave the suggested reforms of George and Waller (we suggest the reader should look at the reforming ideas of others as well) it must be emphasized that statutory measures like those instituted by Lloyd George in his 1908 budget may be counter-productive. In an attempt to break the 'land monopoly' Lloyd George introduced an Incremental Value Duty and Undeveloped Land Duty which had the effect of causing one-quarter of the surface of England to change hands in the four-year period 1918–22. Henry George was well aware of the dangers of such partial measures. By interesting a slightly greater number in the continuance of the existing system, the lobby opposing land reforms assumed greater rather than less power.[4]

Clearly, before any schemes for land reform can be fully implemented it will be necessary to decide on a method of finding out what the community wants with the land. In practical terms county and district councils might be the best vehicles for administering the reforms, especially if they were given the short-term responsibility of administering planning controls over farming and forestry activities. Nevertheless, there will be real difficulties in weighing local priorities against national ones, for example over the use and development of National Parks.

The real attraction of the land tax is that once again it would be the community which really determines the fate of the land rather than either private individuals or the state. As George puts it, 'rent being taken by the state in taxes, land, no matter in whose name it stood or in what parcels it was held, would be really common property, and every member of the community would participate in the advantage of ownership.'

Of course, reform of landownership must be accompanied by reform in the way we use the land. Michael Allaby has suggested that if we reduced the use of chemicals and machines and turned to muscle power, we would have to increase the farm labour force dramatically. If the labour force was increased to the EEC average as a proportion of the total working population we would create another 1·2 million jobs. Allaby suggests that such a shift would account for a movement of 4 million people into the countryside when one adds in the future workers' families. The final shift, he predicts, could be around 8 million when one adds in the mechanics doctors, shopkeepers, etc. who will service the population.

To some, the ideas of Waller, George and Allaby may seem abhorrent; to others, utopian. Others still will dismiss them as unworkable. However, the only factor which is likely to thwart land reforms (and we already see this with the opposition to planning controls over farming and forestry) is the power of landowners and vested interests. As Galbraith suggested in *The Affluent Society*, 'Few things have been more productive of controversy over the ages than the suggestion that the rich should, by one device or another, share their wealth with those who are not. With comparatively rare and normally eccentric exceptions, the rich have been opposed.'

Accountability in Government and Freedom of Information

From our survey of the workings of the agricultural, forestry and water industries it is clear that many of our important decision-makers are unaccountable to the public. We are often denied important information about industrial activities and we are excluded from the decision-making processes which determine the fate of our natural resources. (It is also clear that our political leaders are often deprived of vital information, so they are sometimes in the same boat as the rest of us, albeit on a higher deck.) All this should be seen in the context of the workings of the technological imperatives which influence the decisions taken by our political leaders.

We find the water industry justifying its activities through spurious forecasting techniques, the energy industries expanding at their own predetermined rate and the agricultural industry doing likewise. The public is given no opportunity to challenge official forecasts, either in public inquiries or elsewhere, and both the government and major industries make it as difficult as possible for us to gather information which will help us challenge the ethos, economic desirability and workings of the users of natural resources. 'Ignorance of others is bliss' seems to be the appropriate aphorism guiding the administrative civil service and government.

Our major political parties pay lip-service to the ideal of community participation, yet behind the locked doors of Whitehall the civil service is doing its best to deny public participation in planning issues of both local and national importance. The PI system is fast losing its credibility and in most circumstances it is little more than an elaborate placebo. The government is presently dismantling the planning system, not through parliamentary vote but by the backdoor method of issuing circulars and regulations which amend the working of existing Planning Acts. And as we suggested in the first section, the powers of local planning authorities are being steadily eroded by central government.

O'Riordan has capably summarized the defects of the Whitehall civil service:

> The major faults of the senior British Civil Service appear to lie in its inability to root out mistakes, its arrogance in assuming it can master any topic no matter how technical, its failure to relate expenditure to policy outcome and public benefit, and its general lack of accountability whether to politicians or to the public.

We can only offer the briefest suggestions for some of the immediate changes needed in the way in which decisions are made if our present land-use policies are to be reformed. The danger of brevity is obvious: our suggestions may seem trite. Nevertheless, we can say with certainty that we sorely need legislation along the lines of the American Freedom of Information Act. People are not in any position to make decisions about the desirability of a development or an official policy if they are denied information. At present we are expected to acquiesce with the ideas and information fed to us by government and industry through the media. Needless to say, experience has proved that this is often nothing more than raw propaganda, biased in favour of what ministers, civil servants or industrial leaders want.

However, a Freedom of Information Act will be of little use on its own. The Americans have found that though information may be technically available to members of the public, government bureaucracies make it as difficult as possible for people to get hold of. The dissemination of information determining or impinging on government policy must be coupled with institutional reform. After all there is no point in our having all the information enabling us to make our own decisions if we are then to be denied the right to participate in the decision-making processes. It is for this reason that many of the green parties in Europe have campaigned (in some instances successfully) for the use of referenda on major issues. As important as the introduction of referenda is the need for the civil servants in MAFF, the Forestry Commission, and the CEGB and the policy-guiders in the National Water Council, IDBs and similar organizations (we include the NCC and the Countryside Commissions) to be made accountable for their decisions, not just to MPs but to the general public. At present it is official secrecy and the lack of accountability of decision-makers which is thwarting the reforms championed by environmentalists as much as anything else. Everything, including the minutes of their meetings, that does not have to remain secret for strictly defined reasons of national security, should be available for public inspection.

New Life for Old Watchdogs

After the last war Parliament established separate government conservation agencies to look after the needs of wildlife and landscape. From our criticisms of the NCC and the Countryside Commissions, it should be evident that we believe urgent changes are needed in these institutions.

At present we have two weak organizations, the NCC and the Countryside Commission, acting separately, one looking after nature and the other after amenity and landscape. Malcolm and Ann MacEwen have pointed to the absurdity of the situation, one which is repeated nowhere else in the world: 'In theory at least, the

Commission's job is to conserve both nature and beauty, although in practice it tends to lose interest in nature unless it believes it to be beautiful. What then is the job of the Nature Conservancy? It is to conserve nature, but not its beauty!' The MacEwens, like many others, believe that the state conservation agencies should be amalgamated. We agree. Bryn Green, a former NCC regional officer, has argued that the merger between the Council and the Commission would help the two bodies to tackle government agricultural policies, and the MacEwens believe that the extension of the common ground between them would lay the basis for common action, directed towards two objectives:

The first must be to secure fundamental changes in government policy, so that conservation of natural resources and natural beauty is built into the entire apparatus of subsidies, grants, tax incentives, farm development plans and dedication agreements for agriculture and forestry. The second must be to enable the agencies and the voluntary bodies to unify their forces, and to concentrate their influence and their support where it will do most good – above all, perhaps, in helping, persuading, informing and in some cases thwarting, the owners and users of land – both public and private.

The amalgamation of the Conservancy and the Commissions must be accompanied by other measures. The state conservation effort must receive considerably greater financial and labour resources if it is to carry out the duties with which it is charged under Parliamentary Acts. It is no good the government grumbling about the inflationary effects of public spending. The real issue concerns the government's priorities. Doubling the budgets of the NCC and the Commissions would mean that the Chancellor has to take another £20 million out of his pocket. This sum, seen in the context of, say, the massive defence budget, is a mere drop in the ocean. If the government wants conservation (it says it does) then it must expect to pay something for it. There is one point we must add here. At the time of writing the DoE is busy cutting the staff and funds of the Countryside Commissions. Many Commission and NCC officers fear that this is a preliminary to amalgamating the Conservancy and the Commissions, thus creating not a single strong body instead of two weak ones, but a single weak organization.

Another reform is needed if the old watchdogs are to be given a new set of teeth. The state conservation effort is doomed to failure if those charged with determining its policies continue to fail to challenge those interests which are destroying the countryside. The majority of members on the NCC council and the majority of Commissioners are failing to do this either because they are scared of tackling the agricultural and forestry lobbies or because they themselves have vested interests in farming and forestry. These people, however honourable and well-intentioned, must be replaced by people more representative of the 3 million environmentalists – or the 50 million other people – who have a vested interest in the survival of the British countryside. We would not suggest that the Ministry of Agriculture or the Department of Energy should be run by conservationists; by the same token we do not believe that farmers and foresters should be asked to run the NCC or the Commissions.

At an international conservation conference in London in October 1981 Ian Prestt, the Director of the RSPB, had the following to say about the NCC's Council: 'At a time when we are working towards more open government we find the Council of the NCC hiding behind closed doors. They meet often but we scarcely ever hear from them. Even their own employees often know nothing of what happens. Their silence has become a fob.' As the dispensers of public money we would expect the Councillors and Commissioners to be more accountable for their decisions, just as we expect the same from MAFF, the National Water Council and any other public body.

The Environmental Revolution: A Question of Faith

Max Nicholson coined and popularized the term the *Environmental Revolution* in his book of that title published in 1970. In the foreword he wrote: 'Awareness of the decisive importance and of the disturbing vulnerability of man's environment is bursting upon most alert and public spirited people.' The problem has been translating this awareness into action.

Over the last few pages we have indicated some of the fundamental changes which we believe are needed if the environmental revolution is not to become a short-lived and spent-out force. However, it is very easy to be an armchair revolutionary: saying that we need something is very different from going out and fighting for it. Land reforms, the introduction of planning controls, changes in agricultural policy and an end to civil servant secrecy will only come about through intense pressure and parliamentary lobbying.

Schemes to improve the local environment will only follow from the action of individual members of the community. Appendix 2 deals with the subject of how to start a pressure group, who to lobby and how to use the press. The following pages can be seen as either a lengthy foreword to that appendix or as a lengthy footnote to the last three sections of this chapter. It is about the pitfalls of trying to change the 'system', thereby pushing the environmental revolution a bit further along the path to success.

In his *Maxims for Revolutionaries*, George Bernard Shaw wrote that 'The golden rule is that there are no golden rules.' This applies as much to the environmental revolution as any other.

Ten years on from Nicholson's declaration of the environmental revolution, many would-be revolutionaries are beset by worry and doubt. As Timothy O'Riordan suggests, the environmental movement is suffering from two complementary anxieties. First, there is a feeling that time is running out and something has to be done very fast: 'This is the realization of scarcity – scarcity of certain wild species and landscapes, scarcity of low-cost (or at least low-environmental-cost) energy, food, and other raw materials; scarcity of public amenity and a growing scarcity of reasonably priced private amenity.' The second anxiety about the future concerns 'a pervasive uncertainty that has all but replaced the beguiling self-confidence which has characterized the ruling elite in western democracies ever since the industrial revolution'.

There are undoubtedly many who believe that the environmental revolution is no longer making the headway of the late 1960s and early 1970s. Some claim that environmental reforms (particularly in the United States) came at a time when they could be afforded as a 'luxury'. According to the gloomier observers of the environmental movement the boom in environmental awareness at the time Nicholson wrote *The Environmental Revolution* has had few lasting benefits. They point to the policies of Mrs Thatcher's monetarist government and Ronald Reagan's savage war against the environmental safeguards introduced by his predecessors. Yet despite all this, it is too early to pull down the curtain on the environmental revolution.

The conservation movement does face real problems but there is plenty of room for optimism. Since 1970 the membership of conservation organizations in Britain has risen from around 600,000 to over 3 million. At the same time the increasing influence of younger members of the environmental movement has drawn together the two fringes of nature conservation and environmentalism by linking the problems of habitat destruction and wildlife extinctions with problems of development. The Club of Rome's *Limits to Growth* (1972) and the *Ecologist's Blueprint for Survival* (1972) sent up the first smoke signals which unnerved political leaders. Once it became clear that economic growth in the affluent 'North' was faltering, the 'unrealistic' future foreseen by eco-freaks began to appear not only attractive but feasible. Nature conservationists gradually began to take a more political view of the development of industrial society and today's economists and politicians are at least paying lip-service to environmental concerns. Doomsday may have been postponed; it has yet to be cancelled.

The publication during 1980 of the *World Conservation Strategy* and *Global 2000* was a watershed in this process. Both documents recognized that inequality between and within nations, and the resultant poverty which afflicts much of the 'South', are the roots of environmental destruction and resource-misuse. These documents were important not just for what they were saying but who was saying it. The *Strategy* came from scientists of the IUCN in collaboration with the Food and Agriculture Organization and the United Nations Environmental Programme, while *Global 2000* came from the advisers of the most powerful leader in the Western world, the then President of the United States, Jimmy Carter.

The voluntary bodies have become increasingly sophisticated, both in the way they state their arguments and in their lobbying of politicians. Ten years ago few would have thought that proposals to introduce planning controls over farming and forestry activities would gain acceptance within Parliament by today, yet we now have the Labour Party committing itself to exactly that. At the same time a growing number of teachers and educationists are introducing environmental themes into school curricula.

Galbraith believes that one of the essential conditions for a successful revolution is that the other side must be weak: 'All successful revolutions are the kicking in of a rotten door.' As far as most environmentalists are concerned the door is very rotten though it has yet to be knocked from its hinges. They no longer have faith in what Max Nicholson termed 'the vainglorious religions of Big Capitalism and Big Communism' and the conventional economics of both Left and Right have done little to sort out environmental problems or the misery which has become the lot of many in the 'South' and a growing minority in the 'North'. Conservationists have won the battle to establish the seriousness of environmental problems; the fact that many of them do not yet seem to realize this may be preventing the environmental movement from pressing more more vigorously for reforms. It is very much a question of faith, above all in their ability to bring about the changes they champion.

Influencing the 'System'

Anyone who has fought on a conservation issue, be it to save a local wood, to curb badger gassing or stop the culling of seals, will have sometimes felt quite powerless to do anything against 'the powers that be'. Often it is difficult to find out exactly who and where the powers are without undertaking lengthy and difficult research. Having found out in which particular corner of Westminster, White-hall or the local authority planning department they reside, it will cost even more time and money to have any influence.

Max Nicholson in his book *The System* asked the question which occurs to many environmentalists: 'How can the system prove so disastrous when so many of those who have served and developed it have personally been so good?' Nicholson was particularly well-placed to answer the question. He had been chief official adviser to a Deputy Prime Minister, organizer of allied dry cargo shipping during the Second World War, a founder of Oxford University's Political and Economic Planning Unit, Director-General of the Nature Conservancy and a key figure in the World Wildlife Fund, the United Nations International Biome Programme, European Conservation Year and the International Union for the Conserva-tion of Nature. According to Nicholson, the system is 'held together and driven by a triple fear – fear of facing new facts, fear of facing the people and fear of facing the future ... The system hates the thought of what the British people will choose to do if they are allowed to be themselves.' Nicholson reserves his strongest criticism for the civil service. Its members, more than any other group of individuals, are the core of the system.

We have already had a good deal to say about civil servants, either directly in terms of their policy-making role in government depart-ments like MAFF, or tangentially, in their relationship to the big business lobbies which influence their decisions. It would be pointless for us to try to explain further the real nature of the system; indeed anyone who has seen the uncannily realistic BBC series 'Yes, Minister' will have a good appreciation of how it works.

There is, however, scarcely any conservation campaign which will not, at some point, pass into the orbit of the system. Its main characteristics should not be forgotten; without some dramatic changes it will always be there in roughly the same form, regardless of which political party is in power. And as Nicholson says, it hates the thought of what people would choose had they the choice. For that reason it will do its best to deny you the information or help which you require.

O'Riordan has pointed out that despite their cash problems and high turnover of workers, many environmental organizations 'have not only endured but have become strategically more sophisticated and truly well informed. In many cases they have access to friendly moles in the most important political and administrative offices and hence are kept well aware of impending developments in government policy and civil service advice.' But, as he warns,

information is one thing and power is quite another. In order to gain any influence on the political order, many of these groups have to play the system to demonstrate their trustworthiness and respectability. The price of influence is accommodation, at least in the short term, to a way of doing things which is often fundamentally disliked, and which in the long term may prove environmentally counterproductive.

This is an argument which we rehearsed in some detail in *Vole* magazine in April 1981 in a critique of Friends of the Earth (FoE). We argued that the British environmental movement gains much of its strength from its diversity. Some groups rely on direct action while others argue their case with facts and attempts to participate in official policy-making by sitting on government committees and liaising with civil servants. These two extremes of action – one arguing a rationalist case, the other inflaming public opinion – reflect a divided perspective. The gradualists believe that reforms can only be created by bringing about incremental changes in official policy. The radicals, if we can use that term, do not believe that rational arguments always win (a proposition for which there is plenty of evidence) and are more likely to resort to direct action. They would argue, with good reason, that government committees are not the places where government (or the system) will relinquish its authority to pressure groups. To give just one example, FoE were enticed on to the government's Waste Management Advisory Committee in the mid-1970s. Many observers saw this as a neat way in which government dissipated the head of steam which FoE had built up – much to the embarrassment of industry – in its early campaign for recycling prior to the formation of the committee. They were right. Before its recent dissolution, the committee produced a major report which was so much at variance with FoE thinking that the Friends refused to associate themselves with it and produced a separate minority report. Five years of committee-sitting had evidently been in vain. FoE were beaten by the very system they tried to join.

The moral is clear: do not be fooled into thinking that the system will agree with you because it appears to hear your arguments. Or as Nicholson told a group of conservationists, 'Never put your trust in the State and observe that I say this to you when for practical purposes in this field I am the State!' Once inside the system an organization must be more, not less, intransigent. This is a lesson which older groups like the CPRE have learned well. The CPRE, where necessary, is prepared to fight the Countryside Commission (as over Halvergate Marshes, where a new pumped drainage scheme was proposed) as well as the Ministry of Agriculture and other government departments.

The voluntary sector must also be wary of the state's conservation agencies. The DoE, as paymaster, frequently lays down the law for the line to be taken by the NCC and the Commissions on rural affairs. Yet when publicly confronted with direct questions on the subject of countryside conservation, the DoE Rural Affairs Directorate passes the buck back to the quangos. The myth here is the 'disinvolvement' of the civil service: 'We merely advise.' As we have seen they can exert considerable indirect influence on the behaviour of the Conservancy and the Commissions by appointing the 'right' men for the job of running them.

Party Games and Coalitions

One of the most enduring myths about conservation is that it is apolitical. Nothing could be further from the truth. The conservation case is frequently expressed in terms of social justice. Here, for example, is an extract from a speech by the Duke of Edinburgh:

'a poor environment affects the less well-off much more directly ... It is the poor districts which suffer from pollution and the lack of amenities; it is the crowded industrial urban areas which need space for recreation. The rich can escape from the noisy and dirty places, it is the poor who get stuck with them.'

So far most conservation organizations have specifically avoided, with good reason, aligning themselves with any one political party. There are, of course, some exceptions, but these have mainly been groups which have arisen from within a party: for example, the Socialist Environment Resources Association (SERA), has its roots in the Labour Party, and the Ecology Party is itself a political party. Organizations like the Ramblers' Association have a very obvious leaning towards the Left and its history is closely intertwined with the labour and cooperative movements. It would have been counter-productive, however, for it to make too much play of this as it is also keen to attract members whose sympathies lie outside the labour movement. If a conservation body goes so far as to express explicit support for one party, rather than for particular policies of that party, it will undoubtedly alienate many of its members. However, the unwillingness to enter straight party politics in no way implies that the groups should or do act apolitically.

One of the principal aims of the conservation movement is to influence the political system by convincing the major parties to take on board environmental policies. (Over the last fifty years the Labour Party has proved much more responsive to environmental demands than the Conservative Party, but that is no great accolade in itself.) Obviously the greater the support for environmental reforms the greater the likelihood of a political party accepting and implementing the reforms. Environmental groups, in common with professional organizations such as the British Medical Association (BMA) or the trade unions, are pressure groups. They differ, however, in an important way. The BMA and the NFU represent specific and clearly identifiable sectors of society. As Andrew Colman points out in *The Psychology of Influence*, they 'tend more often to be able to engage in genuine bargaining than do purely promotional or cause groups which do not speak for any specific interest other than society at large, such as the Campaign for Nuclear Disarmament, the Aid Lobby or the Friends of the Earth'. Most environmental pressure groups are *influencing* groups: their success depends on them marshalling support for their causes and, in the case of those which lobby governments for reforms, convincing politicians both that their cause is just, right and beneficial to society, and that it has significant popular support. Direct action has the interesting consequence of turning pressure groups from influencing into bargaining organizations. The threat to thwart, say, the dumping of waste or the culling of seals, is analogous to the withdrawal of labour by a trade union or the refusal to handle 'blacked' goods.

For both environmental influencing and bargaining pressure groups, public support is essential. Examples of the former would include the RSPB, CPRE and the Ramblers' Association; all rely to a large degree on the financial support of their members. The Animal Liberation Front and Greenpeace might be considered examples of environmental bargaining groups; for them public sympathy (and media sympathy) may be as important as public membership (when such groups have a membership) and the funds raised by membership.

In some situations a pressure group can be much more influential when acting in cooperation with other groups pursuing similar ends. This is particularly true when lobbying government for legislative change. During the passage of the 1981 Wildlife and Countryside Act through the two Houses, Wildlife Link played a key role in putting across the conservation case. The Link acted as spokesman for over twenty voluntary bodies, including such diverse organizations as the RSPB, the Ramblers' Association, the Youth Hostels' Association, the British Herpetological Society and the FoE. The success of Wildlife Link owed much to its chairman Lord Melchett, who managed to bring the various wildlife, amenity and animal welfare groups together as a joint lobby for the first time. It was no mean achievement. None of the groups involved was precluded from doing its own individual lobbying, but there is no doubt that the united front of the Wildlife Link added much strength to the campaign to force the government to produce an improved piece of legislation. As it happened the Act has turned out to be exceedingly weak, but there is no doubt that the Labour Party would never have advocated planning controls over agricultural and forestry activities had it not been for the lobbying of such groups.

There are many other examples of successful coalitions in environmental politics. Nature conservation, animal welfare, nuclear disarmament, soft energy, anti-motorway and food and health campaigners have much in common and there are encouraging signs that powerful marriages of convenience are being made between such groups on some issues. For example a meeting held in early 1982 brought together such seemingly different groups as the British Association for Nature Conservation, the National Centre for Alternative Technology and anti-heart disease campaigners to formulate plans to produce an alternative agricultural strategy. These coalitions are by no means permanent but they can be highly effective.

However, much of the strength of the environmental movement comes from its diversity. Coalitions, particularly on specific issues, are useful, but each environmental group has its own constituency and a shotgun marriage between one that attracted radicals and another which had tapped conservative support would probably prove to be disastrous. Chris Hall, the former Director of the CPRE, was pragmatic enough to realize that CPRE had to become more effective *without* upsetting its traditional support: 'CPRE can tap a constituency that groups such as Friends of the Earth could never reach. Surely we should try to involve as many people as possible in the environmental lobby regardless of their backgrounds.' The environmental researcher Tom Cairns carried out a study of environmental groups in the city of Bath, in which he found that there were significant differences (in terms of attitudes, values and socio-economic standing of members) between organizations whose aims and activities appeared very similar. He found fundamental social distinctions between pairs of groups which might seem to be natural bedfellows; for example between FoE and the Conservation Society, the National Trust and CPRE, and Bath Natural History Society and the RSPB. Interestingly, there were greater social similarities between groups (like, for example, the RSPB and the Ramblers' Association) which have very different fields of interest.

There is a clear message here. Coalitions between different environmental groups can add great strength to specific campaigns, but it is vital that the individual organizations maintain their separate identities and do not succumb to the temptation of forming mergers in order to increase their size. There is, of course, no reason why activists within environmental groups should not become *individually* active within a specific political party and attempt to influence the policies of that party. The move of environmental campaigners in large numbers into the New Left parties in some European countries is a good example of the fruits that can be born from direct involvement within the party political system. In Italy, for example, there are few environmental pressure groups but the Radical Party – a loose coalition of environmentalists, feminists and young radicals – has become one of the principal vehicles for environmental campaigning.

Bringing Conservation Home

'Conservation,' wrote Richard Mabey in the *Common Ground*, 'begins precisely where the pain and destruction of modern development are most keenly felt – in the parish, that indefinable territory to which we feel we belong, which we have the measure of.' He goes on to say that for existing wildlife groups, their 'economic and administrative activity will be pointless – and quite likely fruitless – if it does not have the support and active involvement of the whole community'.

Many voluntary bodies have fallen into the trap of trying to emulate the government conservation agencies. This is all the more extraordinary when, as we have seen, the approach of the state conservation bodies has hardly proved a roaring success. We find, for example, the RSPB basing its policy on 'the need' to concentrate its resources on acquiring places which are of 'international importance' for bird species. (A site is considered to be of international importance when it supports a certain percentage of the world or European breeding or wintering population of a species.) There are clear arguments in favour of saving such sites, and thus the creatures they support, but the rigidity of such acquisition strategy often ignores what local people think and want.

The RSPB is essentially mimicking the NCC's strategy of taking a supposedly *consistent* national view of conservation priorities. The NCC claims that this is essential to maintain respect among landowners, other land-users and the government for its programme of SSSI designation. As we suggested in an earlier chapter (see p. 62) the scientific approach to conservation is very restrictive.

The County Naturalists' Trusts have frequently based their priorities on the NCC's local lists of SSSIs, acquiring these sites, or parts of them, whenever they come on the market at a price which can be afforded.[5] During the 1960s and 1970s many trusts acquired holdings in suburban areas but their outlook remained thoroughly elitist and rural-oriented. They refused to become involved in what they saw as 'amenity issues' and continued to swallow the NCC doctrine of 'scientific importance' hook, line and sinker.

The consequences of this narrow approach were frequently ludicrous and would have been amusing had they not, in the long term, stifled the general support of the sort to which Mabey alluded. Searching for support from sympathetic organizations, people would often approach groups like the trusts with requests for help to fight off developments to which they were opposed. It might be the felling of a row of old trees, or the proposal to build a road which prompted these people to seek help. More often than not they would be turned away on the grounds that the site with which they were concerned had no 'scientific importance' or 'conservation value'.

It is a great mistake to believe that the judgement of the public on environmental matters necessarily carries less weight with the planners and local government politicians than that of the so-called experts. Politicians have to be sensitive to public opinion to survive, and the local planning authorities are ruled over by elected representatives who are often more open to suasion than the professional officers. The strength of the environmental lobby owes much less to the 'experts' than it does to the popularizers.

The case of Walthamstow Marshes in East London's Lea Valley Regional Park highlights many of the problems and consequences of not involving local people in conservation campaigns.

A group of naturalists had already spent some time 'ranking' the various parts of the Lea Valley for conservation purposes, in conjunction with the Lea Valley Authority planners, when in 1979 local people began to object to plans for gravel extraction at Walthamstow Marshes, one part of the Valley. These Marshes are old flood meadows. They are much used for local recreation and have a flora typical of such places (rich in sedges for instance) but few large winter concentrations of birds, because of disturbance.

The Lea Valley Authority wanted to extract 38 ft of gravel and leave it as a sailing lake. The Lea Valley Conservation Group's plan for the whole Valley placed a strong emphasis on birds, and being produced in conjunction with the RSPB it saw the Lea Valley's national status as a bird haunt as its most important feature. All the existing local conservation groups were represented on it at officer level (NCC, County Naturalists' Trusts, etc.). There was a natural tendency to identify 'key sites' for conservation, an approach in line with zoned-use which also suited the planners. In effect, Walthamstow Marshes might be sacrificed in order to save other places of 'greater scientific importance'. In drawing up such a local strategy, the Conservation Group were making an implicit judgement about local support. They might claim to be asking for what was *reasonable* but, like the NCC nationally, they were really asking for what they felt they were likely to get.

The lobbying powers of the Conservation Group stemmed from its officers' own activities, but these were inevitably limited once they had become committed to a 'close working relationship' with the planning authority. Their influence stopped there because their organization's membership, though large, was passive. Consequently, once the list of priorities was drawn up the conservation organizations were jointly committed to pursuing them to the exclusion of all else. It was then that the trouble began.

An assorted group of local teachers, amateur botanists and others convinced of the conservation case, decided to try to save the Walthamstow Marshes. They had never heard of SSSIs, the Lea Valley Conservation Group or the NCC. To their amazement, they found that these groups were as hostile to their pleas as the would-be developers. They formed the Save the Marshes Campaign.

Their intense activities soon attracted the attention of the local and the national press and some eminent naturalists expressed their support for the Campaign. The Lea Valley Authority told the Campaign that the Marshes couldn't be important as they hadn't been declared an SSSI by the NCC. The NCC, when pressed, at first refused to give the Marshes SSSI status. However, public opinion was clearly behind the Marshes Campaign. The Waltham Forest Council and the Greater London Council minerals sub-committee both came down in favour of the conservation case. Their decision to reject the application for developing the Marshes has saved the area, for the time being at least. However, the arguments that saved the Marshes were not scientific. In their publication *Walthamstow Marsh: Our Countryside Under Threat*, the campaigners had written:

This marsh lies in East London, still real marsh and wild ... a wonderful, open, wild place to be in ... for such pastimes as walking, picnicking, jogging, enjoying the fresh air, taking the dog for a walk, seeking out peace and quiet ... Kids mess about in it. People pick flowers in it. The people living in the houses and GLC flats that overlook it from the Hackney side enjoy it.

In short, it was for these reasons that the Marshes have been saved.

Ultimately the NCC found a way to designate the Marshes as an SSSI. Without admitting to it, the NCC tacitly acknowledged that local opinion had to be taken into account: 'Walthamstow Marshes like some other SSSIs and even National Nature Reserves are not in pristine condition. [However] contact with nature can make an important contribution to the quality of life.'

What happened at Walthamstow Marshes, and at places like Birmingham's Moseley Bog, has been described as part of the 'urban nature conservation' movement. This unprepossessing phrase can be misleading. Until recently it was used to describe the transfer of what conservationists did in the countryside into the suburbs and cities. Conservationists had condescendingly acknowledged that the black redstarts and rare weeds found in old bomb sites were of 'scientific importance'. Hampstead Heath, Kenwood and other relics of the countryside were also thought worthy of conservation. People, however, often never entered the equation. This attitude is at last changing.

A survey of wildlife in the towns of the West Midlands by the NCC's George Barker and naturalist Bunny Teagle resulted in the much-acclaimed book *The Endless Village*. They found a rich flora and fauna thriving alongside canals, under motorway bridges and on old wasteland. Although the approach of the survey still tended to be scientific, the NCC was at last recognizing that conservation doesn't come to an abrupt halt where the fields turn to houses.

Cynics have claimed that the NCC's interest in towns and cities was spurred on by a suggestion from Dennis Howell, a former Environment minister. He told the NCC that projects in cities and towns might attract more financial support than projects in the remote countryside. Cleaning up and improving the urban environment clearly had good political mileage.

In the late 1970s the NCC commissioned Lyndis Cole to look at the potential of wildlife conservation in urban environments. She had been closely involved in the establishment of the William Curtis Ecological Park in 1977. The park is run by the Ecological Parks Trust and was the brainchild of the indomitable Max Nicholson. Within a few years, a couple of acres of bare hard-standing, which had formerly been a lorry park in the shadow of London's Tower

Bridge, had been converted into a thriving wildlife sanctuary. Each year it is visited by thousands of schoolchildren and others interested in nature.

Cole's report, *Wildlife in the City*, emphasized the importance of creating new wildlife sites in built-up areas. A great deal can be achieved by practical habitat creation in parks or on derelict land. Cole quite rightly saw that for any project to be successful local people must be involved. 'It's no use naturalists telling people that rose-bay willowherb is a beautiful plant,' she says, 'when they associate it with wasteland, dereliction and housing problems.'

Land must be seen to have a use, in order for people to enjoy and respect it. Having a use does not imply that it must be conventionally farmed, built on or dug up. But nature must be accessible. In the green belts and fringes of Britain's towns and cities there are great stretches of land which are unused or under-used by agriculture. As far as groups like the Land Decade Council (see p. 28) are concerned, this land is 'blighted'. The conventional response of local authorities to this no-man's-land between the city and the country is to landscape and 'parkify' it. This often results in even greater waste of land. Rather than applying cosmetic management techniques, we should be using the land more adventurously, for allotments or smallholdings, for labour-intensive coppiced woodland and other activities which are inimical neither to wildlife conservation nor to public recreation.

This brings us on to the important question of conservation management providing employment for much greater numbers of people than it does at present. Taken all together Britain's conservation organizations manage around 2–3 per cent of our land surface. Management, where it does occur, is nearly always geared towards retaining certain features of sites (for example burning cycles to keep heather moorland in good health, grazing to maintain chalk downland, etc.) rather than to making an economic gain from their resources. There is undoubtedly great potential for conservation groups to harvest certain crops from their land while at the same time retaining all the features for which the land is valued. A particularly good example concerns coppice woodland. Coppicing involves the regular cutting of trees down to their bole. It not only provides a frequent crop of wood but increases the longevity of the trees. Let us look briefly at the employment possibilities for conservation groups of their coppices.

In *Trees, Woods and Man*, H. Edlin notes that hazel coppice was traditionally managed so that one man took a year to 'work up' 3 acres. Thus if coppice was to be managed on a seven-year rotation he would need only 20 acres to keep him in permanent employment. In 1977 there were some 3,000 ha of County Naturalists' Trust woodland in their Nature Reserves. If all this were to be coppiced, there would be enough land, using Edlin's figures, to provide work for 340 people.[6] Taking into account other forms of estate management – for example, pollarding, felling of standards, ditching and so forth – the figure might be doubled to around 700.

This is just one small example of how conservation groups could create jobs. There are many other ways in which their properties could be managed to produce saleable products and provide work. Obviously some market research is required to evaluate the feasibility of using conservation areas in this way, and the whole scope of the subject is too vast to consider in this book. The point we wish to make is that much of the land presently managed by conservation groups has a potential which has yet to be realized. Many of our Nature Reserves, for long considered by the scientists as their outdoor laboratories, could become the work places of the future without in any way damaging their wildlife interest.

Direct Action: the Last Word

This book would be incomplete without a mention of the role of direct action in the field of environmental reform. During the last ten years some environmental groups have adopted an increasingly belligerent stance against what they see as the Machiavellian policies of governments and industries. Direct action – action outside and beyond the ordinary channels of political protest – rather than compromise and cooperation is now coming to the forefront.

As we have already suggested, the reputation of groups like the FoE was built on dynamic campaigning and expert use of the media with what were, in the early 1970s, the new ideas and arguments. Subsequently FoE's influence waned as it allowed itself to be lured on to government committees and commissions. As we wrote in *Vole* on the occasion of FoE's tenth birthday in 1981, 'Poland Street [the London HQ] has been annexed by the establishment ... it has forsaken passion, which lies beyond government control, for reason, which can be ignored.' The signs are that FoE is once again turning to more radical action as it sees the success of the direct action tactics of groups like Greenpeace.

The resort to direct action and civil disobedience by environmental groups has been infrequent enough to turn a few occasions of dissent into *causes célèbres*. The ramming of the illegal whaling ship, the *Sierra*, by the *Sea Shepherd* off the coast of Spain on 15 July 1979 concluded the whaler's nefarious activities, and this incident has become an appropriate symbol of the willingness of some environmentalists to take direct action. (Two years earlier HRH the Duke of Edinburgh anticipated such action: 'Certain governments simply ignore the rules ... it is virtually impossible to do anything about it – short of sinking their whale catchers and factory ships.') Paul Watson, the leader of the *Sea Shepherd*, told a reporter before leaving Boston: 'Of course we expect violence. We are going to confront them physically to stop them and expect them to retaliate.' Indeed, for ships like the *Sea Shepherd* and groups like Greenpeace confrontation has become the key to their actions, whether they concern the prevention of seal culls in the Orkney Islands or harrying ships which are dumping nuclear and other wastes at sea.

Britain, however, has yet to see environmental dissent on the magnitude of scale and degree of violence which occurred in the struggle to prevent the building of Japan's Narita Airport between 1966 and 1978. In their battle to stop the construction of the airport, and later its use, peasant farmers, students and militant radicals resorted to paramilitary tactics more usually associated with the police forces who break up such demonstrations. During 1980/81 the authorities in Germany met with similar resistance to their plan to destroy a large area of woodland on the outskirts of Frankfurt to make way for an airport.

Nevertheless, British environmentalists have periodically been roused into taking direct action. We have already mentioned the great 'mass trespasses' of the 1930s, whose purpose was to challenge Britain's primitive access laws (see p. 15). Walking on to private moorland today might not be considered an act of direct action but for those who climbed on to Kinder Scout, it certainly was: the five ringleaders were banished to prison. More recently direct action at Crymlyn Bog in South Wales, led by local FoE campaigner Andrew Lees, finally won increased safeguards for the site from the NCC in 1981. People of all ages from a nearby housing estate formed a picket across the entrance to the bog, turning away lorries loaded with waste which was to be tipped there.

It is far from easy to gauge the success of direct action but the same applies to other forms of conservation strategy, including even land acquisition. Laws and regulations can be ignored and repealed as indeed they are being in the United States where, for example, in 1980 the Reagan administration suspended regulations which banned oil and gas exploration in nature sanctuaries off the Californian coast. Similarly, environmental argument may win through at a PI but the refusal of planning permission for a development may prove only temporary. As FoE Director Graham Searle pointed out when Rio Tinto Zinc's plans to mine copper in Snowdonia in the early 1970s were thwarted, 'RTZ withdrew but there is no guarantee that they won't return in the future.'

To those who claim that direct action does not work, one can only point out that it was through civil disobedience that the Chartists won the rights of trade unions and universal suffrage; it was through direct action that the suffragettes won the vote for women; and it was largely the mass trespasses of the 1930s that led to an Act which opened up some moorland for public recreation. In short, 'rights' which we now take for granted came about not through compromise, cooperation and consensus, but through direct action.

Direct action inevitably provokes strong reactions. During the Second Reading of the Laboratory Animals Protection Bill in the Lords on 18 December 1980, the Earl of Halsbury, reacting to incidents such as the Animal Liberation Front (ALF) raid on the Agricultural Research Council Institute of Animal Physiology at Babraham, near Cambridge (dubbed Frankenstein Farm by the press), claimed that 'we live in abnormal times in which any advocates of minority opinion now feel free to emphasize their opinions by civil commotion and violence at a time when the judiciary seem to have lost their faith in punishment as a deterrent'. Halsbury referred to the 'disturbed personalities' involved in the animal liberation movement as 'neurotic' and 'psychotic'. They were, he said, afflicted by 'vicarious paranoia', yet he himself claimed that 'if they could not protest about animals, they would be protesting about putting fluoride into drinking water or something like that'.

Lord Houghton suggested during the debate that Halsbury had got 'vandalism on the brain', and proceeded to explain the frustration which has driven individuals in the ALF to direct action:

the noble Earl has no understanding at all of the mood, the outlook and the desire for idealism and action of the young people of Britain today. With great respect to him, he is an 'old square'. It is not a bit of good lecturing magistrates and criticizing the judiciary and virtually asking them to send these people to remand homes or institutions for reform and better order and discipline. None of that is going to carry any influence with young people. They are disenchanted with the society which has been created for them by their elders. They do not like what they see; they want to change it. They want to be where the action is. Unfortunately where the action is is usurped by the older people in the community who stand in the way of the attainment of the life and vision they want to see.

Disorder, then, looks like being the order of the day for some environmental groups in the 1980s. The ALF is already attracting the attention of Special Branch policemen, who are now said to be regular attenders at film shows about the laboratory use, or abuse, of animals. It is to be hoped that government does not completely misjudge widespread public concern for both conservation and animal abuse by trying to squash it through brute force. If there is a lesson to be learnt from some of the violent 'green' battles in Europe it is that establishment intransigence or the refusal to listen to objectors has encouraged the infiltration of the environmental movement by those who wish to use it as a front for terrorist activities. Threatening harsh discipline will not, as Houghton realizes, deter the genuine campaigners. Members of the ALF have shown that they are willing to go to prison for their 'crimes', as were the trespassers of the Peak District half a century before them. Chris Hall, at a time when he was director of the CPRE (one organization we can be sure will not resort to direct action), predicted that civil disobedience and confrontation with the law are likely to increase in the future if environmentalists believe that they are not getting a fair hearing. The warnings of Hall and Houghton should not be ignored, yet the present government is pursuing and introducing policies which further damage our environment. It would have been pleasant if the problems of land-use conflict had been solved by compromise and cooperation. But, as we have seen, they have not been.

Postscript

Since this book was written a Conservative government has been re-elected. Rural reforms remain as far off as ever. However, in recent months certain events have taken place which are worth noting.

Sir Ralph Verney, who unwittingly did so much to highlight the conflicting claims on the countryside, was replaced as Chairman of the NCC by William Wilkinson in May 1983. Wilkinson is an ex-treasurer of the RSPB, a farmer and an accomplished business-man.

Verney's replacement as chairman was remarkable because, far from being prompted by pressure from conservationists, he was effectively sacked by the then Secretary of State for the Environment, Tom King, for fighting too hard for conservation interests. Verney had fallen foul of agricultural interests when the NCC tried, some-what belatedly, to protect what remained of the Somerset Levels, in particular the area known as West Sedgemoor. Against the advice of the NFU and the CLA, Somerset farmers made no secret of their outright opposition to NCC's plans to designate the area as an SSSI under the Wildlife and Countryside Act. Indeed the NFU's efforts to encourage a compromise solution and get farmers to accept the promised handouts under the Act's compensation mechanism were brought to an abrupt halt when local farmers threatened to leave the union. Local landowners enlisted the help of local Tory MPs John Peyton and Edward du Cann, both of whom attacked Verney and his staff (described in one famous letter to the minister as 'minions and zealots'). Nevertheless the NCC designated the area and local farmers responded by burning effigies of Verney, the NCC Regional Officer and an RSPB representative. Soon afterwards King refused to accept Verney's offer to continue as NCC chairman for another three-year spell.

In recent months we have had ample time to assess the working of the compensation mechanisms of the Wildlife and Countryside Act. They are scandalous. While responsible owners or occupiers of land with SSSIs get not one penny for conserving them voluntarily (as many have in the past been willing to) anyone who now has the wit to claim a desire to develop an SSSI can get compensation for profits forgone by not doing so. Lord Thurso, scarcely a pauper, received over £250,000 for agreeing not to plant conifers on a famous peat bog in the north of Scotland. Viscount Cranbourne, MP, stood to receive a sum running into six figures for not converting the ancient and very rich Boulsbury Wood to conifers. Another farmer, in the North Kent marshes, signed an agreement with the NCC not to convert any more of the traditional grazing marsh on his Isle of Sheppey land to arable. His land – Elmley Farm – is to become a National Nature Reserve, under a Nature Reserve Agreement, and the yearly cost under the loss-of-profits calculation is £100,000.

It is quite clear that the Act is impractical as it transfers responsibility for channelling public funds to the farmer from MAFF and the EEC purse to the tiny and impoverished NCC. The Act panders to the presumption that the landowner's principal concern should be to maximize profit whatever the costs to the environment and it compounds this by rewarding the landowner who threatens destruction rather than the landowner who genuinely wishes to conserve. It has further driven conservationists and land users apart, and judging from agreements reached since the passage of the Act between NCC and landowners it is clear that it is those who least need public money who are getting it. The Act does nothing to help the thousands of small farmers and sympathetic woodland owners who are struggling to make a living and often help conservation, despite government policies pushing them in the opposite direction.

The Act must be reformed. One short-term measure might involve the re-writing of its financial guidelines. But if it has done one good thing, albeit inadvertently, it has been to draw out into the open the unjustifiable level of public subsidy which *some* farmers and foresters enjoy, both directly through grant-aid and indirectly through price support. Indeed the Common Agricultural Policy is under attack from so many different quarters that it is difficult to see it surviving in its present monstrous form. In 1983 annual CAP expenditure was expected to be around £10,000 million. This massive spending will only be increased with Spain joining. (During the House of Lords' Select Committee on the European communities assessment of the 1982–3 Farm Price Settlement – of which the Committee took an exceedingly dim view, so large was it – Lord Raglan remarked: 'We have taken some evidence on olive oil where we were startled to find that should Spain join, it may let the Community in for 1,600 million ECU [approximately £1,000 million]. I do not know where I am with all these buggling figures ...')

Two other events worthy of inclusion here have been the establishment of a European Environment Fund by the EEC and the publication of the UK response to the World Conservation Strategy.

The Environment Fund is a certain target for conservation lobbyists, not just for funds but more to get it increased from its present £300,000 to a much greater figure. It is unfortunately typical that it was the British government that fought against the Fund being set up and then objected to proposals to make it big enough to be significant. With adequate finance, the Fund ought to be a principal agent in helping to realize the aims of the World Conservation Strategy by making conservation a fundamental part of development: without it, the use of EEC funds by agencies such as the Ministry of Agriculture and the Department of Agriculture and Fisheries Scotland (for example in the Integrated Development Programme for the Western Isles and similar schemes in the Highlands) will only stoke the fires of conflict.

As we write this postscript, the London launch of the British response to the WCS is a recent memory. It remains to be seen how much the 'process' of implementing the WCS will achieve, but at present it looks like very little. The original WCS managed to get closer to real issues that the British one, which makes up in length and unnecessary research what it lacks in government commitment or short-term proposals. Among a bevy of worthies at the launch, HRH Prince Charles was remarkable for being about the only speaker to come down to earth, pointing out to landowners that if they didn't mend their ways, and if MAFF's grant policies weren't changed, some public agency would step in to take control.

Indeed despite out natural misgivings about laws and regulations, it does seem certain that some better protection for wildlife and countryside – probably some form of planning controls to protect features – is needed. Even before the CAP is adequately reformed,

MAFF could help things along by putting an embargo on all grant-aid for new drainage, reclamation of saltmarsh, stump grubbing, moor gripping, re-seeding of old pastures and so on. The British tax-payer should no longer tolerate farmers taking his or her money to produce most of what already exists in surplus at the expense of the remarkable beauty and richness of the countryside.

Appendix 1

National Nature Reserves and

RSPB Reserves in Britain

(a) National Nature Reserves in Britain

The maps on pp. 161, 167 and 173 show some of the 180 or more National Nature Reserves (NNRs) run by the NCC. (In addition there are a number of Local Nature Reserves (LNRs) run by local authorities and other groups, some 1,300 mainly rather small reserves run by County Naturalists' Trusts, and an assortment of Nature Reserves or refuges in the control of the National Trust, the British Association for Shooting and Conservation, and other organizations. For information concerning the County Naturalists' Trust reserves contact the Royal Society for Nature Conservation, The Green, Nettleham, Lincs.) Updated lists of both NNRs and RSPB reserves (see pp. 183 and 187) are available from the respective organizations. It is advisable to contact the RSPB or the relevant Regional Office (below) of the NCC before planning a trip to any reserve. Most reserves are accessible to some degree, and ◗ is used to denote partial or restricted access and ◗◖ where there is open access on NNRs. The brief details concerning some NNRs given below come from the free NCC Information Sheets available on receipt of a stamped addressed envelope at NCC, 19 Belgrave Square, London SW1X. Number given in brackets (e.g. (64)) denote size of National Nature Reserves in ha; O denotes a NNR owned by the NCC, L leased and NRA where there is merely a Nature Reserve Agreement.

Scotland

North-East Region

(Wynne Edwards House, 17 Rubislaw Terrace, Aberdeen, AB1 (tel: 0224–572863))

1. Hermaness (964) NRA ◗◖
2. Keen of Hamar (30) NRA ◗
3. Haaf Gurney (18) NRA ◗◖

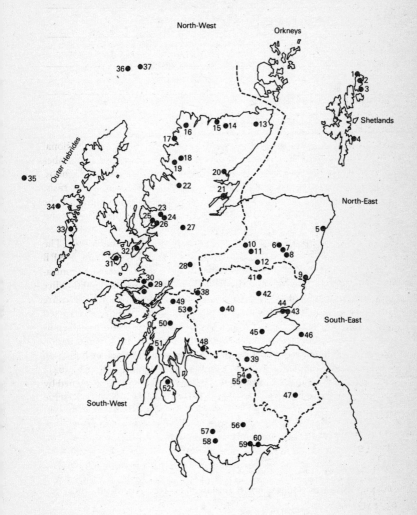

Map 8 National Nature Reserves in Scotland

4. Noss is an island reserve 4 miles east of Lerwick. With its great sand-stone cliffs this is one of the most spectacular sea-bird colonies in Europe. The horizontally bedded planes of Old Red Sandstone provide suitable nesting ledges for thousands of guillemots, kittiwakes and gannets as well as a wide variety of other sea-birds. A colony of 200 great black-backed gulls breeds on the reserve, while the moorland contains important breeding colonies of great and Arctic skua. A ferry service to the island where there is a visitor centre is operated across Noss Sound by the NCC during the summer. (Leaflet 10p.) (313) NRA ⬛⬛

5. Sands of Forvie (718) L ⬛
6. Muir of Dinnet (1415) NRA ⬛⬛
7. Dinnet Oakwood (13) NRA ⬛
8. Glen Tanar (no information) ⬛
9. St Cyrus (92) NRA ⬛⬛
10. Craigellachie (Highland Region: Badenoch and Strathspey District) lies immediately west of Aviemore, and contains one of the largest birch woods in the Spey Valley, and open moorlands rising to 1,700 ft. Schistose rocks of the Moine Series outcrop in steep cliffs, including the famous Craigellachie Rock, and the soils support a rich flora. Ornithological and entomological interest is considerable and geo-logical features include examples of rock-folding and mountain-building processes. (260) NRA ⬛⬛
11. Cairngorms (Highland and Grampian Regions): this reserve is the largest in Britain (25,947 ha), a granite mass reaching an altitude of over 4,300 ft between the Spey and Dee valleys. Glacial action has carved out many high corries, some of which contain Arctic-Alpine lochs, and has left extensive sand and gravel deposits on the lower slopes. The summit plateau represents the largest area of high ground in Britain; the Arctic-Alpine communities of plateau, cliff and scree lead down into extensive heather moorland, bog and mire com-munities at lower levels, with large tracts of native pinewood present in some areas. The flora is characteristic of acid soils, with more diverse communities found where outcrops of schistose rocks occur. The fauna includes a wide range of species typical of the Scottish Highlands; red deer is the largest mammal and ptarmigan one of the commonest birds of the high tops. Access unrestricted (beware autumn deer culling at Loch-an-Eilein). (Visitor centre and nature trail. Leaflet 10p.) (25,947) O/NRA ⬛⬛
12. Morronne Birkwoods (225) NRA ⬛

North-West Region

(Fraser Darling House, 9 Culduthel Road, Inverness, IV2 (tel: 0463–39431))

13. Achanarras Quarry (no information) ♦�
14. Strathy Bog (49) L ♦�
15. Invernaver (552) NRA ♦�
16. Gualin (2,522) NRA ♦
17. Loch a'Mhuilinn Wood (no information) ♦�
18. Inchadamph (1,295) NRA ♦
19. Inverpolly is a wild, remote, almost uninhabited area on the north-west coast near the Sutherland border which includes three summits over 2,000 ft and the whole of Loch Sionascaig. There is a great diversity of habitats: lochs, streams, bogs, moorland, woodland, screes, cliffs and summits. On the east boundary is the classic geological locality of Knockan Cliff which exposes a section of the Moine Thrust zone. The reserve contains relatively untouched relics of primitive birch-hazel woodland and the fauna of the reserve is typical of the West Highlands. Permission is required, from Assynt Estate Office (Lochinver 203), to visit Drumrunie in late summer and autumn. (Summer-manned display/information centre, nature and geological trails. Leaflets: *Knockan Cliff Geological Trail* 5p, *Knockan Cliff Nature Trail* 10p, general leaflet 15p.) (10,586) NRA ♦
20. Mound Alderwoods (267) NRA ♦
21. Nigg and Udale Bays (673) L/NRA ♦▊
22. Corrieshalloc Gorge, Highland Region (Ross and Cromarty) adjoins the south side of the Garve–Ullapool Road just west of the road to Dundonnell at Braemore. About a mile long, the reserve is a magnificent example of a box-canyon, formed by cutting back of river (Abhainn Droma) through hard, horizontal rocks. Its width varies between 50 and 200 ft and the walls are mostly 100–150 ft high attaining 200 ft and approaching the Falls of Measach. The tree growth in the walls is generally scanty and dwarfed, except the upper levels, the principal species being wych elm, birch, hazel, sycamore, Norway maple and beech. The plant communities, including certain mosses, are of much interest. (5) O/L/NRA ♦
23. Loch Maree Islands (200) NRA ♦
24. Ben Eighe, Highland Region (Ross and Cromarty) is located 45 miles west-north-west of Inverness and 24 miles north-east of Lochalsh. This was the first NNR to be declared in Britain; and was acquired primarily for the preservation and study of remnant Caledonian pinewood. The mountain slopes of Ben Eighe are also of great geological, physiographical and floristic interest. Visitors are requested not to enter fenced enclosures. Contact the warden for

further information. (Summer-manned display/information centre; two nature trails. Leaflets: *Mountain Trail* 10p, *Glas Leitre Trail* 25p.) (4,758) O/NRA ♣

25. Rassal Ashwood (85) NRA ♣♣
26. Alt Nan Carnan (7) NRA ♣♣
27. Strathfarrar Pinewoods (2,189) NRA ♣♣
28. Glen Roy (1,168) O ♣
29. Loch Sunart Woodlands (254) O ♣♣
30. Claish Moss (563) O ♣
31. Rhum is 7 miles south of Skye. The small mountains along the east coast of the island rise at three points above 2,500 ft and are of exceptional geological interest owing to their volcanic origin and their composition of rare ultra-basic rocks. Rhum is an outstanding area for geological and botanical research and for studying red deer. Important experiments and investigations into the restoration of woodland are also being carried out by the Council. Permission is required to visit parts of reserve away from Loch Scresort area. (Leaflet 20p, also available in French, German and Spanish: nature trail leaflet, *Kinloch Glen Nature Trail*, 3p.) (10,684) O ♣
32. Coille Thocabhaig (80) NRA ♣
33. Loch Druidibeg (1,677) O/NRA ♣
34. Monach Isles (577) NRA ♣
35. St Kilda (853) L ♣
36. Sula Sgeir (129) NRA ♣
37. North Rona (129) NRA ♣

South-East Region

(HQ for Scotland, 12 Hope Terrace, Edinburgh E H9. (tel: 031-447-4784))

38. Rannoch Moor (1,499) O ♣
39. Blawhorn Moss (no information) ♣
40. Ben Lawers (3,974) NRA ♣♣
41. Caenlochan (3,638) L/NRA ♣
42. Milton Wood (no information) ♣
43. Tentsmuir Point (505) O/NRA ♣♣
44. Morton Lochs (24) O ♣
45. Loch Leven is located in the plain of Kinross midway between the Firths of Tay and Forth. The loch is world-famous for its trout fishing and the most important freshwater area in Britain for migratory and breeding wildfowl. In autumn thousands of pink-footed geese and hundreds of greylag geese arrive at Loch Leven and later disperse over Britain. Many thousands of ducks winter on the Loch, and those which breed include mallard, tufted duck, gadwall, teal and shoveler.

Access is confined to Kirkgate Park, Findatie, Burleigh Sands and Loch Leven Castle, with permission needed elsewhere. (1,597) O/NRA ◢

46. Isle of May (57) NRA ◢▮
47. Whitlaw Mosses (15) NRA ◢

South-West Region

(The Castle, Loch Lomond Park, Balloch, Dunbartonshire G83 (tel: 0389–58511))

48. Loch Lomond reserve is at the south-east corner of Loch Lomond near Balmaha and consists of five islands: Inchcailloch, Torrinch, Creinch, Clairinsh and the Aber Isle, with part of the mainland shore and marshy hinterland around the lower reaches of the River Endrick. The islands lie along the Highland Boundary Fault, one of the two major structural features of Scotland. The four larger islands bear fine examples of semi-natural deciduous woodland, with oak dominant. The slow-moving rivers and lagoons of the mainland are especially rich in aquatic invertebrates. The area is also noted for several botanical rarities and is of regional importance for the numbers of wintering wildfowl. Access to Inchcailloch where there is a nature trail, is unrestricted to the casual visitor, but larger organized groups should seek permission from the Regional Office. Permission is needed to camp on Inchcailloch. To visit the mainland portion other than the Shore Wood contact the Reserve Warden, 22 Muirpark Way, Drymen by Glasgow G63 0DX. (Leaflets: general, free; *Inchcailloch Nature Trail*, 25p.) (416) O/NRA ◢
49. Glasdrum Wood (169) O ◢
50. Glen Nant (59) NRA ◢
51. Taynish (370) O/L ◢
52. Glen Diomhan (10) NRA ◢
53. Ben Lui (798) O/NRA ◢▮
54. Braehead Moss (no information) ◢▮
55. Clyde Valley Woodlands (no information) ◢
56. Tynron Juniper Wood (5) L ◢▮
57. Silver Flowe (191) L ◢
58. Cairnsmore of Fleet (1,314) O/NRA ◢
59. Kirkconnel Flow (155) NRA ◢
60. Caerlaverock is 8 miles south-east of Dumfries and extends along 6 miles of coastline between the estuaries of the River Nith and Lochar Waters. A complete range of low-lying coastal habitats including sandbanks, saltmarsh creeks and freshwater marsh are within the boundary. The merse (saltmarsh) is one of the largest unreclaimed

saltmarshes in Britain and the most northerly breeding site of the
natterjack toad. The foreshore is used as a winter roost by thousands
of geese including the entire Spitsbergen population of the barnacle
goose. Access to part of the reserve is restricted. (Leaflet free; booklet
on the natterjack toad 25p.) (5,501) NRA ◢

England

North-East Region

(Archbold House, Archbold Terrace, Newcastle upon Tyne NE2 (tel:
0632–816316/7))

61. Lindisfarne. This reserve has some of the best saltmarsh and mud-flat
    habitats in Britain while the flocks of ducks, geese, swans and waders
    which frequent the area, especially in winter, make it of international
    importance. No permit is required to visit the reserve but you should
    check when the island is accessible via the tidal causeway. (3,278)
    L ◢▮

62. Coom Rigg Moss (36) L ◢
63. Upper Teesdale (3,497) L/NRA ◢
64. Forge Valley. This site retains many of the features of pre-historic
    forest of the region despite long-established human use. An iron
    industry was established here in the thirteenth century which led to the
    felling of native trees and the introduction of sycamore to supply
    timber for the smelting process. The older part of the woodland has a
    canopy of oak and ash with a well-developed under-storey of shrubs
    and a rich herb layer. A woodland walk has been established.
    (Leaflet 10p.) (63) NRA ◢▮

65. Ling Gill (5) O ◢▮
66. Colt Park Wood (8) O ◢
67. Scar Close (93) L ◢

North-West Region

(Blackwell, Bowness on Windermere, Windermere, Cumbria LA23 (tel:
09662–5286))

68. Glasson Moss (58) O ◢
69. Moor House (3,894) O ◢
70. Asby Scar (166) O ◢
71. Blelham Bog (2) L ◢
72. North Fen (2) L ◢
73. Rusland Moss (24) O/L/NRA ◢
74. Roudsea Wood and Mosses, lying on the eastern flank of the Leven
    Estuary. This low-level woodland and surrounding raised sphagnum

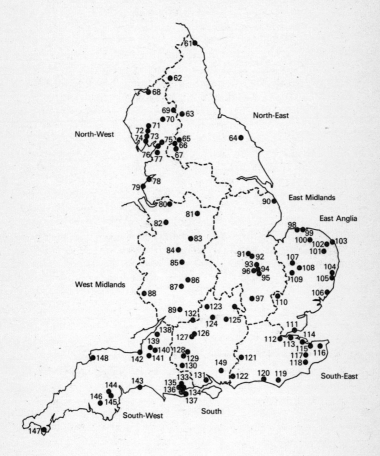

Map 9 National Nature Reserves in England

bogs contain a number of diverse habitats. Limestone and slate outcrops support rich and characteristic native woodland, flora and fauna.
The reserve has been subject to intense management for over twenty
years converting coppice back to high forest. 276 ha in total area, the
woodland was declared in 1955 and the Mosses extension acquired in
1978. A permit is required. (116) L/NRA ◢

75. Park Wood (no information) ◢
76. Clawthorpe Fell (14) NRA ◢
77. Gait Barrows contains the most important single example in Great
Britain of low-level carboniferous limestone pavement with clint and
grike structure. The pavements are surrounded by a woodland of
mixed native trees and shrubs, yew being the dominant species. The
reserve also includes the small tarn of Little Haweswater. Fed by lime-
rich springs it embraces herb-rich wet meadow, sedge fen, alder and
willow carr. An area of 70 ha, it was declared on 31 May 1977 to
commemorate the Silver Jubilee of Her Majesty Queen Elizabeth II.
A permit is required away from the public right of way. (69) O ◢
78. Ribble Marshes (no information) ◢
79. Ainsdale Sand Dunes is the finest example of a sand dune system on the
north-west coast. It consists of 493 ha of foreshore, dunes, slacks and
woodland. Since the end of the eighteenth century this diverse area
has been famous for its variety of plants and animals. The pinewood,
planted earlier in the century to stabilize mobile sand, is managed to
improve the wildlife habitat. Concessionary pathways and rights of
way are open to the public. The reserve was declared in 1965 (492)
O ◢

West Midlands Region

(Attingham Park, Shrewsbury, Salop SY4 (tel: 074377–611))

80. Rostherne Mere: a deep lowland lake of outstanding importance for
wildfowl and used for research in freshwater ecology. As the main
purpose of the reserve is to provide an undisturbed refuge for wildfowl it is not possible to allow public access. However, there is a bird
observatory which provides a wide view over the mere. Permits, valid
for a year, are obtainable from the Manchester Ornithological Society.
(152) O/NRA
81. Derbyshire Dales (174) O/L/NRA ◢
82. Wynbury Moss (permit required) (11) O
83. Chartley Moss (permit required) (42) L
84. Mottey Meadows (permit required) (no information)
85. Wrens Nest (30) NRA ◢▮
86. Chaddesley Woods (102) O ◢

87. Wyre Forest (240) O/L/NRA ♣♠
88. Moccas Park (permit required) (no information)
89. Cotswolds Commons and Beechwoods (part formerly Workmans Wood) (118) NRA ♦

East Midlands Region

(Godwin House, George Street, Huntingdon, PE 18 (tel: 0480–56191))

90. Saltfleetby/Theddlethorpe Dunes (140) O/L ♣♠
91. Barnack Hill and Holes (23) L ♣
92. Castor Hanglands (90) L ♦
93. Holme Fen (259) O ♦
94. Woodwalton Fen (208) L ♦
95. Chippenham Fen (104) L ♦
96. Monks Wood (157) O ♦
97. Knocking Hoe (research only) (9) NRA ♦

East Anglia Region

(60 Bracondale Road, Norwich, Norfolk (tel: 0603–20558))

98. Scolt Head Island (except in spring) (737) L ♣♠
99. Holkham covers 3,953 ha of the Norfolk coast between Overy Staithe and Blakeney. West of Wells, it consists mainly of sand dunes and reclaimed saltmarsh now used for agriculture, while to the east it includes one of the largest saltmarshes in England. There are also extensive inter-tidal sand and mud-flats. It is the largest coastal Nature Reserve in England. Access is open except for farmland. (Leaflet 10p.) (3,925) L/NRA ♣♠
100. Swanton Novers Woods (closed) (60) NRA
101. Hickling Broad is a large shallow lake (base rich and slightly saline) surrounded by extensive reedswamp, sedge beds and alluvial marsh-land of great floristic and entomological interest. The reserve is of out-standing importance for its populations of marsh-birds, several of which are rare in Great Britain. The Norfolk Naturalists' Trust manage the reserve which is open daily (April to November) to holders of permits obtained from the Warden's office, Stubb Road, Hickling, Norwich NR12 0BW (tel. Hickling 276). Information about nature and water trails can also be obtained from the Warden. 487 (NRA) ♣♠
102. Bure Marshes, Norfolk, consists mainly of unreclaimed fenland and includes four broads. The waterways contain freshwater and are noted for their abundance of plant, animal and bird life. (Nature trail open early May to mid September and accessible only by boat: Hoveton

Great Broad Nature Trail (booklet 15p and leaflet 5p).) A permit is required except for walking the nature trail. (412) NRA ◢

103. Winterton Dunes (105) NRA ◢▉
104. Walberswick (514) O/L/NRA ◢
105. Westleton Heath (47) O ◢
106. Orfordness-Havergate (see RSPB also) (225) O/NRA ◢▉
107. Weeting Heath (137) NRA ◢
108. Thetford Heath (98) NRA ◢
109. Cavenham Heath (152) O/L ◢
110. Hales Wood (8) L ◢
111. Leigh (257) L ◢▉

South-East Region

(Zealds, Church Street, Wye, Ashford, Kent TN25 (tel: 0233–812525))

112. Swanscombe Skull Site (2) O ◢
113. High Halstow (52) NRA ◢
114. The Swale (165) O/L ◢
115. Blean Woods (67) O ◢
116. Stodmarsh (163) O/NRA ◢
117. Wye and Crundale Downs holds one of the best remaining examples of chalk downland in Kent, rich in flowers and insects. (Unmanned display, nature trail, leaflet 10p, paths open.) (101) O ◢
118. Ham Street Woods (97) O ◢
119. Lullington Heath (63) L ◢
120. Castle Hill (47) L ◢
121. Thursley Common (319) O ◢▉
122. Kingley Vale was mainly established to maintain what has been described as the finest natural yew forest in Europe. It also includes a wide variety of other plants and animal communities. (Manned display/information centre and nature trail, leaflet 10p.) (146) O/L ◢▉

South Region

(Foxhold House, Thornford Road, Crookham Common, Newbury, Berks RG15 (tel: 063523–429/439/533))

123. Wychwood (262) NRA ◢
124. Cothill (2) L ◢
125. Aston Rowant comprises an attractive stretch of the Chiltern escarpment. The 130 ha encompass fine examples of the semi-natural habitats characteristic of the Chiltern Hills, particularly beech woodland, mixed and juniper scrub and grazed chalk grassland.

(Unmanned display/nature trail, leaflet *Beacon Hill Escarpment Trail*, 20p.) Permit required away from public rights of way and nature trail. (105) O/L/NRA ◢

126. Fyfield Down (248) L ◢
127. Pewsey Downs (149) O/NRA ◢
128. Parsonage Down (no information) ◢
129. Wylye Down (no information) ◢
130. Prescombe Down (no information) ◢
131. North Solent (no information) ◢
132. North Meadow Cricklade (39) O ◢

South-West Region

(Roughmoor, Bishops Hull, Taunton, Somerset TA1 (tel: 0823–83211))

133. Holton Heath (no information) ◢
134. Arne (3) L ◢
135. Morden Bog (149) L ◢
136. Hartland Moor (258) L ◢
137. Studland Heath contains a wide variety of habitats including sand dunes, heathland, woods, boggy ground and a lake. (Two nature trails, The Sand Dunes Nature Trail (leaflet 10p) and The Woodland Trail (leaflet 20p.)) Observation Hut open at weekends. Unrestricted access on foot and on public bridleway. (174) L ◢▮
138. Avon Gorge (64) NRA ◢▮
139. Rodney Stoke (35) O ◢
140. Ebbor Gorge includes a fine example of a Mendip Valley carved out of the carboniferous limestone by an ancient river. (Marked walks, unmanned display, leaflet, 3p, nature trail, particularly designed for the wheelchair disabled.) (41) L ◢▮
141. Shapwick Heath (222) NRA ◢
142. Bridgwater Bay (2,559) O/L/NRA ◢
143. Axmouth–Lyme Regis Undercliff (321) O/L/NRA ◢
144. Bovey Valley Woodlands (73) O/L ◢
145. Yarner Wood is managed to conserve examples of Dartmoor woodland habitats. (Nature trail, leaflet 10p, and a woodland walk, leaflet 10p, unmanned display.) Permit required away from the marked walks. (150) O ◢
146. Dendles Wood (30) O ◢
147. The Lizard (84) O ◢
148. Braunton Burrows (604) L ◢▮
149. Old Winchester Hill (no information)

Wales

South Wales

(44 The Parade, Roath, Cardiff, CF2 (tel: 0222–48511))

150. Oxwich is an unspoilt piece of Gower countryside with a great variety of different habitats. The 2-mile-long sandy beach of Oxwich Bay ends in a rocky shore around the exposed headland of Oxwich Point. The Burrows consist of a dune system displaying several stages in the processes of dune formation. A small saltmarsh lies behind the northern end of the dunes, which together enclose a large freshwater marsh with several freshwater pools. Woodland covers the slopes of Oxwich Point, parts of the dunes furthest from the shore, and the south-facing slopes of Nicholaston and Crawley Woods. The plateau above the reserve is a parkland. (Display and information centre, various leaflets.) A permit is required to visit those areas off footpaths away from the beach. (261) O/L/NRA ◀

151. Gower Coast (Peninsula) is rich in plant and animal life, and with many important geological features. A number of reserves have been established in South Gower to safeguard these special qualities. These reserves consist of rocky shores and limestone cliffs stretching for almost 10 km (6 miles) from Rhossili to Port-Eynon in the south-west corner of Gower. The tidal island of Worms Head and two parts of the mainland cliffs comprise the Gower Coast National Nature Reserve, declared in 1958. The shore and cliffs near Rhossili are owned by the National Trust, while cliffland and a shingle beach near Port-Eynon have been acquired by the Glamorgan Naturalists' Trust. (Leaflet 10p.) (47) L ♣

152. Whiteford (782) L ◀

153. Cwm Clydach (20) L ◀

Dyfed Powys

(Plas Gogerddan, Aberystwyth, Dyfed SY23 (tel: 0970–828551))

154. Ogof Ffynnon Ddu (413) O ◀

155. Craig y Cilau (64) L ◀

156. Craig Cerrig-gleisiad (282) NRA ◀

157. Stackpole (no information) ◀

158. Skomer lies at the southern end of St Bride's Bay and is principally a tableland, 200 ft above sea-level, part of a platform cut by the sea in pre-glacial, Pliocene times. The island is the home of many birds which include Manx shearwaters (the most numerous), storm petrels, fulmars, puffins, razorbills, kittiwakes and guillemots. Grey seals are present around Skomer at all times of the year and it is the second

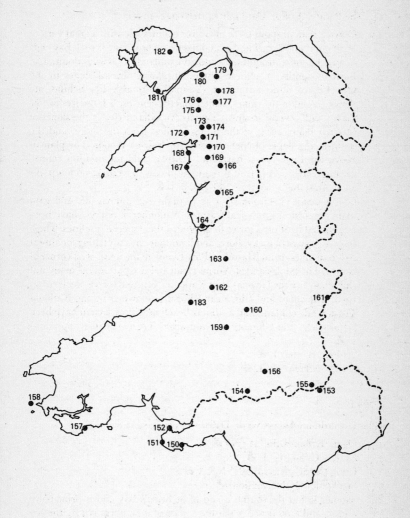

Map 10 National Nature Reserves in Wales

most important breeding site in the south-west. The island is leased by NCC to the West Wales Naturalists' Trust (Leaflet, 25p.) There is a landing fee for visitors and a permit is required to visit parts of the Island other than the nature trail. (307) O/L ◢

159. Allt Rhyd y Groes (62) O/L ◢
160. Nant Irfon (136) O ◢
161. Stanner Rocks (no information) ◢
162. Cors Caron (no information) ◢
163. Coed Rheidol (43) O ◢
164. Dyfi is a river estuary, a dune system and a raised bog. The estuary is the most important station for wildfowl and migrant waders in Cardigan Bay and has a range of estuarine habitats, with sand banks, mud-flats, saltmarsh, river channels and creeks. The dunes form an important part of the estuarine complex and have great botanic interest. The raised bog, Cors Fochno, although subjected to extensive reclamation around its margins, is one of the most extensive tracts of unmodified raised bog vegetation in Great Britain. There is un-restricted public access on foot into the Ynyslas section, but a charge is made for parking cars on the edge of the dunes in the spring and summer. There is limited access to the foreshore at the western end of the estuary along public footpaths on the banks of the River Leri and River Clettwr, but the tides and soft mud can be dangerous. Access to Cors Fochno is by permit only. The Reserve Warden may be con-tacted at Llwyn Awel, Talybont, Aberystwyth (tel: 097086–485) (1,608) O/L ◢▙
183. Cors Tregarron (768) NRA

North Wales

(Plas Penrhos, Fford Penrhos, Bangor, Gwynedd LL57 (tel: 0248–55141))

165. Cadair Idris is situated about 2 miles south of Dolgellau. This reserve is of great interest to geologists for its Ordovician lavas and ashes in which there is a band of igneous rocks together with fossil-bearing mudstones and slates. The various minerals in these rocks, and the diverse soils, slopes and heights, give rise to a wide range of habitats and plant communities. Cadair Idris is one of the most southern areas in Britain for Arctic-Alpine plants. A permit is required to visit the enclosed woodland. (392) O/NRA ◢▙
166. Coed Ganllwyd (24) L ◢
167. Morfa Dyffryn (202) NRA ◢
168. Morfa Harlech (491) L ◢
169. Rhinog (598) O ◢▙
170. Coed Camlyn, opposite Coed Maentwrog, oak woodland with bilberry (64) O ◢

171. Coed y Rhygen (28) O/L ◢
172. Coed Tremadoc (closed) (20) O/L
173. Coed Maentwrog, oak woodland with bracken. (Leaflet 10p.) (68) O/L ◢
174. Coed Cymerau (26) L ◢
175. Y Wyddfa-Snowdon, 9 miles north of Bangor, is the largest reserve in Wales, with a wide range of habitats from the oak woods near Llyn Dinas at 176 feet above sea-level, through the intermediate sheep-walk grasslands to the main Arctic-Alpine plant communities on the calcareous cliffs and the windswept sub-Arctic heath of the exposed summits at over 3,000 ft. There are also many geological features of outstanding interest. (Two trail guides: *Miners Track* 5p; *Cwm y Llan* 25p; permit needed to enter experimental plots and enclosed woodlands.) (1,677) NRA ◢▙
176. Cwm Idwal is situated 5 miles west of Capel Curig, and was the first reserve to be declared in Wales with an outstanding Arctic-Alpine flora. It is a 'natural amphitheatre' of Ordovician rocks, both volcanic and sedimentary up to 3,200 ft. (398) L ◢
177. Cwm Glas Grafnant (15) NRA
178. Coed Dolgarrog (69) L ◢
179. Coed Gorswen (13) L ◢
180. Coedydd Aber 147 O/L/NRA ◢
181. Newborough Warren/Ynys Llanddwyn, on Anglesey's southern tip, one of the largest and richest sand-dune systems in western Britain. A four-ridge dune system created by westerly winds, including a large and growing saltmarsh and all stages of dune formation. The reserve also has parts of two estuaries, a varied flora and avifauna. (Display centre leaflet 5p.) (633) O/L ◢
182. Cors Erddveiniog 31 (L) ◢

(b) RSPB Reserves

Since it is RSPB policy that both the Society's membership and the public should be able to visit its reserves where this does not conflict with bird conservation, most reserves are open in one way or another. A detailed leaflet is available from the RSPB Reserves Department, The Lodge, Sandy, Beds.

RSPB reserves fall into the following habitat groups:

Sea-Bird Colonies
Sites with cliff-nesting species

1. Noup Cliffs; 2. Marwick Head; 3. North Hill (Papa Westray); 4. Copinsay; 5. Fetlar; 6. Handa; 7. Fowlsleugh; 8. Bempton Cliffs; 9. St Bees

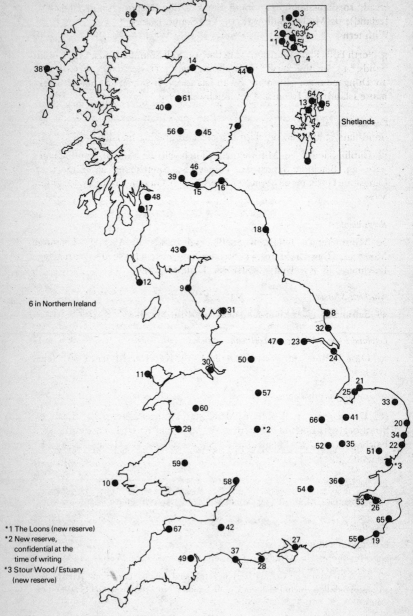

Shetlands

6 in Northern Ireland

*1 The Loons (new reserve)
*2 New reserve,
confidential at the
time of writing
*3 Stour Wood/Estuary
(new reserve)

Map 11 RSPB Reserves in Britain

Head; 10. Grassholm; 11. South Stack Cliffs; Rathlin Island Cliffs (N. Ireland); 12. Mull of Galloway; 13. Yell Sound Islands;*
With terns

3. North Hill (Papa Westray); 5. Fetlar; 13. Yell Sound Islands;* 14. Cublin Sands;* 15. Inchmickery;* 16. Eyebroughty; 17. Horse Island; 18. Coquet;* 19. Dungeness; 20. Minsmere; Swan Island (N. Ireland); Green and Blockhouse Islands (N. Ireland);* 21. Titchwell

Coastal Marshes
(mud-flats, saltmarsh, brackish lagoons and grazing marshes)

14. Cublin Sands;* 20. Minsmere; 21. Titchwell; 22. Skinflats* and Havergate; 23. Blacktoft Sands; 24. Tetney; 25. Snettisham; 26. Elmey; 27. Langstone Harbour; 28. Arne; 29. Ynys-hir; 30. Gayton Sands; 31. Leighton Moss

Reedswamps

20. Minsmere; 21. Titchwell; 23. Blacktoft Sands; 28. Arne; 31. Leighton Moss; 32. Hornsea Mere; 33. Strumpshaw Fen; 34. North Warren; 35. Fowlmere; 36. Rye House Marsh; 37. Radipole Lake

Northern Marshes

38. Balranald; 39. Loch of Kinnordy; 40. Insh Marshes

Lowland Flood Meadows and Alluvial Marshes

41. Ouse Washes; 42. West Sedgemoor; 43. Ken-Dee Marshes; 66. Nene Washes

Winter Wildfowl Waters

19. Dungeness; 31. Leighton Moss; 32. Hornsea Mere; 44. Loch of Strathbeg; 45. Loch of Kinnordy; 46. Vane Farm (by Loch Leven); 47. Fairburn Ings; 48. Lochwinnoch; Shanes Castle (by Lough Nee) (N. Ireland)

Lowland Heath

20. Minsmere; 28. Arne; 34. North Warren; 49. Aylesbeare Common

Woodland

Lowland deciduous
20. Minsmere; 28. Arne; 29. Chapel Wood; 50. East Wood; 51. Wolves

* There is no visiting at Coquet Island, Yell Sound Islands, Green and Blockhouse Islands, Skinflats, Inchmichery or Cublin Sands. Visiting is free to members at other sites.

Wood; 52. The Lodge and Sutton Fen; 53. Northward Hill; 54. Church Wood; 55. Fore Wood; 65. Blean Woods; Castlecaldwell (N. Ireland); Shane Castle (N. Ireland)

Upland oakwoods
29. Ynys-hir; 56. Killiecrankie; 58. Coombes Valley; 58. Nagshead; 59. Gwenffrwd and Dinas; 60. Lake Vyrnwy

Native pine forest
61. Loch Garten

Moorland

5. Fetlar; 59. Gwenffrwd and 60. Lake Vyrnwy; 62. Birsay Moors Cottasgarth; 63. Hobbister; 64. Lumbister

Appendix 2

Organizing a Campaign and Using the Media

Groundwork

Check that an existing group is not already doing what you want to do, but if you do find one, lobbying on the same issue in a different way, for instance, do not be put off. Go ahead and start your own group. To find out about other local groups your local library and information service of the council (district or borough) are the best starting places. Even if you disagree with the other groups' methods you might join them, as you can always raise your point at the Annual General Meeting if need be!

Organization

The views of an individual can be ignored or dismissed by planners or landowners as those of self-interested cranks. The views of a group carry weight in proportion to its size. Try to get mass support, whatever your cause. If your organization wishes to enter into any agreement concerning land, you will need a proper constitution (the National Council for Voluntary Organizations, 26 Bedford Square, London WC1 may be able to provide advice, or your local Citizens' Advice Bureau).[1] You should keep records of all members, have a Treasurer and arrange for the accounts to be audited. Securing the services of a sympathetic solicitor is very useful. For reasons of accountability, your organization should be democratic.

Lobbying

If your campaign is for a particular piece of land try distributing leaflets in the immediate area, particularly if houses overlook it or if people use the site for recreation. A cheaply duplicated typed sheet (try a community centre or CAB, school, college or library for access to a Roneo or Gestetner machine) can put your case. It can also be used to announce the formation of a group and the first meeting. At any first meeting be sure to have a few people ready to propose and second the three key officers (Chairman, Secretary, Treasurer). A local worthy can be added as President or Patron at a later date. Keep the name of your group short.

The key to successful lobbying lies in using the media effectively.[2] A campaign can often be started with a letter to the local newspaper. Local papers are always hungry for news and have a well-established system of passing on suitable items to the regional or national press. The phone numbers of the press will be listed in your telephone directory. Check through newspapers to discover which journalists are interested in, or sent to cover, environmental matters. Local radio and television are also potential allies. Only experience can teach you which things are newsworthy or not, but obvious points are that TV requires something striking or unusual to film (and your most convincing and attractive group member to make your case) and will only devote a few minutes to even the most major cases. Radio can go into depth but will usually be concerned with 'balance' and will try to present your case as having an equal and opposite case against it, even where this isn't so. Aim at a large number of short radio pieces rather than one or two lengthy ones. Both radio and TV therefore require a stream of 'events', such as letters released to the press (these are also ideal for newspapers if they receive them just before copy day), petitions handed in, people demonstrating or occupying a site or sitting up trees, and so on. You must manufacture these events as part of your campaign. Bear in mind that developers, government departments and so on can have a press-release sent out to every news outlet in your area within an hour and they can spend vastly greater sums than a voluntary organization on lunches, drinks, press packs and press conferences.

Human interest stories (for instance the children who use a wood for school projects), animals and, these days, even rare plants are particularly newsworthy. Pollution, too, can provide good copy as does bungling, obstinate or unjust local bureaucracy, which is a favourite with local newspapers. Find a keen local photographer to produce a slide-set for talks to other local groups, and black-and-white pictures for the press.

The press-release is a vital weapon in your armoury, and it goes to TV and radio as well as to newspapers. It is best addressed to known individuals, and should be followed up with a polite telephone call inquiring if more information is needed (to jog the conscience of a reporter and make him or her actually read it). Try to have a striking logo on the top of the paper.

The press-release should be typed, double-spaced and kept very short. Good press stories contain the information Who, Where, When and What, in the first paragraph, so put them in and add Why afterwards. Be sure to give a telephone number where someone can be contacted, both in the day and in the evening. Don't try to write news, that is the job of a reporter. It helps if your press-release covers only one side of the paper, otherwise it is less likely to be read. Minor points should always be left out (imagine you are writing a telegram) as these can be given to the reporter later to help colour the story. Useful embellishments may be a quote by your best-known member or Chairman, for example: 'This is a colossal failure by the Council. They have reneged on our agreement. There is trouble ahead.'

The angle of your stories can be measured to suit the newspaper you are dealing with (TV and radio are markedly less political than newspapers). There are many local newspapers but there are interesting variations within the national press.

The Times, for instance, regards itself as a 'newspaper of record' and will carry all sorts of strange information if it is of the coldest, tallest, widest, first-ever variety, or if it is in some way official. It is also conservative and read by the establishment who call it 'the Paper'. Its letters column is important as a target for your Patron or President. The *Telegraph* is, if anything, more conservative but harbours a strong dislike of 'tea-drinking bureaucrats'. It is good for anti-bureaucracy stories and probably contains more minor news stories than most other national newspapers added together. It is widely read by middle-class conservatives and freemasons. The *Guardian* is the establishment paper of the union hierarchy, intellectuals and the education system. It is liberal rather than left-wing and has a high proportion of features rather than news. (Features editors will be as useful to an environmental group as news editors.) It is keen on vogue causes and issues of social concern. Of the tabloid press, the *Mirror* has a well-established interest in conservation, and is the conventional paper of the old-style Labour Party. The *Observer* is a much smaller, less bureaucratic paper than the *Sunday Times* and generally gives conservation issues more serious treatment, although the latter is a good vehicle for Sunday morning shock-disclosures if you are in the business of giving politicians indigestion over their breakfast tray. Whichever branches of the media you deal with, send press releases to them all and do not openly cultivate favourites. Also, do not forget the many monthly or weekly magazines.

Conservation Organizations in Britain

Philip Lowe has estimated that there are in the region of 100 national conservation groups in England, Wales and Scotland. Many of these have little interest in wildlife and landscape conservation while others confine their business to very specific activities. Save Britain's Heritage (SAVE), for example, is preoccupied solely with the conservation of buildings, and the British Butterfly Conservation Society is an example of an organization with a very narrow and well-defined objective.

This section gives a brief outline of the activities and objectives of those groups most involved with landscape and wildlife conservation. The majority have already been referred to in the text.

Throughout, we have tried to emphasize the diverse nature of the environmental movement. The appearance of the movement as a united front is more often than not illusory, though as will become clear from the short descriptions we give, there is much cross-fertilization between groups with the same individuals cropping up time and again on the councils, committees and lists of dignitaries associated with the groups.

Most of the detailed information – for example, the key individuals running the groups – comes from a survey carried out in early 1980. Some changes may have occurred since, but the information gives a firm indication of the nature of the organizations involved in conservation. In each section we indicate whether or not groups have a public membership and how they can be contacted. For those interested in learning more about the history of the groups we provide a list of references. One of the most interesting studies of environmental groups was carried out by Tom Cairns, then a research student at University College, London, in the city of Bath in 1979. Bath, of course, is not Huddersfield or Hartlepool and there is a danger of using Cairns' findings for Bath as an indicator of national characteristics of environmental groups. However his summaries of the organizations which he studied (through interviews of their members) are illuminating and we incorporate some of his findings in our analysis.

By now it will come as no surprise to the reader to find that our analysis of conservation groups is not without criticism. Statements of the formal aims of the groups are available from each organization while purely factual directories already exist. The opinions are, of course, our own.

The Satellites of State

The government's conservation agencies – the NCC, the Countryside Commission for England and Wales and the Countryside Commission for Scotland – come under the umbrella of the DoE and its Scottish equivalent, the Scottish Development Department (SDD). Anyone who reads a daily paper will be aware that the DoE and the SDD are primarily concerned with the servicing and planning of the urban environment. It is no exaggeration to say that the Environment Departments regard the NCC and the two Commissions as very small fish in a very large pond. (The DoE handles Ulster's conservation affairs from an office in Stormont.)

At the launch of the World Conservation Strategy in London in March 1980 Michael Heseltine, the Secretary of State for the Environment, said:

> It is not the way of politics to guarantee that all the decisions taken by this government will fall on the conservation side; but I can promise a philosophical approach totally in line with a sensible conservation policy. And I can promise, too, a personal commitment that starts from a simple premise: in any individual decision, the starting point will be to conserve what matters. Those who have a contrary objective must bear the onus of proof.

Fine words, perhaps, but in practice Mr Heseltine's own party so emasculated the 1981 Wildlife and Countryside Act that it is weak to the point of being worthless. The conservation agencies have been pruned back and the government has shown negligible interest in conservation.

The Nature Conservancy Council (NCC)

The NCC is the government's wildlife conservation agency. It was reformed from the old Nature Conservancy by Parliamentary Act in 1973. The Conservancy was a child of post-war reconstruction, set up under the 1949 National Parks and Access to the Countryside Act, which also established the National Parks Commission, later to become the Countryside Commission. The NCC manages 181 National Nature Reserves covering a total 138,918 ha.

The founding fathers of the Conservancy included the zoologist Julian Huxley and ecologists Arthur Tansley and Charles Elton. From 1953 to 1966 Max Nicholson was Director-General and he shaped the Conservancy into an accomplished technocratic institution. During the 1960s and the 1970s, before its research functions were idiotically split off by government into the separate Institute of Terrestrial Ecology (ITE) in 1973, the Conservancy pioneered work on the effects of pesticides on wildlife and much besides. Since 1973 the Conservancy's authority, confidence and capability have gone into sharp decline.

From the time when Sir David Serpell – an ex-MAFF Permanent Secretary – was appointed Chairman of the NCC in 1974, the ruling council (whose members are appointed by the Secretary of State for the Environment) has been obsessively secretive. In contrast, its pre-1973 counterpart allowed its deliberations to be widely known. The Council's secrecy has annoyed and alarmed other conservation groups who see it as a parallel with the Conservancy's reluctance to speak out forcefully against the Ministry of Agriculture and the Forestry Commission.

The shift from a Council served by naturalists and ecologists to one dominated by career civil servants, foresters, farmers and industrialists has distressed conservationists. Sir Ralph Verney, the last Chairman, is the epitome of the new breed of members. As Chris Hall (former Ramblers' Association and CPRE leader) pointed out in *Ecos* in 1981, 'Just in case we were in any doubt which way [government] policy was pointing, Sir Ralph Verney, Forestry Commissioner and ex-President of the CLA, was appointed Chairman of the NCC.' Indeed, his appointment, like others to the Countryside Commission, owed much to direct lobbying by the CLA and NFU.

Partly as a result of its Council's composition, the NCC has failed to speak out effectively or to make full use of its legal powers (for example compulsory purchase) to act against the destruction of key sites by modern farming and forestry activities. There are signs of disenchantment with the Council among the NCC's own 585 officers but as government servants they cannot speak out effectively. The Advisory Committees for Wales and Scotland, and to a lesser degree England, are similarly constrained by members with vested interests in other land-use activities. In 1981 Michael Heseltine's office conducted a 'trawl', looking for suitable Council candidates, as a result of the alarm being expressed by voluntary conservation bodies at the composition of the Council. Unfortunately, as candidates must meet the established criteria – representing different landowning interests, etc. – few changes will be made.

The NCC has eight regions in England, three in Wales and four in Scotland. There are national HQs at Banbury, Bangor and Edinburgh, although the Banbury office may be merged with the UK HQ at Belgrave Square, London. Within each region there is a Regional Officer (RO), supported by a deputy and a number of Assistant Regional Officers (AROs). The NCC also employs wardens to look after the reserves. AROs carry out surveys, liaise with local authorities and other interest groups, and formulate management policies for the reserves in conjunction with wardens. The NCC has a small education branch which provides literature on wildlife conservation and the expertise for displays in the visitor centres on its holdings.

Budget: 1981/2 £10,047,000
1982/3 £11,270,000
Chairman: Sir Ralph Verney, replaced by William Wilkinson in 1983.
Vice-Chairman: Lord Arbuthnott

Director-General: R. C. Steel
Address: 19/20 Belgrave Square, London sw1x 8py (tel: 01–235 3241)

The Countryside Commissions

The Countryside Commission for England and Wales was set up under the 1968 Countryside Act as a replacement for the National Parks Commission. The Countryside Commission for Scotland was established under the 1967 Countryside (Scotland) Act. The Commissions are the government's amenity agencies. Unlike the NCC, the Commissions own no land. But like the NCC the Commissions have appointed members, many of whom have a stronger interest in farming and forestry than in conservation. From 1 April 1982 the Countryside Commissions gained public service status, like the NCC.

The Commissions are frequently criticized by voluntary bodies for their weak stance against commercial agriculture and forestry and the Commissions are seldom consulted by any government ministries outside the DoE on major issues which should be their concern. Both Commissions appear to be hampered by their lack of a regional organization, the southern one being based at Cheltenham and the northern counterpart at Battleby in Perthshire.

The main aims of the Commission for England and Wales are as follows: to help formulate policy for the National Parks; and to provide grants for public access to open countryside, wardens, footpaths, nature trails etc. It also helps in the creation of country parks and the designation of Areas of Outstanding Natural Beauty (AONBs) and Heritage Coasts. The Commission has similar functions in Scotland although there are no National Parks there. It has been responsible for the designation of the controversial National Scenic Areas (see p. 205). Both Commissions have advisory roles and may be consulted by both public and private landowners on amenity matters. Possibly one of the southern Commission's most successful projects has been the establishment of a Demonstration Farms Programme. The Commission has taken ten farms on which it can be demonstrated to farmers and other land users that farming economically does not have to preclude the conservation of wildlife and landscape.

Countryside Commission

Budget: 1981/2 £8,216,000; plus £6,861,000 direct to National Parks, AONBs, long-distance footpaths, etc. (this figure does not pass through the Commission's hands but is allocated by the DoE on advice of Commission)
Chairman: Derek Barber (ex-Chairman of the RSPB)
Director: Adrian Phillips
Staff: 100 (intention at February 1982 was to cut to 93)
Address: John Dower House, Crescent Place, Cheltenham, Glos (tel: 0242–21381)

Countryside Commission for Scotland

Budget: 1981/2 £3,750,000
Chairman: Dr Jean Balfour
Director: John Foster
Staff: 55
Address: Battleby, Redgorton, Perth PHI 3EW (tel: 0738–27921)

The Voluntary Organizations

National Trust

Established in 1895, the Trust is one of the largest landowners in the UK, with 400,000 acres of land (about 1 per cent of the land surface of England and Wales). There is a separate National Trust for Scotland. The Trust owns and manages many areas of outstanding nature conservation value in addition to many fine houses and estates. Famous nature sites owned by the Trust include the Farne Islands, Lundy Island, Ebbw Gorge and Wicken Fen. The Trust is the only private body whose land is inalienable (that is, it cannot be dispossessed of its land by local authorities without approval from Parliament). Among the Trust's most successful operations has been Operation Neptune to save the coastline of England and Wales (the Trust now owns over 350 miles of coast). The Trust owns one-quarter of the Lake District and in such areas it leases much of its land to tenant farmers.

The Trust's relationship to conservation is analogous to the relationship of the Vatican to Christianity: it is always in the rearguard. The Trust studiously avoids the pressure group image, which it scarcely needs considering its immensely powerful connections within the corridors of power. There are over 130 associations for National Trust members. Of the Bath Group, Tom Cairns wrote: 'The picture emerges of a Trust member who is affluent, urban and urbane, upper-middle-class, female, elderly and conservative but who has a strong aesthetic appreciation and equally strong desire to see Britain's heritage preserved in perpetuity.'

1981/2 Income: £29,560,000 (of which 29 per cent from subscriptions)
1981/2 Expenditure: £29,560,000
Director-General: Jack Boles
Membership: over 1,460,000 by January 1982
Address: 42 Queen Anne's Gate, London SWI (tel: 01–222 9251)

The Royal Society for Nature Conservation (RSNC) and the County Naturalists' Trusts

The RSNC is the umbrella body for the forty-two County Naturalists' Trusts. It owes its cumbersome title to starting life as the Society for the Promotion of Nature Reserves (SPNR), established in 1912 by aristocrat N. C. Rothschild. It was an elite pressure group which attempted to persuade the National Trust to buy Nature Reserves. The Trust found reserves an unwelcome encumbrance and the SPNR had little success for the next three decades. The SPNR became the SPNC in 1977 and won its royal prefix in 1981. The RSNC, like the SPNR and the SPNC, remains essentially undemocratic.

In 1957 the SPNR became the trusts' coordinator. The first trust was founded in Norfolk in 1926; it was followed by Yorkshire (1946) and Lincolnshire (1948). Trusts vary greatly but are almost all dominated by the 'county set' (or at least people who aspire to it!). The trusts are good at raising money to acquire small Nature Reserves. Recently established urban-based trusts have a markedly less conservative outlook and it remains to be seen whether they will be fully integrated into the RSNC system. Some of the trusts are totally undemocratic (notably Norfolk) but members don't seem to mind. Tom Cairns found that with the Bath branch of the Somerset Trust 'The overall picture of the average member is of an affluent, car-owning, urban, middle-class professional who is strongly committed to nature conservation based upon the application of technical expertise but who is strongly conservative and disapproves of pressure groups activity.'

The RSNC has a handful of professional staff and maintains an uneasy relationship with the constituent trusts, whose eagerness to retain a great deal of independence has prevented the RSNC developing a powerful centralized role. In recent years power seems to have shifted from the old caucuses of volunteers to the full-time officers. Between them the trusts manage over 1,300 Nature Reserves covering about 145,000 ha. Joint membership is 129,000. Total staff of trusts is around 150.

Finance: Income of SPNC for 1979 was £130,000. This included a government grant of £42,000 and earnings of £29,000.
Patron: HRH Prince of Wales
President: Christopher Cadbury
Secretary: Franklyn Perring
Address: The Green, Nettleham, Lincoln LN2 2NR (tel: 0522–52326)

The Royal Society for the Protection of Birds (RSPB)

The RSPB is Europe's largest conservation pressure group with over 340,000 members. The Young Ornithologists' Club, the junior branch of the RSPB, has over 110,000 members. The RSPB runs eighty bird reserves covering 37,000 ha. It employs a staff of 300.

The RSPB grew from the Society for the Protection of Birds (obtaining a royal charter in 1904), which itself was descended from the Fur, Fin and Feather Folk, a ladies' tea club established in Croydon in 1889. The ladies aimed to curb the plume trade and members pledged to 'refrain from wearing the feathers of any bird not killed for the purpose of food, the ostrich only excepted'. Contemporary bird societies like the British Ornithologists' Union refused to allow women to become members and so, remarks historian David Allen, 'the anti-plumage bodies became greater hothouses of emotion than they might otherwise have been'. In America's more progressive social climate the mixed-sex Audubon Society moved rapidly into the field of combat, and by 1902 three of its wardens had already been shot by plume hunters!

Like the RSNC, the RSPB has always attracted aristocratic patronage. By 1925 it was already pressing the government on matters such as oil pollution, calling for a debate on the subject at the League of Nations. More democratic than the RSNC, the RSPB has always had a more popular following and its membership cuts through the class divisions. Cairns had the following observations to make of the Bath Group of the RSPB: 'A profile . . . emerges of the typical member as being youngish, unsophisticated and not highly educated, urban-dwelling but who enjoys the escape to the "world of birds" as often as possible and is above all extremely organized and serious about the way in which he or she approaches this interest.'

Run by a staff with a reputation for professionalism, the RSPB is expert at enlisting the support of both key environmentalists and public figures. The organization carries covert political weight and it often seems to be aware of government intentions before the NCC. In recent years the RSPB has taken an increasingly strong stand against activities which it sees as inimical to conservation and its impatience with the timorous NCC has sometimes been quite obvious.

The RSPB has regional offices in Northern Ireland, Wales, Scotland and England.

Finance: Income for 1979 was £2,106,556
President: Max Nicholson
Chairman: Michael Hare
Director: Ian Prestt
   Council members include popular figures like Robert Dougall, Bill Oddie of the Goodies and the radical peer, Lord Melchett
Address: The Lodge, Sandy, Bedfordshire (tel: Sandy 80551)

Council for the Protection of Rural England (CPRE)

CPRE was founded as the Council for the *Preservation* of Rural England in 1926. It is a pressure group whose prime concern is landscape conservation: 'to ensure that not a single acre of land is lost unnecessarily through greed, indifference or bad planning'. CPRE has considerable political influence. In its early years it concentrated on the broad strategy of getting legislation for National Parks and AONBs on to the statute books. After the 1949 National Parks Act it turned its attention to specific issues. It now has forty-one county-based branches and fifty-one constituent bodies. Despite having constituent organizations like the CLA and the NFU, CPRE has led calls for greater controls over agriculture and forestry practices. Though its

30,000 members are predominantly rural, middle-class and middle-aged, CPRE has become a more aggressive and outspoken organization in the last decade. Much of the credit for this must go to former director Chris Hall and the current director Robin Grove-White, who has involved CPRE in policy issues of transport and energy. Tom Cairns' summary of the Bath group is very appropriate: 'The CPRE member appears as an affluent, upper-middle-or upper-class, individualistic and highly educated and professionally qualified member of the "county set" yet curiously activist and even somewhat radical in outlook, a most interesting combination.'

Finance: Income for 1981 was £137,000
Patron: H M the Queen
President: Sir Colin Buchanan
Chairman: R. Wade
Director: Robin Grove-White
Address: 4 Hobart Place, London sw 1 (tel: 01–235 9481)

Ramblers' Association

Established in 1935 by a coalition of ramblers' federations. Much loathed by farming organizations. The Ramblers have strong links with the urban labour movement, from which it draws many of its 37,000 members. It is primarily concerned with the fight for legislation to give access to uncultivated countryside. Most of its funds go towards defending rights of way, and protecting and improving access (on the ground as well as in the courts). It has been one of the main advocates of long-distance footpaths.

Though not concerned specifically with nature conservation the Ramblers have been active in opposing potash mining in the North Yorks Moors National Park and various road schemes such as the M25 across the North Downs. The Ramblers make aggressive and effective use of the national press. There are 455 affiliated clubs and societies.

Finance: Income for 1981 was £187,000, mainly from members' subscriptions
President: Lord Melchett
Secretary: Alan Mattingly
Address: 1–5 Wandsworth Road, London sw8 (tel: 01–582 6826)

World Wildlife Fund (UK) (WWF)

Financially the WWF is one of the heavy mob. It was the idea of a group of businessmen and was founded in 1961 with Max Nicholson being involved in its early years. The international HQ is at Gland in Switzerland. The principal purpose of the WWF is to raise money for wildlife conservation projects. The IUCN is heavily reliant on WWF funding. Projects to save the tiger, gorilla and panda are vital for publicity and attracting funds, but WWF money is also used for habitat conservation. WWF sees itself as the banker of the conservation movement and is concerned at the lack of credit it receives compared to bodies like the RSPB and the County Naturalists' Trusts which run the projects.

Recent problems for International WWF – the disgrace of its former President HRH Prince Bernhardt over the Lockheed scandal, and more recent revelations that some of the world's leading environmental wreckers may have contributed to it – appear to have left the independent WWF (UK) unscathed.

Finance: Income for 1978 was £1,208,660. Much of Fund's income comes from industry. It has had successful fund-raising projects with firms like Brook Bond Tea (PG Tips), Spillers (Kattomeat) and United Biscuits (Penguins). Membership is around 35,000

President: HRH Duke of Edinburgh

Vice-President: Sir Peter Scott. Trustees include David Attenborough, Grenville Lucas, Richard Fitter and the Lords Craigton, Dulverton and Melchett

Director: George Medley

Chairman: Sir Arthur Norman

Address: Panda House, 12–13 Ockford Road, Godalming, Surrey

Council for Environmental Conservation (CoEnCo)

Formed in 1969 as the Committee for Environmental Conservation in the wake of the 'Countryside in 1970' conferences (like the Royal Society of Arts Committee for the Environment), CoEnCo is an umbrella body for twenty-four conservation groups, ostensibly putting united viewpoint to MPs, ministers and civil servants. Its effectiveness is questioned by many conservationists but the organization has few staff and limited resources. It has a remarkably poor record of using the media. Its approach is 'establishment-oriented' with a heavy reliance on funding from industrial sources. CoEnCo has sub-committees and working parties looking at various issues – energy, transport, pollution and conservation. Its future now looks uncertain.

Finance: Income for 1979 was £29,390. Main sources are grants from private trusts (such as the Dulverton Trust) and donations/sponsorship from industry (for example BP, Shell, Metal Box, Unilever, United Biscuits, Whitbread). Constituent members also contribute to CoEnCo.

Chairman: Lord Craigton

Vice-Chairman: Gerald McGuire

Secretary: Edward Dawson

Address: Zoological Gardens, Regents Park, London NW1 (tel: 01–722 7111)

Wildlife Link

This is a committee of CoEnCo worthy of mention in its own right. It is the phoenix which rose out of the ashes of the quietly but indecently interred Council for Nature in 1980. It acts as spokesman for thirty-two voluntary conservation bodies. For its first year it was mostly preoccupied with the Wildlife and Countryside Bill. The group has working parties on subjects like the conservation of whales, grey seals and U K involvement with I U C N and the Convention on International Trade in Endangered Species. It is funded from members' subscriptions.

Since early 1983 Wildlife Link has been a separate organization, chaired by Lord Melchett with a Vice-Chairman in Stanley Johnson, a Conservative Member of the European Parliament.

Chairman: Lord Melchett
Secretary: Hazel Phillips
Addresses: as for CoEnCo

Royal Society of Arts Committee for the Environment

Like CoEnCo and W W F this group has strong links with industry. It was formed in 1971 following the third 'Countryside in 1970' conference of which the Royal Society of Arts (R S A) was a co-sponsor. It organizes conferences and seminars on major environmental topics – e.g. forestry, energy, wasteland – but its preoccupation with bringing environmentalists and industrialists together precludes it from taking a hard line on any issue. Like the Land Decade Educational Council and CoEnCo, it receives money from the Dulverton Trust (Lord Dulverton is a member of the Wills family (of tobacco fame) and a large landowning forester who has served on an N C C committee, see pp. 75–6).

Finance: Income for 1979 £12,000, from private trusts and parent R S A
President: H R H Duke of Edinburgh
Chairman: Lord Nathan. Committee members include Lord Craigton (as CoEnCo Chairman), Sir Peter Parker (Chairman of British Rail) and three members nominated by the Duke: Sir Ralph Verney (past Chairman of N C C), Max Nicholson and Professor Sir Norman Rowntree.
Assistant Secretary: Timothy Cantell
Address: 8 John Adam Street, London w c2

The Conservation Society (ConSoc)

ConSoc is the environmental movement's equivalent to a Victorian philosophical society, dedicated to solving problems through the joint grinding of minds and the prolific publication of pamphlets and proceedings. It was spawned during the doomwatch era in 1966. It drew its greatest impetus from concern about population growth and resource depletion. In recent years its fortunes have waned as the membership has developed factional views on the fundamental issues to which the Society addresses itself.

Conservation News carries an active correspondence from members and with its sibling Conservation Trust ConSoc produces a large amount of other literature on population, waste paper, energy, etc. ConSoc is decentralized, democratic and *serious*. Like the United Nations and CoEnCo it sets up working parties on subjects like land-use planning, pollution, lead in petrol (it deserves much credit for its work on this topic) and, more recently, transport. According to Cairns' Bath survey, 'The typical Conservation Society member ... appears as a middle-aged, married, male, pessimistic, upper middle-class executive or professional whose interest in the environment is man-oriented and whose approach to environmental problems is intellectual rather than practical with a stress on education.' Despite its name, ConSoc has taken no part in countryside conservation, perhaps because NCC made it secret policy to blackball it soon after it was established. The Conservation Trust is an allied sales organization.

President: Lord Avebury. Other notables include Ted Heath
Address: HQ is at 12 Guildford Street, Chertsey, Surrey (tel: Chertsey 60975)

Woodland Trust

Established by Kenneth Watkins in 1972 with the specific aim of protecting natural deciduous woodland. It is said to be a product of frustration with a local naturalists' trust (Devon). The Woodland Trust is growing fast and it plants a tree for each new member. Over 1,200 members by 1982. Its latest project involves community woodlands.

Finance: Main source of finance from members' subscriptions
Patrons include Earl of Bradford, Dame Sylvia Crowe, Lord Denning, Henry Moore and Max Nicholson. Richard Mabey is an adviser
Development Officer: John James
Address: 34 Westgate, Grantham, Lincolnshire (tel: 0476–74297)

British Association for Shooting and Conservation (BASC)

BASC was formerly WAGBI (Wildfowlers' Association of Great Britain and Ireland). Despite its best efforts to persuade us otherwise there is a lot more shooting than conservation with this group. WAGBI was founded in 1908 as the shooting man's pressure group. Following the last war it enlisted the help of Max Nicholson and various other conservationists and the stress on conservation is partly a result of their influence.

BASC appears to have a good working relationship with the NCC. This is perhaps not surprising as Lord Arbuthnott, WAGBI's 1979/80 President, is now Vice-Chairman of the NCC, and NCC's past Chairman, Sir Ralph Verney, is a shooter himself. Nevertheless, it is by far the most responsible wildfowling organization.

Finance: Income for 1979 just under £300,000. It has around 10,000 members. NCC gave WAGBI a grant of £10,000 in 1979.

British Trust for Conservation Volunteers (BTCV)

This is the 'Conservation Corps', a group sometimes unkindly described as the boy scouts of conservation. Volunteers do all sorts of practical conservation management on Nature Reserves and other sites. It is increasingly active in urban areas and has become very professional. However, BTCV has run into problems with its huge voluntary committee structures and full-time staff of thirty. The National Conservation Corps was founded in 1959 and incorporated into the Trust in 1970. There are 120 local groups affiliated to the Trust. Over 40,000 members managed over 70,000 days of work during 1979 and early 1980. The Trust was formerly under the influential directorship of Charles Flower. The BTCV is increasingly looking for a role as a Manpower Services Commission agent, utilizing the unemployed to increase its scale of activities.

Finance: Income for 1980/81 was £410,000 from local authorities, central government, earnings, subscriptions and private trusts
Patron: HRH the Duke of Edinburgh
President: C. Morrison. Vice-Presidents include R. E. Boote (alias Robert Arvill and former Director-General of NCC), Sir John Cripps (ex-Chairman of the Countryside Commission), Lord Craigton, Spike Milligan and Sir Peter Scott
Director: Colonel Ian Branton
Address: 10–14 Duke Street, Reading, Berkshire RG1 4RU (tel: 0734–596171)

Land Decade Educational Council

Established in 1979 with its main interest in land waste (see Chapter 2), the Land Council is an unashamedly right-wing pressure group. It is viewed with some suspicion and considerable fear by most other groups with the exception of the CLA (whose prospectus claims that 'without the CLA [the individual landowner's] interests would be overwhelmed by the claims of the urban and industrial majority'). It is difficult to see exactly what the Land Council is up to although it intends to promote a third land-utilization survey. It is fervently anti-planning.

The Land Council is an unholy alliance of peers, geographers, landed gentry and others wary of public intervention in land management. It has a part-time secretary, housed in the offices of the *Architects' Journal*.

Finance: mainly from Dulverton Trust

The Land Council has the blessing of the Duke of Edinburgh. Its patrons include the Lords Buxton, Dulverton, Hunt and Shackleton, Sir Nigel Strutt and Professor R. W. Steel. Council members include Alice Coleman (who undertook the second land-utilization survey of Britain), Leslie Fairweather (editor of the *Architects' Journal*) and Lord Lever of Manchester

Address: c/o 9 Queen Anne's Gate, London SW1 (tel: 01–222 4333)

Friends of the Earth (FoE)

Though FoE now appears to be suffering from a bout of premature senility, it was one of the leaders of the environmental movement throughout the 1970s. It has recently suffered from considerable internal turmoil. There are a number of reasons for this. Past directors have been strikingly autocratic and FoE workers at the London HQ have not been subject to any proper system of accountability. In addition the HQ has discouraged local groups (of which there are over 250) from participating in national decision-making.

FoE's main interests have been energy conservation, transport, endangered species and waste. Individuals may join either a local group or, as 20,000 have, the national organization (or both). Campaigners estimate that there are about 2,500 local activists. Some groups have been particularly successful in mobilizing public opinion and action within their areas. There are some indications that FoE (national group) is on the road to recovery and may once again become a powerful force in the environmental movement.

Finance: Turnover around £250,000 p.a.
Campaign Director: Steve Billcliff
Address: 377 City Road, London E C I (tel: 01–837 0731)

Greenpeace

Greenpeace began life in Canada in 1971 and now operates in ten countries. The U K Greenpeace was set up in 1976. The most vigorous and effective of the direct action campaigning groups. Principal campaigns are against commercial whaling, commercial sealing, the dumping of radioactive and toxic waste at sea and the testing of nuclear weapons.

Addresses: Greenpeace Ltd, 36 Graham Street, London N I (01–251 3020)
   International Council of Greenpeace, Temple House, 25/26 High Street, Lewes, East Sussex
Board of Directors: Peter Wilkinson, Bryn Jones, Tony Marriner
Finance: Projected gross income 1983, £250,000 (Greenpeace U K)

Wildfowl Trust

The Trust was founded in 1946 by Sir Peter Scott and runs wildfowl refuges in Amberley, Washington New Town, Solway Firth and at Slimbridge in Gloucestershire. It has a strong research wing with professional biologists. Some of its workers are penitent hunters and all members tend to be *aficonados* of park wildfowl collections.

Address: Slimbridge, Glos G L2 7B T

British Trust for Ornithology (B T O)

The BTO is the expert equivalent of the R S PB but takes no direct action in conservation. It runs the bird-ringing scheme to study bird migration and populations, the Common Bird and other censuses, and has carried out notable surveys including that of the heron. It has compiled the *Breeding Bird Atlas*. The BTO is almost entirely amateur but it has a small professional staff based at Tring.

Address: BTO, Beech Grove, Tring, Herts

Institute of Terrestrial Ecology (ITE)

ITE was formed in 1974 following the decision by the government to split the research from the conservation functions of the old Nature Conservancy. It undertakes ecological research for both government and non-government bodies. One criticism is that essential conservation research, such as that undertaken on pesticides at Monks Wood in the early days of the Conservancy, is going by the board as it does not produce immediate financial gain. ITE has a series of research stations across Britain and staff work at both the research stations and at universities.

HQ is at 68 Hills Road, Cambridge CB2 1LA (tel: Cambridge 69745)

Botanical Society of the British Isles (BSBI)

BSBI perhaps exemplifies natural history and conservation combined at its best. The BSBI apparently manages to accommodate the interests of both amateurs and professionals, though many of its amateur members are experts. It has played a leading role in lobbying for and providing expert advice on wildlife legislation. It has around 2,500 members.

Address: c/o Botany Department, British Museum, Cromwell Road, London SW7

British Ecological Society (BES)

An academic body which has undergone years of fierce internal turmoil and debate about its role in conservation. Critics point to its embarrassingly large profits and the small sums which it gives to conservation projects. The maximum grant is £450.

Address: Piccadilly, London W1 (tel: 01-434 2641).

British Association of Nature Conservationists (BANC)

Founder members include the authors. Established in 1979 to fund a journal, *Ecos: A Review of Conservation*. This quarterly journal aims to increase communication within the conservation world and it publishes material on policy and other matters which would otherwise never see the light of day. It has attracted mainly professional conservationists though it is open to anyone. BANC also holds regular seminars and discussion meetings on conservation topics.

Finance: Income about £4,000 a year from 500 individuals and libraries
President: Duncan Poore
Vice-Presidents: Ian Prestt, Max Hooper and David Goode

Chairman: Nigel Ajax-Lewis
Address: Carla Stanley, Membership Secretary, Rectory Farm, Stanton-St John, Oxford.

European Environment Bureau (EEB)

This is a Euro-umbrella comprising sixty non-governmental organizations (NGOs). It was set up in 1974 with a Brussels-based secretariat. It keeps a watching brief on activities of the EEC, which it alternately advises and castigates about environmental policy. Hubert V. David is its charismatic driving force. The EEB publishes a bulletin and occasional papers.

Address: 31 Rue Vautier, B-1040 Bruxelles, Belgium

Farming and Wildlife Advisory Group (FWAG)

FWAG was formed after the famous Silsoe conference in 1969 when a group of conservationists got together to discuss wildlife protection on farmland with farmers and representatives from MAFF, the NFU and the CLA. There is now a FWAG group operating in every county in England and Wales giving advice to farmers on all aspects of conservation. The group's influence appears to be growing, although there is nothing they can do about the small numbers of farmers bent on wrecking the environment. At the time of writing two full-time advisers are about to start work and before long other counties may follow suit. The strength of the group lies in its farming roots.

Chairman: Norman Moore
Director: Eric Carter
Address: as for RSPB

Appendix 4

Labelling the Land

The purpose of this Appendix is three-fold. First, to look at the various types of conservation and amenity designations in Britain; second, to point out the weaknesses of the designations; and third, to look at the accessibility of the countryside to the general public.

Nature Reserves and Sites of Special Scientific Interest (SSSIs)

National Nature Reserves (NNRs) and Sites of Special Scientific Interest (SSSIs) are the corner-stone of the Nature Conservancy Council's conservation strategy. Under the 1949 National Parks and Access to the Countryside Act the Conservancy was given the power to establish NNRs either by buying land, leasing land or entering into management agreements (Nature Reserve Agreements, NRAs) with owners. Parliament's intention may have been to create legislation to conserve the countryside and make much of it accessible to the non-landowning members of the public (provision for establishing National Parks came under the same Act), but the powers given to the Conservancy were set in a framework of scientific jargon which had a profound effect on the subsequent tenor and development of British government conservation.

The Act contained a rather vague power for the Conservancy to notify local planning authorities of 'any area of land, not for the time being managed as a nature reserve, [as being of] special interest by reason of its flora, fauna or geological or physiographic features'. Only in the margin of the text does the Act refer to 'scientific interest'. Rather than calling these places Areas of Special Interest, as the Act does, the fledgling Conservancy coined the term Sites of Special Scientific Interest (SSSI). Perhaps this was because 'science' was thought to carry great weight with landowners, government agencies and even the public, or perhaps the sites really were thought of as of interest to science: there is evidence to support both cases, and today it is difficult to tell which was the real intention. Unfortunately, like the Conservancy itself, Parliament had failed to foresee the massive changes in agricultural practice which were soon to sweep the countryside, and as a result the SSSI designation proved singularly useless at heading off the main threats to habitats, relying as it did on notification to planning authorities when planners had no control over agriculture or forestry (both were totally exempted under the 1947 Town and Country Planning Act).

The Conservancy interpreted the phrase 'by reason of its flora, fauna or geological or physiographic features' to mean that SSSI-designation should be made because a place was of interest to botanists, zoologists, geologists or geomorphologists, and this automatically excluded the interests of ordinary naturalists and country lovers. It also replaced a common set of values with one expressed in the terminology of a science. It was not long before the Conservancy began acting as if conservation was a branch of applied science, so NNRs were referred to as 'outdoor laboratories' and the Conservancy promoted conservation as 'for science' rather than 'for the public'. To justify its work, the Conservancy turned not to popular appeal but to objectivity. The 1979 Policy Procedure Guidelines of the NCC state their intention to be 'to provide a logical and consistent rationale for SSSI selection throughout Great Britain by establishing the scientific importance of each site in its national context'. In practice the scientific tail has started to wag the conservation dog.

The SSSI system grew out of a minor power originally intended as a stop-gap measure for sites on their way to becoming Nature Reserves. As history turned out, the finances were never sufficient for all deserving sites to be made reserves, and the lengthy elaboration of a complicated scientific framework for SSSI-designation has proved ultimately futile. Scientists have transferred their interests from classifying vegetation types, for which a representative series of Nature Reserves are perhaps useful, to such things as competition between plants grown in pots, for which they are not. And the general public, for so long ignored because they were unscientific, have only been able to watch from a distance while the SSSI-designation has itself proved ineffective against agriculture and forestry.

Nevertheless, the areas designated SSSI are invariably parts of the best countryside and wildlife habitats. Unfortunately, the NCC is reluctant to extend its 1,361,404 ha (in 3,877 sites) for fear of upsetting landowning interests. Thus areas outside the SSSI system remain totally unprotected. The bulk of Britain's remaining wildlife habitats are also to be found outside Nature Reserves. There are some eighty RSPB reserves covering 37,388 ha and 1,300 County Naturalists' Trust reserves amounting to 44,515 ha. Local authorities run eighty reserves covering 12,234 ha (see below). This compares with the 30 per cent of Britain's land surface which is not taken up with housing, intensive agriculture, roads, forestry or industry, and much of which is essential in maintaining the character of our countryside and species living within it, some 36 million ha.

The NCC itself has 181 National Nature Reserves covering 138,918 ha although, like SSSIs, this impressive-sounding total is misleading as many lie in northern Scotland where land is cheap and pressures on its use are fewer, but where species are few as well. National Nature Reserves (NNRs) range in size from small worked-out medieval quarries to large areas such as the 64,000-acre Cairngorm NNR. Bill Adams and Philip Lowe have established that many sites suggested by natural historians, eccentric Edwardian entomologists, biologists and ecologists as being worthy of strict protection cropped up repeatedly in separate lists drawn up by various committees in 1915, 1929, 1943, 1945, 1947 and 1949. Many of these subsequently featured in the 1977 publication *A Nature Conservation Review* written by the NCC, a massive work described by Adams and Lowe as 'the apotheosis of scientific nature conservation'. Although these lists overlap a great deal in their choice of key sites, they were devised by methods which ranged from '100 per cent science' to the personal recommendation of one naturalist. Adams and Lowe argue that this only goes to show that science is an accessory to conservation rather than its basis.

Marine Nature Reserves

Although it failed to allow for the establishment of marine SSSIs, the 1981 Wildlife and Countryside Act makes provision for the establishment of Marine Nature Reserves (MNRs). Previously, no Nature Reserve had legal status below the high-water mark, a boundary that is not respected by plants, animals, or pollution. Despite a number of ploys, including an extended 'consultative period' that lasted beyond the life of Parliament, the DoE, which was very wary of the idea of MNRs, was finally forced to include MNR powers in the 1981 Act (see below for other habitat protection in the Act).

There are nine voluntary marine reserves around our coasts already (including for example, Lundy and Kimmeridge Bay) but they offer no real protection against oil and gas exploration, land reclamation, undersea mining, construction of marinas, dumping, sewage disposal, industrial fishing or even collecting by divers.

NCC powers will operate through the DoE, or in Wales and Scotland with the acquiescence of the appropriate Secretary of State, and can apply to any coastal part of our territorial waters. The actual protection will stem from bye-laws, which may be revoked or amended by the Secretary of State. These can include restriction or prohibition of entry (though not affecting established rights), but not 'discharges from vessels'. Bye-laws can include the cessation of the killing, taking, disturbing or destroying of animals or plants, doing anything to interfere with the sea-bed or dumping rubbish. Before making the appropriate order, widespread public and civil service consultations will take place and it remains to be seen how many sites will get through this stage. Progress may be seen in the next few years around the Scilly Isles, Lundy, the Monarchs, Start Point in Devon, the Isle of Wight's Bembridge Ledges, St Abb's Head and Arisaig in Scotland, and off the Marloes and Lleyn Peninsulas in Wales. However, unless Part II of the 1974 Control of Pollution Act is brought fully into force, many such reserves will be useless.

If the bye-laws do not forbid industrial fishing, the MNRs will be futile designations. Traditional potting and long-lining aside, the use of cockle pumps and clam dredges with heavy booms, which break and maim a high proportion of the catch, wreak havoc on the sea-bed. They leave shattered, dying animals which attract only hordes of scavenging starfish. The plight of our underwater communities is comparable to that of the natural forest before and during its initial clearance. Only in remote rocky inlets do intact communities persist, and even on the rock-strewn 'hard grounds' new techniques of factory fishing and even the hand-picking of clams, crabs and lobsters are eliminating wildlife.

Local Nature Reserves (LNRs) and Forest Nature Reserves (FNRs)

Local Nature Reserves are established by local authorities on land which they own. Some are established partly because the land where they are found is common land or public open space and could not be otherwise developed. Others are established because the authority in question wishes to make some commitment to conservation. However the power to establish LNRs (of which there are eighty-four) is under-used, and no written NCC policy exists, although the Council must agree to any local authority proposals. The average size of LNRs is 127 ha (compared to an average of 12 ha for County Naturalists' Trust reserves). The power to designate LNRs derives from the 1949 Act. Forest Nature Reserves are the result of non-statutory designations made by the Forestry Commission on its own land. They are few and far between although the Commission manages some Forest Parks which are of considerable importance for conservation. The Commission is the organization responsible for running the New Forest, which is one of the most important areas of deciduous woodland left in Western Europe.

Habitat Protection under the 1981 Wildlife and Countryside Act

The 1981 Act attracted a record 2,300 amendments and proved considerably more controversial than the government of the day had anticipated. It was introduced not from any conviction on the government's part that more conservation legislation was needed, but to comply with a directive issued by the EEC Commission. The Wildlife and Countryside Bill became a watershed for both the attitudes and politicization of the voluntary conservation movement. It was during the protracted debates of summer

1981 that the split between farming interests and conservationists widened to a public gulf, and experience may well reveal it as the time when the hitherto very close relationship between voluntary groups and the government agencies came to an end.

The Act finally reached the statute books in autumn 1981. It is composed of three parts. The first is concerned with the protection of individual species, the second deals with habitat protection, and especially SSSIs and the third with access to the countryside. Despite determined and cogently argued pleas by Opposition politicians (notably Lord Melchett and MPs Tam Dalyell and Peter Hardy) for the introduction of statutory planning controls over some forestry and farming operations, and for legally binding protection of SSSIs, the government based its Act on the principle of voluntary restraint. Conservation groups were more or less unanimous in loudly proclaiming that these measures were already in existence, and did not work.

Sections 28 and 33 concern the Voluntary Code, which is an adjunct to the Act, and designation and notification of SSSIs; section 29 concerns reserve powers; and section 31 deals with penalties, while sections 30, 32 and 41 concern compensation. It is an extraordinary principle of the Act that landowners of an SSSI can receive 'compensation' for not developing, and so destroying an SSSI (by announcing their intention to the NCC) while responsible owners (such as the National Trust) receive no money to maintain an SSSI intact. Leeds University economist John Bowers, writing in the journal *Ecos* in April 1982, put the case thus: 'The site safeguard provisions (in the Act) make the occupancy of an SSSI analogous to ownership of a listed building. Both are viewed as valuable national assets and consent is required to demolish them. Owners of listed buildings, however, are not entitled to compensation if consent is withheld and indeed are required to maintain them at their own expense.' Owners also get 'compensation' if an MAFF grant is refused for development of an SSSI. Bowers comments, '... the purpose of these grants is to encourage those improvements in agriculture that are thought desirable in the national interest. With SSSIs such improvements are *not* in the national interest: that is the reason for controls. Grant aid is not simply a device for supplementing farm incomes as the right to compensation makes it appear.' In fact through the considerable power of the agriculture lobby in Parliament, and particularly in Cabinet, what was on the surface a piece of conservation legislation had in practice become a device for bolstering the position and finances of landowners and farmers. Before the 1981 Act, all MAFF grants were reviewed, in theory at least, on conservation grounds. After the Act, that only applied to those on SSSIs. Before the Act, the NCC only notified the relevant planning authority about an SSSI and then went on to tell owners (and it is difficult to trace many of them) as soon as its slim resources permitted. The Act placed a statutory duty on the NCC to inform the owners not only of an SSSI's existence, but of what measures might be taken that would damage it, and gave owners a right of appeal against an SSSI being designated.

It was not long before the 1981 Act ran into serious difficulties. At Romney Marsh in Kent a test-case arose on a part of the area known as Walland Marsh when an old pasture and species-rich ditch network was threatened with conversion to arable and drainage in early 1982. In the face of demands for finance (£250,000 purchase on 142 acres or £69,000 compensation to persuade the owner to do nothing for three years), Sir Ralph Verney, NCC Chairman, took the decision to abandon attempts at using the machinery of the Act to safeguard the SSSI intact. The Act had, in fact, set up NCC as an alternative source of grant aid to farmers, so saving the expenditure of the MAFF but without adequate government funding for the NCC. Meanwhile at Halvergate Marshes in Norfolk the protective measures of the Act collapsed in the face of actions by a farmer who ignored them and ploughed up an SSSI. Similar cases began to crop up elsewhere and it was estimated that the NCC was under-funded by between £10 and £200 million.

At the time of writing, it is still not clear exactly how effective the 1981 Act can be. Much clearly depends on how the NCC, backed up by the DoE, uses reserve powers, which can place a twelve-month restraining order on a landowner or occupier to stop an SSSI being developed. But the DoE has indicated that these powers will only apply to a few (40–50) of the 3,877 SSSIs. Fines payable for ignoring these orders (£1,000 maximum and £100 per day) are also very small compared with the possible profits to be made, for example from converting 450 ha of heathland to arable, as happened at Horton Heath in Dorset. The Voluntary Code itself, which proved ineffective at an early stage, amounts to little more than an exhortation to owners and occupiers not to damage SSSIs. Replacing the 1981 Act with some effective legislation, perhaps with powers to give grants for maintenance of habitats and features, as envisaged in the rejected Sandford Amendment put forward by Lord Sandford, or planning controls coupled with resources from the EEC's Less Favoured Areas Directives, should remain high on the conservation agenda in the early 1980s.

The Amenity Designations

The principal purpose of the designations mentioned above is nature conservation. We have already pointed to its institutionalized division from amenity, access and landscape concerns, and designations reflect this. Despite this artificial dichotomy, many of the amenity designations are conferred on areas of high wildlife value, and vice versa. The amenity areas are those most popular with visitors to the countryside. A survey in 1980 found that 22 per cent of the population takes regular walks in the country, of 2 miles or more, and that there are approximately 120,000 miles of public footpaths and rights of way in England and Wales alone. Nevertheless, much land is inaccessible and many footpaths are vanishing as a result of agricultural intensification and building developments. On the credit side some long-distance paths and coastal paths have been created in the last thirty years.

National Parks

There are ten National Parks in England and Wales, covering 13,618 square km. The 1949 National Parks and Access to the Countryside Act laid down legislation which enabled the Countryside Commission's forerunner, the National Parks Commission, to establish the National Parks (for a comprehensive and stimulating account of their successes and failures see Ann and Malcolm MacEwen's definitive book *National Parks: Conservation or Cosmetics*).

John Dower was asked by the Ministry of Town and Country Planning in 1943 to write a report on the problems of setting up National Parks. His definition of what such a park should be is worth quoting at length. Dower claimed it should be

an extensive area of beautiful and relatively wild country in which, for the nation's benefit and by appropriate national decision and action, (a) the characteristic landscape beauty is strictly preserved; (b) access and facilities for open air public enjoyment are amply provided; (c) wildlife and buildings and places of architectural and historic interest are suitably protected, while (d) established farming area is effectively maintained.

Several chapters would be needed to discuss in detail whether Dower's objectives have been met. As far as (a) is concerned, we find it difficult to believe that nuclear power stations, radar early-warning stations and potash mines (all found in National Parks) have contributed to preserving the landscape's characteristic beauty. With regard to (c) we can only point out that with the exception of the Peak District National Park – which has 46,817 acres of moors and hills to which the public have legal rights of access – the hope that all open country would become accessible in other Parks has proved a pipe-dream. There is of course, *de facto* access over large areas but up to 1975, public access under the relevant Part 5 of the 1949 Act had been secured for a mere 91,215 acres – 'a pitiful achievement' as Howard Hill points out in *Freedom to Roam*.

In 1945 the Minister for Town and Country Planning appointed a committee under the chairmanship of Sir Arthur Hobhouse to consider Dower's proposals and it recommended that National Parks should be established in twelve areas. The South Downs and the Broads were dropped, and have suffered as a result (and left the largest centre of population – London – hundreds of miles from a National Park) but the rest are now Parks. These are the Peak District and the Lake District (the only two with special planning boards) and eight others in Dartmoor, Exmoor, North York Moors, Northumberland, Pembrokeshire Coast, Snowdonia, Yorkshire Dales and Brecon Beacons. Each is administered by an executive committee made up of local authority members and appointees of the Secretary of State for the Environment.

Country Parks

Local authorities were given powers to establish Country Parks under the 1968 Countryside Act. One of the main purposes of the Parks is to take the recreational pressure off National Parks and Nature Reserves. The Countryside Commission can recommend whether or not a particular area should qualify for a 75 per cent government grant to be set up and managed as a Country Park. The areas chosen (there are now 170 of an average size of 133 ha) are often close to large urban conurbations. The intention is to give what recreation planners like to call 'a countryside experience' coupled with facilities needed to cater for more intensive recreational use than one would normally find in a National Park or a Nature Reserve.

Areas of Outstanding Natural Beauty (AONBs)

This is without doubt one of the most useless countryside designations. Indeed a recent policy statement by the Countryside Commission (*Areas of Outstanding Natural Beauty: A Policy Statement*, 1980) was so vapid that one was left wondering whether the Commission, which picks the areas, understood the purpose of the designation.

There are thirty-four AONBs scattered around England and Wales covering some 10 per cent of the land surface. The power to declare them came from the 1949 Act. Together with the relevant local authority, the Commission must make a formal submission to the Secretary of State for the Environment if it wishes to designate an area as an AONB. Unfortunately, while the designation provides no real protection against deleterious operations of farming, forestry or industrial activities, the nationalized industries such as the Central Electricity Generating Board (who are required to have 'due regard' under section 11 of the 1968 Countryside Act to the desirability of conserving flora and fauna) use the extent of AONBs as an argument in favour of allowing them to develop elsewhere, even though the designation in any case provides no check on their activities where it does occur. The only extra protection which planning authorities can give an AONB involves bringing a few activities (not farming or forestry operations) under planning control (for example some forms of agricultural building) which are normally exempt by being outside the remit of the DoE's General Development Order, by asking the Secretary of State for what is termed an Article IV Directive. But this only happens on rare occasions.

Marion Shoard and others have argued that AONBs have failed to provide the widespread public access which Parliament intended under the 1949 Act. Of the 5,372 square miles of England and Wales which were designated as AONBs by 1973, local authorities had only used the powers of the Act to provide access (through access orders and management agreements) to 14 square miles! Finally, it is worth noting that when the Commission published its policy statement, the *Guardian* headline reporting the document's findings ran 'New laws not needed to conserve countryside'. Perhaps it said more about the Commission than about AONBs.

Heritage Coasts

At 30 September 1979 Heritage Coasts covered some 1,084 km of coastline in England and Wales. The first was defined by the Countryside Commission in 1973 (Sussex, 13 km). Three have been 'completely defined' – that is, they include a belt of land along the coast – while the thirty others and the ten proposed new Heritage Coasts have only been defined laterally. The Heritage Coasts vary in length from the 92 km Northumberland Coast and the completely defined 63 km long North Norfolk Coast down to the 4 km long Trevose Head Heritage Coast defined in January 1976.

Iwan Richards, a senior planning officer with Anglesey Borough Council, argued in *Ecos* that Heritage Coasts are being destroyed 'due to neglect'. He points out that while National Parks receive annual funding from the Treasury and county councils, Heritage Coasts and AONBs receive comparatively little support, and then only in the form of grant aid for specific projects. As with AONBs, what positive management is undertaken on Heritage Coasts is directed towards providing recreational and interpretative facilities.

National Scenic Areas

There are no National Parks, AONBs or Heritage Coasts in Scotland although there are National Nature Reserves. Instead the Scottish have National Scenic Areas, which are something like a hybrid between AONBs and National Parks. Under the 1980 Restriction of Permitted Development National Scenic Areas (Scotland) Direction, issued by the Secretary of State for Scotland, restrictions are placed on developments such as buildings over 12 m high and all local authority road works outside present road boundaries, costing over £100,000. Through the Countryside Commission for Scotland it is proposed that local authorities should limit developments to retain existing landscapes. Not surprisingly this has caused a great outcry in the depressed Highlands and Islands, particularly as much of the land is owned by absentee landlords who may reap considerable benefits from having their land designated as part of a National Scenic Area as this procures for them exemptions from Capital Transfer Tax.

The proposed areas – forty in all, identified in a 1978 CCS Report – cover

3,868 square miles, or one-eighth of the land surface of Scotland. Graeme Robertson, the editor of the magazine *Habitat Scotland*, has railed against the £500,000 tax benefit that this has given to the Vestey family on its Assynt Estate in West Sutherland, through a management agreement brought in conjunction with the CCS. Jean Balfour, one-time NCC Council member and Chairwoman of the CCS, is also a large landowner in Scotland.

Long-distance Footpaths

Many footpaths are of immense antiquity, running along the same course as the trading routes and drovers' roads which pre-dated the Roman invasion. The laws relating to footpaths are complex and readers are referred to H. D. Westacott's *The Walkers' Handbook* and Ian Campbell's *Practical Guide to the Law of Footpaths and Bridleways* for detailed information. Suffice it to say that many of our footpaths are under threat from agricultural intensification and development, and the NFU wishes to 'rationalize' the network of footpaths and bridleways. This would result in a considerable reduction, particularly in the more intensively farmed lowland areas.

Possibly the greatest success of the Countryside Commission has been its work on creating long-distance footpaths, many of which run through Heritage Coasts, National Parks and AONBs. The Commission helps local authorities to define the line of paths and helps to negotiate with landowners and other interests. Many stretches of long-distance footpaths were already rights of way but often the Commission and local authorities have had to negotiate with landowners and provide compensation. On 30 September 1979 there were 2,528 km of long-distance footpaths, including the Pennine Way (270 miles), the Cleveland Way (100 miles), the Pembrokeshire Coast Path (168 miles), Offa's Dyke Path (168 miles), the South Downs Way (80 miles), the North Downs Way (141 miles), the Ridgeway Path (85 miles) and the South-West Peninsula Coast Path (572 miles).

In 1982 the Commission abandoned its plans to open the Cambrian Way, a route through the Welsh mountains from Cardiff North to the Conway, and it seems improbable that the Cotswold Way in Gloucestershire and the Ribble Way in Lancashire will receive the official status which ramblers had hoped for. The Commission's only two firm commitments are to the 71-mile Wolds Way in Yorkshire and to a path which will link the Peddars Way in Norfolk with a North Norfolk Coastal Path. Adrian Philips, the Commission's director, was quoted in the *Sunday Times* of 7 February 1982 as saying, 'Given our limited resources, we feel we would get better value by concentrating our attention on managing existing paths and the creation of shorter routes.' In 1979/80 the Commission spent £245,000 on long-distance footpaths but only £150,000 in the following year, putting more emphasis on shorter routes. Since that time, the Commission has received swingeing cuts in both staff and resources.

Selected Bibliography

Adams, J., *Transport Planning: Vision and Practice* (Routledge and Kegan Paul, 1981)

Allen, D. E., *The Naturalist in Britain: A Social History* (Pelican, 1978)

Brandt, W., *North-South: A Programme for Survival* (Pan, 1980)

Carson, R., *Silent Spring* (Hamish Hamilton, 1962)

Chapman, P., *Fuel's Paradise: Energy Options for Britain* (Penguin, 1975)

Cole, L., *Nature in the City* (Nature Conservancy Council, 1980)

Conroy, C. and King, A., *Paradise Lost* (Friends of the Earth, 1981)

Council for the Protection of Rural England, *Planning: Friend or Foe?* (CPRE, 1981)

Cousteau, J.-Y., *The Cousteau Almanac: An Inventory of Life on Our Water Planet* (Doubleday, 1981)

Davidson, J. and Lloyd, R. (eds.), *Conservation and Agriculture* (Wiley, 1977)

Duffey, E. and Watt, A. S. (eds.), *The Scientific Management of Animal and Plant Communities for Conservation* (Blackwell, 1971)

Edlin, H. L., *Trees, Woods and Man* (Collins, 1966)

Elkington, J., *The Ecology of Tomorrow's World: Industry's Environment* (Associated Business Press, 1980)

George, H., *Progress and Poverty* (Centenary Edition by Hogarth Press, 1979)

George S., *How the Other Half Dies: The Real Reasons for World Hunger* (Pelican, 1976)

Girardet, H. (ed.), *Land for the People* (Crescent Books, 1976), in which can be found Robert Waller's essay on land reform

Godwin, Sir H. *Fenland: Its Ancient Past and Uncertain Future* (CUP, 1978)

Goldsmith, E., Allen, R., Allaby, M., Davoll, J., Lawrence, S., *Blueprint for Survival* (Penguin, 1972)

Green, B., *Countryside Conservation* (Allen and Unwin, 1980)

Grove, R. (ed.), *Report on Forestry* (Ecos 3, i, British Association of Nature Conservationists/Packard, 1982)

Hall, C., *How to Run a Pressure Group* (Dent, 1974)

Hill, H., *Freedom to Roam* (Moorland, 1980)

Hoskins, W. G., *The Making of the English Landscape* (Hodder and Stoughton, 1955)

International Union for the Conservation of Nature, *World Conservation Strategy* (IUCN, 1980)

Kumar, S. (ed.), *The Schumacher Lectures* (Blond and Briggs, 1980)

Mabey, R., *Common Ground: A Place for Nature in Britain's Future* (Hutchinson, 1980)

Mabey, R. and Evans, T., *The Flowering of Britain* (Hutchinson, 1980)

Macan, T. T. and Worthington, E. B., *Life in Lakes and Rivers* (Fontana/OUP, 1972)

MacEwen, A. and MacEwen, M., *National Parks: Conservation or Cosmetics?* (Allen and Unwin, 1981)

MacEwen, M. (ed.), *Future Landscapes* (Chatto and Windus, 1976)

MacShane, D., *Using the Media* (Pluto, 1979)

Meadows, D. H., Meadows, D. L., Randers, J., Behrens, W. W., *The Limits to Growth* (Universe Books, 1972)

Mellanby, K., *Pesticides and Pollution* (Collins, 1967)

Mellanby, K., *Can Britain Feed Itself?* (Merlin, 1975)

Mellanby, K., *Farming and Wildlife* (Collins, 1981)

Moore, N. W., *Conservation and Farming* (Nature Conservancy Council, 1977)

Moss, G., *Britain's Wasting Acres* (Architectural Press, 1981)

Murton, R. K., *Man and Birds* (Collins, 1981)

Myers, N., *The Sinking Ark* (Pergamon, 1979)

Newby, H., *Green and Pleasant Land: Social Change in Rural England* (Pelican, 1980)

Nicholson, E. M., *The System: The Misgovernment of Modern Britain* (Hodder and Stoughton, 1967)

Nicholson, E. M., *The Environmental Revolution: A Guide for the New Masters of the World* (Pelican, 1972)

O'Riordan, T., *Environmentalism* (Pion, 1976)

Parker, D. J. and Penning-Rowsell, E. C., *Water Planning in Britain* (Allen and Unwin, 1980)

Pearsall, W. H., *Mountains and Moorlands* (Fontana/OUP, 1972)

Pollard, E., Hooper, M. D. and Moore, N. W., *Hedges* (Collins, 1974)

Rackham, O., *Trees and Woodlands in the British Landscape* (Dent, 1976)

Rackham, O., *Ancient Woodlands* (CUP, 1980)

Ratcliffe, D. A. (ed.), *A Nature Conservation Review*, 2 vols. (CUP/NCC, 1977)

Sandbach, F., *Environment, Ideology and Policy* (Blackwell, 1980)

Schumacher, E. F., *Small is Beautiful: A Study of Economics as if People Mattered* (Blond and Briggs, 1973)

Sheail, J., *Nature in Trust: The History of Nature Conservation in Britain* (Blackie, 1976)

Smith, P. J. (ed.), *The Politics of Physical Resources* (OUP/Penguin, 1975)

Stamp, D. and Hoskins, W. G., *The Common Lands of England and Wales* (Collins, 1963)

Stretton, H., *Capitalism, Socialism and Environment* (CUP, 1976)

Teagle, W., *The Endless Village* (Nature Conservancy Council, 1978)

Tyme, J., *Motorways versus Democracy* (Macmillan, 1978)

United States Interagency Committee, *Global 2000* (US Government Printing Office, 1980)

Warren, A. and Goldsmith, F. B. (eds.), *Conservation in Practice* (Wiley, 1974)

Westacott, H. D., *The Walker's Handbook* (Penguin, 1978)

Wigens, A., *The Clandestine Farm* (Granada, 1980)

Notes

CHAPTER 1: INTRODUCTION

1. It was probably true that many commons were over-stocked in that if each commoner had had fewer beasts, the commons may have yielded more. But unless all commoners reduced grazing, any one cheat could benefit greatly. Yet instead of imposing regulations to benefit all the graziers equally, the land was transferred to the big landlords. The term 'tragedy of the commons' is today used by some ecologists to describe the 'inevitable' over-exploitation of resources when they are communally owned. We go to some length to counter this argument in Chapter 3.

CHAPTER 2: AGENTS OF DESTRUCTION: THE FARMING, FORESTRY AND WATER INDUSTRIES

1. Nor do the figures take account of food wastage. Bryn Green suggests that 25 per cent of the food produced in this country is lost in harvesting, processing and domestic garbage.

2. Kenneth Mellanby points out that of the 10·5 million tonnes of barley produced in Britain from 2·4 million hectares each year, 9 million are used for feeding livestock. Half our wheat goes the same way. Were we to eat less meat Britain could easily become self-sufficient in food. The *Cousteau Almanac* points out that one-third of the world's grain harvest is fed to livestock, yet animal foods accounts for only one-tenth of the world's calorific intake. To produce 1 lb. of meat protein one must feed cattle 16 lb. of grain, pigs 6 lb., turkeys 4 lb. and chicken 3 lb. The *Cousteau Almanac* gives a recipe for 'making' one American cow: one 80-lb. calf; 8 acres grazing land; 1·5 acres farmland; 12,000 lb. forage; 2,500 lb. grain; 350 lb. soybeans; 125 gallons gasoline and various petroleum products; 170 lb. nitrogen; 45 lb. phosphorus; 90 lb. potassium; pesticides; herbicides; hormones; antibiotics; and 1·2 million gallons of water, to be added regularly throughout.

3. Details of the administration and system of land drainage are outlined in *Conservation and Land Drainage Guidelines*, published by the Water Space Amenity Commission (WaSaC). The document recommends that 'landscape and wildlife criteria should be built into relevant grant-aided schemes' but it starts with the firm suggestion that 'on balance, there is no sufficient reason for bringing land drainage under planning control'. WaSaC has done little for conservation.

CHAPTER 3: PLANNING: A MUCH-ABUSED SYSTEM

1. One option for groups which believe inquiries are being held for presentational purposes is to boycott them. In a letter to the *Guardian* on 24 February 1982, Peter Wilkinson of Greenpeace explained why his organization was not going to attend the PI concerning the building of Sizewell B Pressurized Water Reactor: 'We will not play the CEGB's games, and intend to boycott the proposed inquiry, believing that a decision to go ahead with the plant has already been made, and that any participation serves merely to give legitimacy to an elaborate piece of window-dressing.'

2. In December 1981 the Conservative government announced its intention to pass a law increasing maximum legal lorry weights; at least twenty Conservative backbenchers threatened to vote against the government at the time.

3. DoT official to road objector (quoted in John Adams's *Transport Planning: Vision and Practice*): 'You people are inanimate objects. We will fill the hospitals if necessary. What you people have got to understand is that the road is going through.'

4. The CLA's promotional brochure *Your Land* says encouragingly: 'Its [the CLA's] leaders have direct access to Ministers and Head Office permanent staff have a close day-to-day working relationship with government Departments.' The leaders of the government's own conservation agencies could not make the same claim. Referring to the Countryside Commission's statutory duty to advise any minister or public body 'on such matters related to the countryside he or they may refer to the Commission, or as the Commission may think fit', former chairman Sir John Cripps commented: 'This duty and the guidelines must have escaped the attention of most Ministers and public bodies outside the Department of the Environment and Welsh Office, for I do not recall a single instance of our advice being sought.' He continues: 'I conclude that the role of the Commission as advisors to Ministers and the Departments is uncertain and can never be secure. They will consult the Commission when it suits them.'

5. John Adams made the following calculation when he found that a Department of the Environment paper asserted that traffic forecasts should be based on an assumption of 3 per cent per annum growth of GNP 'in perpetuity': by 2205 average annual incomes will reach £1 million and half the population of Britain will be needed to drive the 30 million juggernaut lorries.

CHAPTER 4: THE FALTERING CONSERVATION MOVEMENT

1. The Gross National Product (GNP) is a universally used index which reflects only economic growth. It takes no account of non-monetary costs of growth and thus fails to account for the health of a nation's population, the inequalities within the nation, the amount of water pollution and land despoilation, etc. Were the Windscale nuclear plant to blow up our economists would *add* the costs incurred by the disaster to the GNP rather than subtract them. At very best GNP is a distorted measure of growth; as a symbol of progress it is nonsensical. The Canadian Prime Minister, Pierre Trudeau, has rightly pointed out that GNP is 'no measurement of social justice, or human dignity, or cultural attainment'.

2. Henry George, the American economist who wrote the classic study *Progress and Poverty* – to which we refer in our discussion of land reform (pp. 131 ff) – has argued that land should not be classed as 'capital': 'The term land embraces, in short, all natural materials, forces, and opportunities, and, therefore, nothing that is freely supplied by nature can properly be classed as capital. A fertile field, a rich vein of ore,

a falling stream which supplies power, may give to the possessor advantages equivalent to the possession of capital, but to class such things as capital would be to put an end to the distinction between land and capital, and, so far as they relate to each other, to make the two terms meaningless.'

CHAPTER 6: RECIPE FOR A FUTURE

1. Hardin's *The Tragedy of the Commons* essay (*Science*, 162, 1968) should be read in conjunction with his *The Ethics of a Lifeboat* (American Association for the Advancement of Science, Washington, DC, 1974).

2. Labour politicians have reacted more enthusiastically than Conservatives to the Brandt Report, but it remains to be seen whether they will translate rhetoric into hard financial commitments if and when they come to power again.

3. The approach of the so-called Sandford Amendment to the 1981 Wildlife and Countryside Bill was to direct agricultural subsidies to a mix of rural job creation and habitat conservation (for example, payments for hedge management) which could be used as an extension, or adjunct, to the use of planning controls over farming and forestry.

4. During the last century the number of owner-occupiers has increased significantly, as the figures for England and Wales show in the table below:

	Number of Holdings		Area (ha)	
	Owned	Rented	Owned	Rented
1891	69,000	404,000	1·62 m	9·72 m
1974	129,000	80,000	6·07 m	5·26 m

Owner-occupiers have increased by 72 per cent. However, the number of people both owning *and* renting land in 1974 was 45 per cent of the 1981 figure.

5. The Society for the Promotion of Nature Conservation's 1979 *Nature Reserves Study* found that 53 per cent of the County Naturalists' Trust reserves were SSSIs. The RSPB owns a much higher percentage of SSSI land.

6. Obviously not all of the woodland in County Naturalists' Trust reserves is coppice. However in 1977 there were also some 17,600 ha described in the SPNC *Reserve Study* as 'mixed', and at least some of this area was wooded.

APPENDIX 2: ORGANIZING A CAMPAIGN AND USING THE MEDIA

1. Constitutions should be open-ended and permissive, rather than restrictive.

2. Andrew Colman, in an essay entitled *The Psychology of Influence*, emphasizes the marked difference in effectiveness of the various media channels: 'Repeated studies have shown that identical messages produce markedly different levels of attitude change in audiences depending on the channel through which they are communicated. Most effective by far is face-to-face communication, then in descending order of effectiveness come films, television, radio, and least effective of all, the printed word.'

Index